CAMBRIDGE LIBRARY COLLECTION

Books of enduring scholarly value

History

The books reissued in this series include accounts of historical events and movements by eye-witnesses and contemporaries, as well as landmark studies that assembled significant source materials or developed new historiographical methods. The series includes work in social, political and military history on a wide range of periods and regions, giving modern scholars ready access to influential publications of the past.

The Fifty Years' Work of the Royal Geographical Society

In 1880, the Royal Geographical Society commissioned Sir Clements R. Markham, a noted British geographer and the Society's secretary, to write a history of its formation, and of the many expeditions it had supported since 1830, to celebrate the its fiftieth anniversary. Published in 1881, The Fifty Years' Work of the Royal Geographical Society consists of twelve chapters. The first five are a condensed history of the original group of geographers who called themselves the Raleigh Club, and the events leading up to the Society's official formation. Chapters 6 and 7 recount the activities of past presidents, secretaries and leading members of the Society, with the rest of the book detailing the fascinating scientific expeditions the Society sponsored financially from the Arctic to Antarctica, the explorers who took part in them, and the various publications the Society published to advance natural science and exploration.

T0370650

Cambridge University Press has long been a pioneer in the reissuing of out-of-print titles from its own backlist, producing digital reprints of books that are still sought after by scholars and students but could not be reprinted economically using traditional technology. The Cambridge Library Collection extends this activity to a wider range of books which are still of importance to researchers and professionals, either for the source material they contain, or as landmarks in the history of their academic discipline.

Drawing from the world-renowned collections in the Cambridge University Library, and guided by the advice of experts in each subject area, Cambridge University Press is using state-of-the-art scanning machines in its own Printing House to capture the content of each book selected for inclusion. The files are processed to give a consistently clear, crisp image, and the books finished to the high quality standard for which the Press is recognised around the world. The latest print-on-demand technology ensures that the books will remain available indefinitely, and that orders for single or multiple copies can quickly be supplied.

The Cambridge Library Collection will bring back to life books of enduring scholarly value (including out-of-copyright works originally issued by other publishers) across a wide range of disciplines in the humanities and social sciences and in science and technology.

The Fifty Years' Work of the Royal Geographical Society

CLEMENTS R. MARKHAM

CAMBRIDGE
UNIVERSITY PRESS

CAMBRIDGE UNIVERSITY PRESS

Cambridge, New York, Melbourne, Madrid, Cape Town, Singapore,
São Paolo, Delhi, Dubai, Tokyo

Published in the United States of America by Cambridge University Press, New York

www.cambridge.org
Information on this title: www.cambridge.org/9781108004602

© in this compilation Cambridge University Press 2009

This edition first published 1881
This digitally printed version 2009

ISBN 978-1-108-00460-2 Paperback

THE

FIFTY YEARS' WORK

OF THE

ROYAL GEOGRAPHICAL SOCIETY.

THE

FIFTY YEARS' WORK

OF THE

ROYAL GEOGRAPHICAL SOCIETY.

BY

CLEMENTS R. MARKHAM, C.B., F.R.S.,

SECRETARY.

1881.

LONDON:

JOHN MURRAY, ALBEMARLE STREET.

ANALYTICAL TABLE OF CONTENTS.

CHAPTER X.

PUBLICATIONS OF THE SOCIETY—LIBRARY AND MAP ROOM—EDUCATIONAL MEASURES.

CHAPTER XI.

PROGRESS OF THE SOCIETY.

Finance—Members—Meetings—House Accommodation.

CHAPTER XII.

COMPARATIVE VIEW OF GEOGRAPHICAL
KNOWLEDGE IN 1830 AND 1880, WITH
A NOTICE OF THE WORK THAT STILL
REMAINS TO BE DONE.

THE

FIFTY YEARS' WORK

OF THE

ROYAL GEOGRAPHICAL SOCIETY.

BY

CLEMENTS R. MARKHAM,

C.B., F.R.S., SECRETARY.

━━━━━━━━━━━━━━

CHAPTER I.

THE FATHERS OF ENGLISH GEOGRAPHY.

THE Royal Geographical Society completed the fiftieth year of its existence on the 16th of July, 1880, and its fiftieth anniversary meeting took place on the 31st of May, 1880. In order to celebrate this auspicious event, and also to supply a useful means of reference to Fellows, I have been commissioned by the Council to write the present brief history of the Society. My plan is to give, in four introductory chapters, a condensed view of the ways and means by which the work undertaken by the Society was performed previous to the date of its formation, and of the circumstances which immediately led to its being brought into existence. The fifth chapter contains a history of the original formation of the Geographical Society. The sixth and seventh chapters are devoted to memorial accounts of the Presidents, Secretaries, and other leading members of the governing body. The eighth and ninth review the career of the Geographical Society with reference to the expeditions which it has helped, or actively promoted, including grants-in-aid, and awards in recognition of the services of eminent geographers and travellers. The history of the various publications of the Society, of the rise and progress of the library and map-room, and of the educational measures adopted by the Council, forms the subject of the tenth chapter; and the eleventh reviews the progress of the Society as regards members, finances, places of meeting, and

B

house accommodation. A comparative view of geographical knowledge when the Society was founded in 1830, and in 1880, with a notice of the work that still remains to be done, illustrates its career of laborious usefulness, and forms a fitting conclusion of the work.

The original objects of the Society were to collect, digest, and publish interesting and useful geographical facts and discoveries; to accumulate a collection of books on geography, voyages, and travels, and of maps and charts; to keep specimens of such instruments as are most serviceable to a traveller; to afford assistance, instruction, and advice to explorers; and to correspond with other bodies or individuals engaged in geographical pursuits.

It is obvious that as soon as the people of England began to foster and encourage maritime enterprise and the discovery of unknown countries, the need for some provision or other through which these objects might in part at least be attained would be felt and, to some extent, supplied. The record and preservation of the history of adventure and discovery, the utilisation of results, and the instruction of explorers by land and sea, became necessities so soon as England commenced her glorious career as a nation of discoverers and explorers. When Sebastian Cabot began to make the history of English maritime and inland discovery, it would have been strange indeed if some man or body of men had not arisen, at the same time, to write its first pages. The very fact that we can now enjoy the perusal of those early efforts of our countrymen is a proof that there was not wanting the will to perform, even then, the duties since undertaken by our Society. The fathers of English geography, the forerunners of the Geographical Society, who, during nearly three centuries, performed our work with zeal and ability, though often with insufficient resources and scant encouragement, ought not to be forgotten by their successors. In truth, the history of the Society properly commences with the efforts of those industrious geographers who did our work amidst many difficulties, from the time when Englishmen first began to emulate the adventurous deeds of the Portuguese and Spaniards who preceded them in the field of discovery.

Richard Eden is the Father of English Geography. He it was who first conceived the idea of performing, single-handed and with inadequate means, the duties which our Society proposed to itself more than two centuries afterwards. He it was who first collected together the records of geographical work, and provided the means of instruction to explorers and travellers. Coming up to London from Cambridge, where he had been a pupil of Sir Thomas Smith at Queen's College, young Eden was a spectator of the gorgeous public entry of Philip and Mary. He describes himself as nearly lifted out of self-command by the excitement of the scene. He beheld the union of the Sovereign of the Indies with his own Queen, and he resolved, on the spot, to set about some work which might fitly commemorate the event.

Eden wrote his 'Decades of the New World' in 1555—a little black-letter volume, which he found great difficulty in getting printed, but which is a laborious and very precious collection of the geographical work of his day. He was the first Englishman who supplied to his countrymen the means of studying, in a collected form, the marvellous history of discovery which was then exciting the wonder and admiration of the age. Eden desired that England should emulate the deeds of those who were first in the field. He gave his countrymen translations from Peter Martyr, Oviedo, Gomara, Ramusio, Pigafetta; and added the earliest narratives of English voyages to Guinea and to the north. His laudable object was that " some memory thereof might remain to posterity, if contempt of knowledge should hereafter bury in oblivion so worthy attempts." Eden was the intimate friend of Sebastian Cabot, and attended him in his last moments; and he also knew the Arctic navigators Chancellor and Borough. It was at the request of Stephen Borough that Eden designed his translation of the 'Art of Navigation' by Martin Cortes, "for the increase of skilful pilots whereof then there were very few." So that he strove to do the work now undertaken by the Geographical Society, both by preserving the records of accomplished work and by providing the means of performing efficient service, and of receiving instruction. A new edition of his 'History of Travayle' was published with additions by Willes in 1577, and his translation of Cortes went through ten editions between 1561 and 1615.

The mantle of Eden fell upon a better known but not more zealous and conscientious worker in the cause of geography. Richard Hakluyt came of an old Herefordshire family, was educated at Westminster School, and elected a student of Christ Church in 1570. He very early took a deep interest in voyages and travels, and in all things connected with the naval glory of his countrymen, and he was indefatigable in collecting information. "His genius," says old Fuller, "inclined him to the study of history, and especially to the marine part thereof, which made him keep constant intelligence with the most noted seamen of Wapping, until the day of his death."

Hakluyt, like Eden, has given us an interesting account of the origin and growth of his love for geography. "I do remember," he says, " that being a youth, and one of Her Majesty's scholars at Westminster, that fruitful nursery, it was my hap to visit the chamber of my cousin, a gentleman of the Middle Temple, at a time when I found lying upon his board certain books of cosmography, with an universal map. He seeing me somewhat curious in the view thereof began to instruct my ignorance. From the map he brought me to the Bible, and turning to the 107th Psalm, directed me to the 23rd and 24th verses where I read that they which go down to the sea in ships, they see the works of the Lord and His wonders in the deep. Which words of the Prophet, together with my cousin's discourse, took me in so deep an impression that I would, by God's assistance, prosecute that knowledge and kind of literature, the doors whereof (after a sort) were so happily opened before me."

From that time Hakluyt devoted his life to the cause of geography. At an early age he was appointed to read lectures at Oxford on that branch of knowledge, and " he was the first that produced and showed both the older and imperfectly composed, and the new lately reformed mappes, globes, spheres, and other instruments of this arte, for demonstration, in the common schooles, to the singular pleasure and general contentment of his auditory." In 1584 he went to Paris as chaplain to the Embassy, returning to England in 1588, and becoming Archdeacon of Westminster in 1602. While in Paris he translated the ' History of Florida' from the French, and was indefatigable in collecting geographical information. His great work, 'The Principal Navigations, Voyages, and Discoveries of Englishmen made by sea or over land to the most remote and farthest distant quarters of the earth,' was published in 1589; and the large edition in three volumes in 1598–1600. Under his auspices also appeared the translations of Peter Martyr by Lok, of Leo Africanus by Pory, of Pigafetta's Congo by Hartwell, and of Mendoza's China by Parke. Hakluyt corresponded with Ortelius and Mercator, and worked as hard at the educational interests of geography as at the preservation and utilisation of its records. Personally acquainted with the leading travellers and explorers, he was also foremost in the encouragement of science and in promoting the construction of good maps and charts. He took a leading part in establishing the courses of lectures on navigation which were delivered at Sir Thomas Smith's house in Philpot Lane, by Edward Wright and Dr. Hood. It was for Hakluyt that Wright prepared the famous map of the world on the new projection in 1600, and it was Hakluyt who helped Molyneux in the construction of his famous globes. He it was, too, who as Historiographer of the East India Company, prepared instructions and drew up lists of commodities to be obtained from and in demand at the various ports of the East.

Hakluyt had one great advantage over Eden. In the days of Elizabeth the interest of the nation was fully aroused on all questions relating to geographical research. Those were the times when the merchants of England were as liberal as they were wealthy; when no man asked the fatuous question *cui bono?* but when all, high and low, generously applauded the efforts of explorers, and when it was the highest ambition of the flower of England's sons to add to her fame by achieving discoveries in distant lands. Nor were the students of scientific geography less zealous or less successful than the adventurers by sea and land. Hakluyt, as President of an Elizabethan Geographical Society, would have gathered around him, for a Council, men of action such as Hawkins, Raleigh, Drake, Frobisher, Lancaster, Jenkinson, Gilbert and Davis; and mathematicians and cosmographers such as Hood and Wright, Digges and Molyneux, Dee and Hues, Harriott and Briggs. These were the fathers of our science.

Hakluyt died on the 23rd of November, 1616, at the age of sixty-three, and was buried in Westminster Abbey. He left behind him a great number of manuscripts, which came into the hands of the Rev. Samuel Purchas, rector of St. Michael's on Ludgate Hill, in about the year 1620. These precious documents, with many others, much abridged and indifferently edited, were published in 1625 in the great work in five volumes, which its compiler entitled 'Hakluytus Posthumus or Purchas his Pilgrimes.' Want of funds is some excuse for the abridgments and deplorable omissions, for Purchas appears to have been in very embarrassed circumstances when he died in 1626, only ten years after Hakluyt's decease.

The forty years which intervened between the death of Purchas and the foundation of the Royal Society were troublous times, and geography could not flourish as in the days of the great Queen. Yet Englishmen were not altogether idle. The lectures at Gresham College were continued, one of its Professors invented the Gunter's Scale and introduced the measuring chain, and the great work of Hondius received an English dress. For this useful service we are indebted to a very gallant soldier. Though trained in camps from his boyhood, Henry Hexham ever cultivated a love for literary pursuits. When quite a young boy, he was the Governor's page during the siege of Ostend, and while Sir Francis Vere. roused suddenly from his bed, engaged a desperate storming party at push of pike, young Hexham calmly went on fastening his master's points in the very thick of the fight. He also recorded the events of that memorable siege. He was at many a hard-fought battle and siege in after years, and he wrote the histories of the operations before Maestricht and Bois le Duc. It is to this military writer that we owe the grandest geographical work of the first Stuart period. The 'Atlas or Geographicke description of the regions countries and kingdomes of the world, represented by new and exact maps,' by Henry Hondius and John Johnson, was translated into English by Henry Hexham in 1636, "enlarged and augmented out of many worthy authors of my own nation." This superb atlas, in two folio volumes, brings the record of geographical work up to the time of the outbreak of the great civil war in England.

CHAPTER II.

THE ROYAL SOCIETY.

THE idea of forming a scientific Society in this country was entertained and partly developed during the Protectorate, and in 1665 the Royal Society was created for the improvement of natural knowledge. In the wide scope of its original objects the science of geography was included, but the share of attention that it received was never in proportion to its importance. From 1665 to 1848 the Royal Society printed 5336 papers in its 'Philosophical Transactions,' out of which only 77 were devoted to geography and topography, or very little over 1 per cent. The proportion in which the various sciences have received attention from the Royal Society is as follows:—

	Papers.		Papers.
Medicine and Chemistry	1949	Mathematics	285
Astronomy	621	Botany	280
Mechanics	461	Optics	206
Zoology	420	Miscellaneous	120
Electricity and Magnetism ..	416	Archæology	117
Geology and Mineralogy	384	Geography and Topography ..	77

These seventy-seven papers include a table of places whose positions have been fixed by astronomical observations, some memoirs on the construction of maps, methods of estimating distances, an account of a lake in Carniola (1669), of the Hudson's Bay Settlements (1770), of the Falls of Niagara (1722), of the Patagonians (1770), the Falkland Islands (1776), the North American Indians (1773 and 1786), and of Bogle's Mission to Tibet (1777). Eden and Hakluyt each did more for geography in thirty years than the Royal Society did in a century.

Still the science of geography owes much to the Royal Society. If little attention was given to the work of explorers, very much was done to improve the scientific methods by which explorers efficiently perform their work. The institution of the Greenwich Observatory in 1676 originated in the extension of navigation and the consequent importance of discovering a means of accurately determining longitude, and the Fellows of the Royal Society were appointed Visitors. The President of the Royal Society was an *ex officio* Member of the Board of Longitude which was established in 1713, and the Commissioners conceived and matured the plan of the Nautical Almanac under the auspices of Dr. Maskelyne, the Astronomer Royal, the publication of which was commenced in 1767 ; while, under their superintendence, the survey of the coasts of Great Britain and Ireland was commenced in 1741. Rewards for northern discovery began to be offered by the Government in 1745, at the instance of the Royal Society, Christopher Middleton having, four years previously, made important discoveries in Hudson's Bay, including the Wager River and Repulse Bay.

But the most important geographical work which was done under the auspices of the Royal Society resulted from the necessity for observing the transit of Venus at far distant points on the earth's surface. The Government granted 4000*l.* to the Society for expenses. In 1769 Captain Cook sailed on his first voyage, accompanied by Sir Joseph Banks, and in 1771 on his second voyage. The transit of Venus also led to the despatch of Mr. Wales to Hudson's Bay in 1769, who wintered at Churchill River, and contributed a paper on the Hudson's Bay Company's Territory to the 'Philosophical Transactions.' Meanwhile the persevering representations of Mr. Daines Barrington induced the Royal Society to submit a memorial to the Government, urging the desirability of sending an expedition to discover how far navigation was practicable towards the North Pole. The expedition of Captain Phipps in 1773 was the result, and thus commenced the glorious history of modern Arctic enterprise, undertaken from the desire of increasing—not wealth, but knowledge. Three years afterwards Captain Cook sailed on his third and last voyage, during which further discoveries were made in the Arctic regions, on the Pacific side. The great African traveller, James Bruce, returned from Abyssinia in 1774 and published his narrative in 1790.

The establishment of our Indian Empire also led to the necessity for surveys, and consequently to great advances in geographical knowledge. The careers of Rennell and Dalrymple were commenced in India, but their love for geography and their zealous devotion to its interests led them to continue their labours after their return home. In very different ways they were both geographers of the Elizabethan type.

James Rennell, as a thoughtful and scientific scholar, stands amongst the foremost in the front rank of English geographers. Born in 1742, he commenced life in the navy, and afterwards took service in the army of Lord Clive and rose to the rank of Major. As Surveyor General of Bengal he mapped the Ganges and Brahmaputra rivers, and surveyed the districts of Bengal and Bahar between 1763 and 1782. His famous map of India was published in 1788, and the memoir followed in 1792. His

great works on the geographical system of Herodotus and on
the retreat of the Ten Thousand appeared in 1800 and 1816 ;
and he devoted many years to the collection of log books, with
a view to investigating the currents of the Atlantic.   After he
had reached his 87th year, Major Rennell still possessed all his
intellectual faculties in full vigour, and devoted many hours of
each day to his favourite pursuit.   He was distinguished for
true, patient, and persevering research ; his critical judgment
was seldom at fault, and his work is always reliable.   He died
on the 29th of March, 1830, a few months before the formation
of the Geographical Society.   Rennell, like Hakluyt, was
buried in Westminster Abbey.

Alexander Dalrymple was remarkable rather for his indefatigable industry in collecting geographical materials than for
original criticism or research.   Born in 1737, he went out to
Madras in 1752, and acquired much nautical experience during
a voyage to the Eastern Archipelago in 1759.   When he
returned home in 1777 he received the appointment of Hydrographer to the East India Company, and his labours are represented by 58 charts, 740 plans, and 50 nautical memoirs.   He
also published translations of voyages in the South Pacific, and
many geographical tracts.   Dalrymple was the first Hydrographer to the Admiralty, a post which he held from its creation in 1795 until a few months before his death in June 1808.

It has been seen that the Royal Society, by encouraging all
investigations and discoveries which had for their object the
advancement of scientific geography, and the improvement of
methods of observation, and also by addressing the Government with a view to the despatch of important expeditions, did
a great deal to advance the special objects of geographers.   It
was in the work of utilising and publishing the narratives of
voyages and travels that the Royal Society failed.   In this
respect the labours of Eden and Hakluyt were continued by
various compilers and publishers through the last century ; for
the demand for such information never slackened, as is clearly
proved by the way in which these collections of voyages and
travels continued to be published. ' Harris's Voyages,' in
two large folio volumes, appeared in 1705, and a new edition
came out in 1764.   In the interval ' Astley's Voyages,' in four
quarto volumes, were published in 1745-47; and ' Churchill's
Collection of Voyages and Travels,' containing several hitherto
unpublished narratives, was issued between 1707 and 1747, and
consisted of eight large volumes. ' Pinkerton's Geography '
was published in 1802, and his ' Collection of Voyages and
Travels,' in seventeen quarto volumes, followed in 1808-14 ;
while ' Kerr's Collection,' in eighteen octavo volumes, came out

at Edinburgh from 1811 to 1824.   There were also three valuable collections having special reference to voyages in the
Pacific and Indian Oceans.   Dalrymple, in two volumes, gave
the 'Spanish and Dutch Voyages in the South Pacific' (1770-
71) ; Admiral Burney, who had served under Cook, supplied a
more complete history of all the Pacific voyages in his valuable
five volumes published from 1803 to 1817; and Dr. Hawkes-
worth gave an account of the voyages of Byron, Wallis, Carteret,
and Cook in his well-known three volumes published in 1773.

During all this period, while the Royal Society and the
publishers and map makers were, between them, doing the
needful work at home, and explorers were actively at work
abroad, there was very urgent need for some central organisation, to guide, control, and advance the business of geography,
and to watch more closely over its interests. The Royal Society
was much occupied with the advancement of other branches of
science, and geography received less of its attention than any
other.   Yet Sir Joseph Banks, so many years the President of
the Royal Society, was not only an ardent geographer, but
also a great traveller ; and it will now be seen that he took
a leading part in the establishment and conduct of a separate
association, with the special object of promoting geographical
discovery.

CHAPTER III.

THE AFRICAN ASSOCIATION.

SIR JOSEPH BANKS, during his long and useful life, was ever a warm and active friend to geography. Born in 1743, of a good Lincolnshire family, he inherited Revesby Abbey when he came of age. While still at Eton and Christ Church his love for natural history, and especially for botany, attracted attention; and in 1766 he made a voyage to Newfoundland with his friend, Lieut. Phipps, the future Arctic explorer, to collect plants. Soon after his return he was appointed naturalist to Captain Cook's expedition, and was absent in the famous circumnavigation of the globe from 1768 to 1771. In 1772 he made a voyage to Iceland, and was elected President of the Royal Society in 1778, from which time he devoted himself to the duties of his office with the utmost zeal. He was habitually consulted by the Government, and was created a Baronet in 1781, a Knight of the Bath in 1795, and a Privy Councillor in 1797. Sir Joseph Banks was the first Englishman upon whom an order of knighthood was conferred for scientific services.

It was in 1788 that a company of ardent geographers, amongst whom was the President of the Royal Society, formed an association for promoting discovery in the interior of Africa. They saw that much of Asia, a still larger proportion of America, and almost the whole of Africa was unvisited and unknown. The very remarkable overland journey of Forster from India had recently added considerably to the stock of knowledge respecting Asia, and valuable additions were also expected from America, while the map of the interior of Africa was still a wide extended blank. A few names of unexplored rivers and of uncertain nations were alone traced upon it, with hesitating hand, on the authority of Edrisi and Leo Africanus. Desirous of rescuing their age from a charge of ignorance, and strongly impressed with a conviction of the utility of thus enlarging the bounds of human knowledge, a small body of geographers formed the plan of an Association for promoting the discovery of the interior parts of Africa. Among the first members were the Earl of Galloway, Lord Rawdon, General Conway, Sir Joseph Banks, Sir Adam Fergusson, Major Rennell, and Mr. Beaufoy. The African Association was formed on June

9th, 1788, and a Committee was invested with its management, and with the choice of persons to whom geographical missions should be assigned. This was the germ of the more fully developed Geographical Society of after years.

The first person who was selected for employment by the Association was Mr. Ledyard, an American by birth, who had been a corporal of marines in Cook's third voyage, and had become known to Sir Joseph Banks. Fired with a zeal for discovery, he afterwards resolved to attempt to make a journey across Europe and Siberia to Kamschatka, and thence overland to the east coast of America. But he was nearly destitute. He landed at Ostend with no more than ten guineas in his pocket, and made his way to Stockholm. Thence he walked northward across the Arctic Circle and round the Gulf of Bothnia to St. Petersburg. He obtained permission to accompany a detachment of stores to Yakutsk, and thence to Okzakoff. But, for some unexplained reason, he was suddenly arrested, hurried into a sledge with two soldiers, conveyed across Siberia again in the depth of winter, and left on the frontier of Poland with a warning that he would be shot if again found on Russian territory. He was quite destitute and, having begged his way to Königsberg, where he ventured to draw a cheque for a small amount on his kind-hearted friend Sir Joseph Banks, he thus succeeded in reaching England again. In this resolute and fearless traveller, Sir Joseph hoped to find the very man to execute the instructions of the Association. On the offer being made to him, Ledyard stated that he had always intended to traverse the continent of Africa as soon as he had explored the interior of North America. He, therefore, set out in June 1788, with orders to make his way from Sennaar to the River Niger. But the career of this remarkable man was brought to a premature close. He died of fever at Cairo, soon after his arrival.

The second emissary of the African Association was Mr. Lucas, who had been captured by a Salee rover, had been three years in captivity, and subsequently was Vice-Consul at Morocco. He undertook a journey to Fezzan, but only got as far as Mesurata, returning to Tripoli in April 1789. Mr. Lucas, however, collected a great deal of information at Mesurata respecting Fezzan and the countries to the south, which he forwarded to the Association. In March 1790 Major Rennell compiled a map of Africa from existing materials, including the reports of Lucas.

The next explorer was Major Houghton, who was to attempt to reach the Niger by way of the Gambia. He left England in October 1790, and news was received of him up to July 1791, but he is believed to have perished miserably on the road to Timbuktu. As soon as the news of Major Houghton's death was confirmed, the Association at once engaged another explorer to follow the same route. This was Mungo Park, a young Scot of no mean talent, who had been regularly educated for the medical profession, and had just returned from a voyage to India. He was also able to observe with Hadley's quadrant, to work by dead reckoning, and was a competent naturalist. He set out in May 1795, and soon afterwards reached the Gambia. On the 2nd of December he started from Pisania for the interior, made a most remarkable journey and returned safely in 1797, after an absence of two years, having discovered the Niger, and collected information as to its course. The geographical illustrations of the journey of Mungo Park were written for the Association by Major Rennell. It is well known that Park was employed by the Government in another expedition in 1805, in which he perished. Many years afterwards his book of logarithms, long preserved by the natives, was brought down to the coast. It was presented by Sir John Glover to the Royal Geographical Society, and is now preserved in the Map Room as a precious relic of one of the glorious band of heroes who have perished in the cause of geography.

From the formation of the Association in 1788 until 1797 Sir Joseph Banks was its Secretary. In the latter year his numerous other avocations obliged him to resign that office. He became Treasurer, while Mr. Bryan Edwards undertook the duties of Secretary. Mr. Edwards died in 1801, and was succeeded by Sir William Young. The Committee for 1797 consisted of the Earl of Moira, Sir Joseph Banks, the Bishop of Llandaff, Mr. Stuart, and the Secretary.

In 1798 Mr. Horneman, a well-trained German, was sent to Cairo, with orders to penetrate across the desert to Fezzan. He made a journey to Sinâh, visiting the temple of Jupiter Ammon, and went thence to Mourzouk, reaching Tripoli in August 1799. Thence he sent home accounts of the desert and the kingdom of Fezzan, respecting which Major Rennell again communicated valuable geographical illustrations. The next emissary was Mr. Nicholls, who furnished an account of Old Calabar, where he died in 1807.

Sir Joseph Banks did not confine his exertions in the cause of geography to the African Continent. He it was who obtained the order for forming a settlement at Botany Bay in Australia. It was also through his intervention that Manning obtained the aid and support of the East India Company, without which he could never have reached the capital of Tibet. Above all it was Sir Joseph Banks who, in conjunction with Mr. Barrow, the Secretary of the Admiralty, induced the Royal Society to resume the consideration of the question of

Arctic research.   The objects were geographical discovery : to circumnavigate Greenland, to ascertain the existence of Baffin's Bay, to solve the question of the continuity of sea round the northern coast of America; and to obtain other scientific results.   They were noble and useful objects, fully justifying the despatch of expeditions to secure them.   So thought the Royal Society, and so thought the Government.   Sir Joseph Banks addressed a letter on the subject to Lord Melville, in November 1817, and the reply was favourable.   This step in the cause of geography was one of the last important acts of the venerable President.   He died on June 19th, 1820, after having presided over the Royal Society during a period of forty-two eventful years.

In the interval of ten years between the death of Sir Joseph Banks and the foundation of the Royal Geographical Society, the tendency of events was to make such an institution a necessity. The commencement of trigonometrical surveys in Great Britain and in British India, and the activity of surveyors both in the Royal Navy and the Bombay Marine, gave an extraordinary impetus to the work of instrument and map makers.   Ramsden, Dollond, and Troughton exerted their ingenuity and talents to meet the requirements of Colby and Lambton; while those able cartographers Arrowsmith and Walker, reproduced the ever-multiplying work of surveyors and explorers.   Sir John Barrow, the Secretary of the Admiralty, took the position vacated by Sir Joseph Banks, as the foremost promoter of geographical research.   Under his auspices the voyages of Parry, Lyon, Clavering, and Beechey, and the land journeys of Franklin were undertaken, which threw such a flood of light over Arctic geography, and excited such general interest in maritime adventure and discovery.   He also procured the despatch of the Congo Expedition under Captain Tuckey, in 1816, and edited the narrative of its ill-fated leader.   With equal interest he watched the journeys of Lyon and of Ritchie to Mourzouk, of Denham and Clapperton from Tripoli to Lake Chad; and of the brave Clapperton in his second expedition, when he died at Sokatu in April 1827, but not until he had completed his route across Africa.   Some heroic adventurers, like Tuckey and Clapperton, laid down their lives in the great cause.   Many more returned home and gave their narratives to the world; and so it came to pass that, year by year, an increasing number of eminent explorers and geographers, as well as of educated men taking an interest in geographical subjects, was assembled in London at one time.   This naturally gave rise to a desire for intercommunion and association, and to the formation in the first place of a Club, which was the harbinger of a great and flourishing Society.

CHAPTER IV.

THE RALEIGH CLUB.

CAPTAIN ARTHUR DE CAPELL BROKE was the founder of the Raleigh Travellers' Club, the immediate forerunner of the Geographical Society. The eldest son of Sir Richard de Capell Broke of Great Oakley in Northamptonshire, whom he succeeded in 1829, Sir Arthur Broke, who was born in 1791, had served in the army, and had all the spirit of an adventurous traveller. He was the author of 'Travels through Sweden and Norway' (1823), a work which gives a striking picture of the physical features of those northern lands. He also wrote ' A Winter in Lapland' (1827), and 'Sketches in Spain and Morocco' (1831).

Sir Arthur Broke conceived the idea of forming a most agreeable dining society composed solely of travellers. The world was to be mapped out into so many divisions corresponding with the number of Members, each division being represented by at least one Member as far as it might be practicable, so that the society collectively should have visited nearly every part of the known globe. He first communicated his idea to four friends, Colonel Leake, Mr. Legh, Captain Mangles, and Lieut. Holman, who warmly approved of it. They prepared a general list of the most distinguished travellers, and, a selection having been carefully made in accordance with the above principle, a circular was sent out in the summer of 1826, dated from the Alfred Club in Albemarle Street, and signed Arthur de Capell Broke. The number was at first limited to forty, and the meetings were to take place once a fortnight, commencing in November. The principal object of these meetings was announced to be the attainment, at a moderate expense, of an agreeable, friendly, and rational society, formed by persons who had visited every part of the globe.

The first dinner was held at Grillon's Hotel in Albemarle Street, and the second at Brunet's Hotel in Leicester Square. At the latter meeting it was resolved that the Club should be considered as constituted, and the name of the Raleigh Club, in honour of the illustrious Sir Walter Raleigh, was proposed by Captain Broke and adopted.

Of the original Committee which formed the Raleigh Club,

Sir Arthur Broke was for many years the President. He died at his seat of Oakley in Northamptonshire, in December 1858. His friend Colonel William Martin Leake was an older man. He was born in London in 1777, the grandson of John Martin Leake, Garter King at Arms. Entering the Artillery in 1794, he was appointed on a mission to instruct the Turks. After a residence at Constantinople until 1800, he travelled through Asia Minor, Palestine, and Egypt in an official capacity, making a general survey of the country, the results of which were embodied in a valuable report. He was afterwards commissioned to visit and report upon the European provinces of Turkey, and Greece. Retiring from the army in 1823, he published several valuable works, including 'Researches in Greece,' 'Outline of the Greek Revolution,' 'Topography of Athens,' and 'Travels in the Morea and Northern Greece.' He died on January 6th, 1860, aged 83.

Captain Mangles entered the navy in 1800, serving in the *Narcissus* under Captain Ross Donnelly in the West Indies, and seeing much active service until the peace in 1815. He then travelled in the East with his friend Captain the Hon. C. L. Irby, the results of their tour being privately printed under the title of 'Travels in Egypt, Nubia, Syria, and Asia Minor.' This most popular work was first published in 1844. Devoting himself to the study of geography and hydrography, he published books on these subjects in 1849 and 1851. Captain Mangles died on November 18th, 1867.

Lieutenant J. B. Holman, R.N., was the well-known "Blind Traveller." He was obliged to leave the service owing to an illness resulting in loss of sight, when he was only 25, and he received an appointment as a Naval Knight at Windsor, with permission to travel. From 1819 to 1821 he wandered over various parts of the Continent, and the narrative of his travels passed through four editions. His next journey, from 1822 to 1824, was through Russia and Siberia without any servant, but trusting to his own sagacity, and to the sympathy which never failed him wherever he went, for safe conduct through all emergencies and perils. His book of Russian travels went through three editions. In 1834 appeared his 'Voyage round the World,' which Sir Roderick Murchison pronounced to be an extraordinary literary monument of energy and perseverance. His last journeys were through Turkey in Europe. Lieut. Holman died in 1858.

Sir Arthur Broke and his Committee worked so well during the winter of 1826, that by February 1827 the numbers of the Club were nearly completed. The following is a list of the original Members:—

1. Sir Arthur de Capell Broke.
2. Colonel Leake.
3. Mr. Legh, M.P.
4. Captain Mangles, R.N.
5. Lieut. Holman, R.N.
6. Mr. C. R. Cockerell.
7. Mr. J. Rennie.
8. Mr. G. Rennie.
9. Mr. Mackenzie.
10. Captain Corry, R.N.
11. Captain Owen, R.N.
12. Captain Chapman, R.A.
13. Captain Colquhoun, R.A.
14. Mr. Beechey.
15. Major Abbey.
16. Mr. Wise.
17. Mr. Baillie Fraser.
18. Mr. Bankes.
19. Major the Hon. G. Keppel (now Earl of Albemarle).
20. Mr. Colebrooke.
21. Captain Basil Hall, R.N.
22. Mr. Andrew Knight.
23. Mr. Marsden.
24. Mr. Murdoch.
25. Sir Murray Maxwell, R.N.
26. General Stratton.
27. Captain C. Cochrane, R.N.
28. Mr. John Cam Hobhouse, M.P.
29. Captain Sabine, R.A.
30. Mr. Hanbury.
31. Earl of Belmore.
32. Viscount Strangford.
33. Viscount Corry, M.P.
34. Captain Weddell, R.N.
35. Hon. Henry Corry.
36. Mr. Baily.
37. Mr. Barrow.
38. Captain Marryat, R.N., C.B.

To the first list were soon afterwards added the names of Sir John Franklin, Sir Edward Parry, Captain Beaufort, R.N., Captain Vidal, R.N., the Honourable Mountstuart Elphinstone, Mr. W. R. Hamilton, Captain Beechey, R.N., Sir George Staunton. Roderick Impey Murchison, proposed by Sir John Franklin and seconded by Major the Honourable George Keppel (Earl of Albemarle since 1852), was elected a Member of the Raleigh Club on February 1st, 1830.

The first regular meeting of the Club took place at the Thatched House at 6 o'clock on the 7th of February, 1827, when Mr. Marsden took the chair. The great Orientalist, who died in 1836, was then aged seventy-three, and no doubt the oldest Member present. Sir Arthur Broke presented a haunch of reindeer venison from Spitzbergen, a jar of Swedish brandy, rye-cake (*Flad Bröd*) baked near the North Cape, a Norway cheese (*Gammel Ost*), and preserved cloud-berries from Lapland, for the dinner. It was agreed that each Member should be invited " to present any scarce foreign game, fish, fruits, wines, &c., as a means of adding greatly to the interest of the dinners, not merely from the objects of luxury thus afforded, but also for the observations they will be the means of giving rise to." The evening passed with the greatest enjoyment, and it was agreed that a General Meeting of the Club should take place on the following Tuesday, February 13th, at the Thatched House, for the purpose of deciding upon the rules intended to be proposed. At this General Meeting Mr. Barrow was in the chair; and a set of rules was drawn up and confirmed.

From that time the dinners of the Raleigh Travellers always took place at the Thatched House. At the next one, on

February 19th, Captain Mangles presented some bread, made from wheat brought by him from Heshbon on the Dead Sea. Sir Arthur Broke contributed a brace of capercailzie (*coque de bois*) from Sweden.   On March 5th, 1827, a ham from Mexico was presented for the dinner by Mr. Morier, and the health of that gentleman was accordingly drunk.   At this time a rule was made that, as the object of the Club was that travellers may assemble in social converse, who have visited distant countries, particularly those that have been little explored, it should be required of Members who proposed and seconded a candidate to state his qualification in writing, such statement to be read from the chair when the candidate is proposed, and again when his ballot is about to take place.

In the year 1828 the names, amongst others, of the Honourable Richard Bootle Wilbraham, Mr. Bartholomew Frere, Captain George Back, R.N., Mr. Nicholas Garry of the Hudson's Bay Company, and Captain the Honourable C. L. Irby, R.N., were added to the list of Members.   In 1829 Lieutenant H. Lister Maw, R.N.—the first Englishman who ever went down the Amazon from Peru to the Atlantic—Sir William Ouseley, Colonel Belford Wilson—aide-de-camp to General Bolivar—Francis Baring, Esq., who had just returned from South America, Robert Brown the distinguished botanist, and Captain Blackwood, R.N., became Members of the Raleigh Club.

Thus the most eminent Travellers in London were brought together, an interchange of ideas frequently took place, and the feeling that the creation of a more completely organised institution for the advancement of geography was necessary, gradually took a definite shape.   The Raleigh Club had freshened up old memories, had kept alive an interest in geographical pursuits, and had prepared the way for more systematic work.   It had "lubricated the wheels of science," an expression the origin of which was attributed, by Lord Ellesmere, to Lord Stowell.   For this service the geographers of England are indebted to the happy inspiration of Sir Arthur de Capell Broke.

After the formation of the Geographical Society, the Raleigh Club continued to flourish, becoming more and more closely connected with the Society, until 1854, when the affiliation became complete and, with new rules, the name of Raleigh was dropped, and it became the Geographical Club.   The subsequent history of these dining Clubs thus became a part of the history of the Society.

CHAPTER V.

FOUNDATION OF THE ROYAL GEOGRAPHICAL SOCIETY.

On Monday, the 24th of May, 1830, there was a numerously-attended General Meeting of the Raleigh Travellers' Club, with Mr. Barrow in the Chair. It was then submitted:—

" That a Society was needed whose sole object should be the promotion and diffusion of that most important and entertaining branch of knowledge—geography; and that a useful Society might therefore be formed, under the name of the GEOGRAPHICAL SOCIETY OF LONDON: that the interest excited by this department of science is universally felt, that its advantages are of the first importance to mankind in general, and paramount to the welfare of a maritime nation like Great Britain, with its numerous and extensive foreign possessions; that its decided utility in conferring just and distinct notions of the physical and political relations of our globe must be obvious to every one, and is the more enhanced by this species of knowledge being obtainable without much difficulty, while at the same time it affords a copious source of rational amusement; and finally that, although there is a vast store of geographical information existing in Great Britain, yet it is so scattered and dispersed, either in large books that are not generally accessible, or in the bureaus of public departments, or in the possession of private individuals, as to be nearly unavailable to the public."

These propositions were unanimously accepted as sound and true. It was then suggested that the objects of such a Society would be—

" 1. To collect, register and digest, and to print for the use of Members and the public at large, in a cheap form and at certain intervals, such new, interesting, and useful facts and discoveries as the Society may have in its possession, and may from time to time acquire.

" 2. To accumulate gradually a library of the best books on geography—a complete collection of maps and charts from the earliest period of rude geographical delineations to the most improved of the present time; as well as all such documents and materials as may convey the best information to persons intending to visit foreign countries, it being of the greatest utility to a traveller to be aware, previously to his setting out, of what has been already done, and what is still wanting, in the countries he may intend to visit.

" 3. To procure specimens of such instruments as experience has shown to be most useful and best adapted to the compendious stock of a traveller, by consulting which he may make himself familiar with their use.

" 4. To prepare brief instructions for such as are setting out on their travels, pointing out the parts most desirable to be visited, the best and most practicable means of proceeding thither, the researches most essential to make, phenomena to be observed, the subjects of natural history most desirable to be procured, and to obtain all such information as may tend to the extension of our geographical knowledge. And it is hoped that the Society may ultimately be enabled from its funds to render pecuniary assistance to such travellers as may require it, in order to facilitate the attainment of some particular object of research.

" 5. To correspond with similar Societies that may be established in different parts of the world; with foreign individuals engaged in geographical pursuits, and with the most intelligent British residents in the various remote settlements of the Empire.

" 6. To open a communication with all those philosophical and literary Societies with which geography is connected; for as all are fellow-labourers in the different departments of the same vineyard, their united efforts cannot fail mutually to assist each other."

The meeting then proceeded to nominate a Provisional Committee, consisting of six Members of the Raleigh Club, namely Mr. Barrow, Mr. Robert Brown, Mr. Roderick I. Murchison, Mr. John Cam Hobhouse, Mr. Mountstuart Elphinstone, and Mr. Bartle Frere; to consider and propose resolutions to be submitted to another General Meeting. These six Founders of the Society were representative men, and a history of the Society's origin would be incomplete without a retrospective notice of their previous careers.

John Barrow, who was born near Ulverstone in North Lancashire in June 1764, evinced an ardent love of adventure and travel from his early youth. He quitted his employment as a clerk in an iron foundry to go for a voyage to Greenland in a whaler. Soon afterwards he received an appointment on the staff of Lord Macartney's Embassy, and went to China; the results of his service on that occasion being a Life of Lord Macartney, and a book of Travels in China and Cochin China. In 1797 he accompanied Lord Macartney to the Cape of Good Hope on his important mission to settle the government there, and Mr. Barrow remained as Auditor-General of Accounts. He returned to England in 1803, and published his 'Travels in Southern Africa.' The following year Lord Melville appointed him Secretary to the Admiralty. In this influential position he worked steadily and untiringly for the advancement of science, and especially for the spread of geographical knowledge. After the death of Sir Joseph Banks, it is to Mr. Barrow that all Government aid to geography is due, including the despatch of the Arctic Expeditions and of several exploring expeditions to Africa. In 1830 Mr. Barrow was certainly the warmest and most powerful friend to geographical science in this country.

Mr. Robert Brown was born at Montrose in 1773, the son of the Episcopalian minister of that place. For a short time he was an Assistant Surgeon in an infantry regiment, but, through the kindness of Sir Joseph Banks, his prospects in life were changed, and in 1801 he was appointed naturalist to the scientific expedition which sailed in that year for Australia. Returning in 1805, his collections and discoveries threw an entirely new light on the geographical distribution of vegetable life. Afterwards, as Secretary and President, he was for many years the mainstay of the Linnean Society. Baron Humboldt bore witness to "the vast impulse which Robert Brown gave to the three great objects which must for ever remain attached to his name—the minute development of the relations of organisation in natural families, the geography of plants, and the estimate of their numerical proportions." He was known among scientific men as "Princeps Botanicorum," but he was ever a sincere friend to geography. Robert Brown contributed the botanical appendix to several important works, such as Parry's 'Voyages,' Salt's 'Abyssinia,' and Clapperton's 'Journey.' He died in 1858, at which time he was President of the Linnean Society.

Roderick Impey Murchison was the son of Dr. Kenneth Murchison of Tarradale in Ross-shire, by a daughter of Mackenzie of Fairburn, and was born at Tarradale on the 19th of February, 1792. His mother's dearest friend was Miss Annie Robinson, daughter of the Provost of Dingwall in Ross-shire, the future wife of Mr. John Gladstone, and long before her marriage the mother of the Prime Minister often carried in her arms the child who was hereafter to be our revered President. Roderick Murchison lost his father when he was a child, and his guardians were Colonel Alexander and his godfather Sir Elijah Impey, old Indian friends of Dr. Murchison. His mother married again, and he was sent to school at Durham when he was seven ; but he always attributed the English accent, which he retained through life, to Sally the Dorsetshire lass, who taught him even before he was sent to school. From Durham he went to the military college at Great Marlow, and he was gazetted an ensign in the 36th regiment at the age of fifteen. His uncle General Mackenzie wrote of him as a charming boy, manly, sensible, generous, and warm-hearted. After a short service in Ireland, he sailed for Portugal in 1808, and was present at the battles of Roriça, Vimeira, and Coruña, returning home after Sir John Moore's disaster. In 1814 he exchanged into the cavalry, joining the Inniskilling Dragoons, but was disappointed in his object, which was to be sent to Belgium, where he would have taken part in the Waterloo campaign. His troop did not go, and the war came to an end. So young Murchison retired from the army, and in August 1815 he was married to Charlotte, the daughter of General Hugonin of Nursted House in Hampshire. After passing some time in Italy, the newly-married couple settled at Barnard Castle in Durham, and Roderick Murchison became one of the greatest fox-hunters in the north of England. His devotion to hunting led to their moving to Melton Mowbray, but in 1824 he sold his hunters and passed the winter with his father-in-law at Nursted. It was at this time that he met Sir Humphrey Davy, when staying with his friend Mr. Morritt at Rokeby. The advice of this eminent savant, combined with the persuasions of his wife, finally changed Murchison's career, and he buckled to, with a will, at the study of geology. From that moment he devoted his life to science, first learning chemistry at the Royal Institution. In January 1825 he joined the Geological Society, and in 1826 became a Fellow of the Royal Society, continuing steadily at work both in the field and in the study. In 1828 he explored the volcanic region of Auvergne with his wife and Charles Lyell, continuing his geological tour into the Tyrol and Carinthia. He had accepted the appointment of Secretary to the Geological Society, and was fast rising into fame as a geologist when he joined this Committee of the Raleigh Club.

John Cam Hobhouse, born in 1786, was educated at Westminster School and at Cambridge, and in 1810 was the companion of Lord Byron in his travels through Albania and Greece. He published his well-known 'Journey through Albania' in 1813, and few works of travel have obtained a more lasting reputation. Succeeding to his father's baronetage in 1831, Sir John Hobhouse was the colleague of Sir Francis Burdett in the representation of Westminster from 1820 to 1833. He afterwards held the important posts of Secretary for Ireland, and President of the Board of Control, and he was created Lord Broughton in 1851. He died in his 83rd year on June 3rd, 1869. As Sir John Hobhouse he was a constant diner at the Raleigh Club, and took a keen interest in geography. He was on the Council of the Geographical Society in 1831, and again in 1857–58.

The Hon. Mountstuart Elphinstone was born in 1779, and went to India at an early age, in the Company's Civil Service. After serving during many stirring events in the Dakhan, Lord Minto selected him to conduct the difficult mission to the Afghans, and at Peshawur he collected a mass of new geographical information which was embodied in his 'Account of the Kingdom of Cabul' (1815). In 1810 he became Resident at Poona, and in 1819 was appointed Governor of Bombay. He discharged the duties of this important post with great ability during seven years, and the Elphinstone College is an enduring monument of his rule. After his return to England he devoted several years to the preparation of his admirable 'History of Mogul Rule in India.' He was on our Council in 1831, Vice-President in 1838–39, again on the Council in 1841; but his latter years were passed in literary retirement. He died on November 20th, 1859, in his 81st year.

Bartholomew Frere, brother of the Right Hon. Hookham Frere the intimate friend of Canning, was born in 1776, and educated at Harrow and Cambridge. He then entered the diplomatic service, and was for some time Chargé d'Affaires at Constantinople. He was a well read geographer and a scholar, and these accomplishments, as Sir Roderick Murchison bore testimony, were united with the finest qualities of the heart, a playful wit, and the most engaging manners. He served on the Council of the Geographical Society for nearly twenty years, dying in 1852.

Of these six Members, Mr. Barrow was the senior, and their meetings took place in his room at the Admiralty. They combined great experience and knowledge of the world with profound learning, and in Robert Brown and Roderick Murchison they had colleagues whose practical experience in the working of the Linnean and Geological Societies was of great use. They met several times during the end of May and beginning of June 1830, settled all the preliminary business, and drew up the rules for the new Society.

Meanwhile another Member of the Raleigh Club, Captain W. H. Smyth, R.N., had, early in 1830, not only sketched out a well-conceived scheme for a Geographical Society, but had enrolled many names; and his zealous exertions, now heartily given to the Committee, materially furthered the successful progress of their work.

These then were the seven Founders of the Royal Geographical Society, whose names should ever be had in remembrance by English geographers: namely—

Sir John Barrow.	The Hon. Mountstuart
Sir Roderick Murchison.	Elphinstone.
Mr. Robert Brown.	Mr. Bartholomew Frere.
Lord Broughton.	Admiral W. H. Smyth.

Roderick Murchison went up the Rhine with his wife, and to Vienna in June 1830, and was absent until October; and in the following winter he was elected President of the Geological Society. This is the reason that his name does not appear in the subsequent proceedings, nor on the list of the first Council of the Geographical Society.

As soon as the Committee was ready to submit its Report, another meeting was held at the rooms of the Horticultural Society in Regent Street on July 16th, 1830, when the following Resolutions were adopted, and the Geographical Society of London was constituted.

" 1. That the Society be called the Geographical Society of London.
" 2. That the number of Ordinary Members be not limited, but that the

number of Honorary Foreign Members be limited as shall hereafter be determined.

" 3. That the Council of the Society consist of a President, four Vice-Presidents, a Treasurer, two Secretaries, and twenty-one other Members, to conduct the affairs of the Society.

" 4. That the election of the said Council and Officers be annual.

" 5. That the office of President be not held by the same individual for a longer period than two consecutive years, but that he is eligible for re-election after the lapse of one year.

" 6. That one of the four Vice-Presidents go out annually; he being eligible, however, for re-election after the lapse of one year, but the Treasurer and Secretaries may be annually re-elected.

" 7. That seven of the twenty-one other Members constituting the Council go out annually, at the period of the General Election of the officers of the Society.

" 8. That the Admission Fee of Members be 3*l*., and the Annual Subscription 2*l*., or both may be compounded for by one payment of 20*l*.*

" 9. That such part of the Funds of the Society as may not be required for current expenses be placed in the public securities, and vested in the names of three Trustees, to be hereafter appointed by the President and Council.

" 10. That these three Trustees be Supernumerary Members of the Council.

" 11. That early in November next a General Meeting be held to decide on a Code of Regulations and Bye-laws for the management of the Society, which the President and Council will in the meantime prepare to be submitted to the said meeting.

" 12. And lastly that the following noblemen and gentlemen compose the Council and Officers of the Society for this year (1830) :—

PRESIDENT.
The Right Hon. Viscount Goderich, F.R.S.

VICE-PRESIDENTS.

John Barrow, Esq., F.R.S.	G. Bellas Greenough, Esq., F.R.S.
Lieut.-Col. Leake, F.R.S.	Capt. Sir John Franklin, R.N., F.R.S.

TREASURER.
John Biddulph, Esq.

SECRETARIES.

Capt. Maconochie, R.N.	Rev. G. Renouard (*Foreign and Hon. Sec.*).

COUNCIL.

Viscount Althorp, M.P., F.R.S.	R. W. Hay, Esq., F.R.S.
Francis Baily, Esq., F.R.S.	J. Cam Hobhouse, Esq., F.R.S.
Capt. Beaufort, R.N., F.R.S.	Capt. Horsburgh, F.R.S.
John Britton, Esq., F.S.A.	Colonel Jones, R.E.
W. Brockedon, Esq.	Capt. Mangles, R.N., F.R.S.
Robert Brown, Esq., F.R.S.	Thomas Murdoch, Esq., F.R.S.
Sir Arthur de C. Broke, F.R.S.	Rt. Hon. Sir George Murray, G.C.B., F.R.S.
Hon. Mountstuart Elphinstone.	
Capt. Sir Aug. Fraser, K.C.B., F.R.S.	Capt. Lord Prudhoe, R.N., F.R.S.
Capt. Basil Hall, R.N., F.R.S.	Capt. Smyth, R.N., F.R.S.
W. R. Hamilton, Esq., F.R.S.	H. G. Ward, Esq."

* The Admission Fee and Annual Subscription continue the same. But now (1881) the composition, on entrance, is 28*l*., or at any subsequent period 25*l*., if the Entrance Fee be already paid.

As soon as these Resolutions had been adopted, Mr. Barrow the Chairman, delivered an address explanatory of the general views of the Society. He concluded from the fact that 460 names had already been enrolled on the list of Members that a favourable opinion had been formed of the utility likely to result from the labours of the Society. He spoke in the name of the Foundation Committee, and said that the degree of utility which would be really effected must depend on the attention and assiduity which the President and Council might bestow on the Society's concerns, quite as much as on the stock of knowledge they might bring to the consideration of the several subjects that would come before them. He looked with confidence to aid and zealous co-operation from officers, both of the army and navy. He urged that on the exactitude of the minutest details of hydrography mainly depended the safety of navigation, and looked forward to the completion of surveys and to extended observations on prevailing winds and currents. Every accession to hydrographical knowledge must be of great importance to navigation and therefore a fit object for promulgation by the Society. But he added that the Committee hoped that many valuable contributions on geographical subjects would be received from other individuals than those who are thus professionally qualified and invited to furnish them. Mr. Barrow went on to suggest the various branches of the subject which should occupy the attention of the traveller; and concluded with the hope that the Society would shortly be in a position to form a valuable geographical library, and a useful collection of maps and charts.

The list of 460 original Members contains 43 naval officers besides the King, 50 officers in the army, and 10 clergymen. It includes most of the leading statesmen of both parties, Wellington and Peel, Aberdeen and Ellenborough, Melville, Goderich, Herries, Bexley, John Russell, Althorp, Huskisson, and a dozen other Members of Parliament. Among botanists, Robert Brown, Bentham, Hooker and Lindley; among geologists, Buckland, Greenough, Sedgwick, De la Beche, Egerton, Lyell and Murchison enrolled themselves as original Members of the new Society; with Bailey, Whewell, Lubbock and Hallam, and the engineers Brunel and Rennie. With the great surveyors Colby and Everest, appear also the cartographers Arrowsmith and Walker, and the instrument-maker Dollond. With the Hydrographer Beaufort, the marine surveyors are represented by Beechey, Owen, King, Becher, Belcher, Blackwood, Sheringham, Denham, Washington, and Horsburgh, and soon afterwards FitzRoy, Graves, and Stokes. All the leading men of every profession who either saw the importance of advancing the cause of geography, or were actively engaged in its pursuit, had rallied at the call of the Foundation Committee of the Geographical Society; and thus this new organisation, so urgently needed, and destined to work so much for good in the prosperous future that was in store for it, auspiciously commenced its career.

LIST OF MEMBERS

OF THE

GEOGRAPHICAL SOCIETY, AUGUST 4TH, 1830.*

The Right Hon. the Earl of Aberdeen, K.T., F.R.S., P.S.A.
Sir Thomas Dyke Acland, Bart., M.P., F.G.S.
Lieut.-Gen. Sir Frederic Adam, G.C.B.
John Adamson, Esq., F.S.A.
William Ainsworth, Esq.
James Alexander, Esq., M.P.
Captain J. E. Alexander.
J. M. Alsager, Esq.
Viscount Althorp, M.P., F.R.S.
10 Sir Edmund Antrobus, Bart.
Captain Archer.
Rev. Dr. Arnold, F.R.S., Master of Rugby School.
Mr. Aaron Arrowsmith.
Mr. J. Arrowsmith.
William Astell, Esq., M.P., Chairman E.I.C.
John P. Atkins, Esq.
Thomas Rose Auldjo, Esq.

Adolph Bach, Esq.
John Backhouse, Esq.
20 Alexander Baillie, Esq.
George Baillie, Esq.
Arthur Baily, Esq.
Francis Baily, Esq., F.R.S.
Sir F. F. Baker, Bart., F.R.S.
Captain Bannister.
Alex. Baring, Esq., M.P., F.H.S.
Francis Baring, Esq.
B. W. Barker, Esq.
Rev. John Barlowe.

30 Thos. Barnes, Esq.
John Barrow, Esq., F.R.S.
Mr. B. B. Bate.
Lieutenant-Colonel Batty, F.R.S.
Captain H. W. Bayfield, R.N.
Captain F. Beaufort, R.N., F.R.S.
Henry de la Beche, Esq., F.R.S.
Lieutenant A. B. Becher, R.N.
The Right Hon. Sir J. Beckett, Bart., M.P., F.R.S.
His Grace the Duke of Bedford, F.S.A.
40 Grosvenor Charles Bedford, Esq.
Henry Bedford, Esq.
Capt. Frederick Beechey, R.N., F.R.S.
Capt. Edward Belcher, R.N., F.G.S.
Frederic Debell Bennett, Esq.
John Joseph Bennett, Esq.
George Bentham, Esq., F.L.S.
R. Bentley, Esq.
Henry Berens, Esq., F.R.S.
Joseph Berens, Esq.
50 Captain J. Betham, E.I.M.
The Right Hon. Lord Bexley, F.R.S.
John Biddulph, Esq., F.H.S.
Jonathan Birch, Esq.
Captain Price Blackwood, R.N.
William Blake, Esq., F.R.S.
Major Blanchard, R.E.
John Bolton, Esq.
John Bonham, Esq.
Captain Bowles, R.N.
60 Lord Brabazon.
Captain H. Rowland Brandreth, R.E.
E. W. Brayley, Esq., F.S.A.

* The names printed in *italics* are those of Fellows still alive at the fifty-first anniversary in 1881.

Earl of Brecknock.
Rev. Dr. Brereton, F.S.A.
Sir Thomas M. Brisbane, K.C.B., F.R.S.
John Britton, Esq., F.S.A.
John Broadley, Esq., F.S.A.
William Brockedon, Esq.
William John Broderip, Esq., F.R.S.
70 Sir Arthur de Capell Broke Bart., F.R.S.
James Browne, Esq., M.P.
Robert Brown, Esq. F.R.S.
Thomas Brown, Esq.
Wade Brown, Esq.
M. I. Brunel, Esq., F.R.S.
Major-Gen. Sir Alexander Bryce, C.B.
J. S. Buckingham, Esq.
Professor Buckland, F.R.S.
J. William Buckle, Esq.
80 C. Bullen, Esq.
Captain F. Bullock, R.N.
Dr. J. Bunny.
Rev. Chas. P. Burney, D.D., F.R.S.
Decimus Burton, Esq., F.S.A.
Marquis of Bute, F.R.S.
Archdeacon Butler, F.R.S.
Captain Theophilus Butler.

B. Bond Cabbell, Esq.
Earl of Caledon, K.P., F.G.S.
90 John Caley, Esq., F.R.S.
John Carey, Esq.
Nicholas Carlisle, Esq., F.R.S.
Ralph Carr, Jun., Esq.
W. Ogle Carr, Esq.
John Bonham Carter, Esq., M.P.
Samuel Cartwright, Esq., F.G.S.
Viscount Castlereagh, M.P.
Francis Chantrey, Esq., R.A., F.R.S.
William Chaplin, Esq.
100 Aaron Chapman, Esq.
Dean of Chichester.
J. George Children, Esq., F.R.S.
Francis Cholmeley, Esq., M.P., F.H.S.
John Christie, Esq.
Earl of Clare.
Dr. Chas. M. Clarke.
Thomas Clarke, Esq.
William B. Clarke, Esq.
William Stanley Clarke, Esq.
110 Sir George Clerk, Bart., F.R.S.
Captain T. H. Shadwell Clerke.
M. Waller Clifton, Esq., F.R.S.
The Right Hon. Sir George Cockburn, G.C.B., F.R.S.
Pepys Cockerell, Esq.
Rev. H. Coddington, F.R.S.

H. Colburn, Esq.
Lieut.-Colonel Colby, R.E., F.R.S.
Viscount Cole, M.P., F.G.S.
Captain J. N. Colquhoun, R.A.
120 Shelton Coulson, Esq.
W. M. Coulthurst, Esq.
Chas. T. Cox, Esq.
Lt.-Col. the Hon. J. R. Cradock.
W. P. Craufurd, Esq., F.G.S.
William Crawfurd, Esq., F.H.S.
J. Crawfurd, Esq., F.R.S.
The Right Hon. J. W. Croker, F.R.S.
Mr. J. Cross.
The Hon. Robert Curzon, M.P.
130 Lieutenant-Colonel H. Custance.

Richard Hart Davis, Esq., M.P., F.R.S.
Lieutenant R. K. Dawson, R.E.
Lieutenant H. M. Denham, R.N.
Francis H. Dickinson, Esq.
Colonel Sir Alexander Dickson, K.C.B., R.A., F.S.A.
John Disney, Esq.
George Dollond, Esq., F.R.S.
Lieut.-General Sir Rufane Donkin, K.C.B., F.R.S.
Captain J. G. Doran.
140 Maj.-Gen. Sir H. Douglas, Bart., F.R.S.
W. R. Keith Douglas, Esq., M.P., F.R.S.
Lieutenant-Colonel Carlo Doyle.
Captain Charles Drinkwater, R.N.
Colonel Drummond, R.A.
Edward Drummond, Esq.
Lieutenant Thomas Drummond, R.E.
Lord Ducie, F.R.S.
Sir George Duckett, Bart., F.R.S.
The Hon. Captain R. Dundas, R.N.
150 Major W. B. Dundas, R A.
Lord Durham, F.G.S.
Vice-Admiral Sir P. C. H. Durham, K.C.B.

A. Earle, Esq.
H. Earle, Esq.
Captain the Hon. W. Edwards.
Sir P. de Malpas Grey Egerton, Bart., F.G.S.
Lord Eliot, M.P.
The Right Honourable Lord Ellenborough, F.H.S.
Edward Ellice, Esq., F.H.S.
160 Captain the Hon. George Elliot, R.N.
The Hon. G. Agar Ellis, M.P., F.R.S.
The Hon. Mountstuart Elphinstone.
Charles Enderby, Esq.

George Enderby, Esq.
Captain George Everest, Surveyor-Gen. E.I.C., F.R.S.

John Fairlie, Esq.
Doctor Falconer.
W. Falconer, Esq.
Lieut.-Colonel Fanshawe, R.E.
170 Alexander Findlay, Esq.
William Henry Fitton, Esq., M.D., F.R.S.
Captain Adolphus Fitzclarence, R.N.
Lieutenant-Colonel G. Fitzclarence.
Edward Forster, Esq., F.R.S.
Captain Sir J. Franklin, R.N., F.R.S.
Captain Franklin, E.I.A.
Colonel Sir Augustus Frazer, K.C.B., R.A., F.R.S.
J. W. Freshfield, Esq., F.R.S.
John Fuller, Esq., F.H.S.

180 John Galt, Esq., F.S.A.
James Gardner, Esq.
Nicholas Garry, Esq., Dep. Gov. Hudson's Bay Company, F.H.S.
Henry Gawler, Esq.
Davies Gilbert, Esq., M.P., P.R.S.
Earl of Glasgow, F.R.S.
Right Hon. Visct. Goderich, F.R.S.
Isaac Lyon Goldsmid, Esq., F.R.S.
James Gooden, Esq., F.S.A.
Adam Gordon, Esq.
190 Major H. W. Gordon, R.A.
Sir I. Willoughby Gordon, Bart., G.C.B., F.R.S.
J. R. Gowan, Esq., F.G.S.
John Edward Gray, Esq., F.G.S.
G. B. Greenough, Esq., F.R.S.
Thomas Green, Esq., M.P.
Col. Greenwell, A.D.C. to the King.
Rev. Richard Greswell.
John Griffin, Esq.
John Guillemard, Esq., F.R.S.
200 Hudson Gurney, Esq., M.P., F.R.S., V.P.S.A.

Captain Basil Hall, R.N., F.R.S.
Lieutenant W. S. Hall.
Henry Hallam, Esq., F.R.S.
Terrick Hamilton, Esq.
William Richard Hamilton, Esq., F.R.S.
George Hammond, Esq.
Lieutenant Harding, R.N.
The Right Honourable Sir Henry Hardinge, K.C.B.

Right Honourable Earl of Hardwicke, K.G., F.R.S.
210 Major-General Hardwicke, E.I.C. F.R.S.
Captain T. G. Harriott.
George Harrison, Esq., F.R.S.
T. Charles Harrison, Esq., F.G.S.
William Harrison, Esq., F.R.S.
George Hathorn, Esq.
Robert William Hay, Esq., F.R.S.
George Heald, Esq.
The Right Hon. John Charles Herries, M.P.
Lord Marcus Hill.
220 H. W. Hobhouse, Esq.
John Cam Hobhouse, Esq., M.P., F.R.S.
Thomas Hoblyn, Esq., F.R.S.
James Hoffman, Esq.
John Hogg, Esq.
Robert Holford, Esq., F.R.S.
Doctor Holland, F.R.S.
Richard Hollier, Esq.
Professor Hooker, F.R.S.
Captain Horsburgh, E.I.C., F.R.S.
230 Vice-Admiral the Honourable Sir Henry Hotham, K.C.B.
Vice-Admiral Sir Wm. Hotham, K.C.B.
John Hudson, Esq.
Rev. Dr. Hunt, F.S.A.
The Right Hon. William Huskisson, M.P.

Sir R. H. Inglis, Bart., M.P., F.R.S.
Captain the Honourable Charles Leonard Irby, R.N.
Lieutenant Thomas J. Irvine, R.N.

Richard Jenkins, Esq.
William Jerdan, Esq., F.R.S.
240 John Heneage Jesse, Esq.
Charles Jones, Esq.
Thomas Jones, Esq., F.H.S.
Colonel Jones, R.E., A.D.C. to the King.
R. W. Jones, Esq.
William Jones, Esq., F.H.S.

Captain Kater, V.P.R.S.
Joseph Kay, Esq.
Lieutenant Edward Kendall, R.N.
Rev. J. Kenrick.
250 *Major the Honourable George Keppel*, F.S.A.

H. Bellenden Ker, Esq., F.R.S.
H. T. Kilbee, Esq.
Captain Philip Parker King, R.N., F.R.S.
Chas. Knight, Esq.
H. Gally Knight, Esq., F.L.S.

Aylmer Bourke Lambert, Esq., F.R.S.
Edward Copleston, Lord Bishop of Llandaff, F.S.A.
Lieutenant Larcom, R.E.
William J. Law, Esq.
260 Colonel W. M. Leake, F.R.S.
John Lee, Esq., LL.D., F.S.A.
Stephen Lee, Esq.
Thomas Legh, Esq., F.R.S.
John Lindley, Esq., F.R.S.
J. A. Lloyd, Esq.
William Horton Lloyd, Esq.
Edward Hawke Locker, Esq., F.R.S.
Professor Long.
John Wilson Lowry, Esq.
270 J. W. Lubbock, Esq., F.R.S.
George Lyall, Esq.
Charles Lyell, Esq., F.R.S.
John M'Arthur, Esq.
Major J. Macfarlane, E.I.C.
Alexander Mackenzie, Esq.
Harry Mackenzie, Esq.
The Right Hon. Sir James Mackintosh, M.P., F.R.S.
Edward Magrath, Esq.
Captain Mangles, R.N., F.R.S.
280 Edward Marjoribanks, Esq.
William Marsden, Esq., F.R.S.
Alexander Marsden, Esq.
J. Marshall, Esq., M.P.
Rev. J. W. Martin.
Joseph Martineau, Esq., F.H.S.
G. F. Mathison, Esq.
Doctor Maton, F.R.S.
Acheson Maxwell, Esq.
George Mayer, Esq.
290 The Right Hon. Lord Viscount Melville, K.T., F.R.S.
Viscount Milton, F.R.S.
Dr. Charles Mitchell.
Captain M'Konochie, R.N.
Sir Charles Monck, Bart.
Moses Montefiore, Esq.
Aristides Franklin Mornay, Esq., F.L.S.
James Moyes, Esq.
Captain R. Z. Mudge, R.E.
Captain William Mudge, R.N.

300 Roderick Impey Murchison, Esq., F.R.S.
Thomas Murdoch, Esq., F.R.S.
Lieutenant Hastings Murphy, R.E.
Lt.-Gen. the Right Hon. Sir George Murray, G.C.B., F.R.S.
John Murray, Esq.
T. Laurie Murray, Esq.
T. M. Musgrave, Esq.
T. Myers, Esq., LL.D.
Captain Lord Napier, R.N.
Professor Napier.
310 Sir George Nayler, K.G.H., F.R.S.
William Nicholson, Esq.
George Nicholson, Esq.
Alexander Nimmo, Esq.
Lord Nugent, M.P., F.S.A.

Nathaniel Ogle, Esq.
George Ormerod, Esq., F.S.A.
Thomas J. Ormerod, Esq.
The Right Hon. Sir Gore Ouseley, Bart., G.C.H., F.R.S.
Doctor Outram, R.N.
320 Captain William Fitzwilliam Owen, R.N., F.H.S.

F. Page, Esq., F.G.S.
G. Palmer, Esq.
Lieutenant-Colonel Parker, R.A.
Captain Sir William Edward Parry, R.N., F.R.S.
Francis Charles Parry, Esq., M.D., F.R.S.
Lieut.-Colonel Pasley, R.E., F.R.S.
J. Pattison, Esq.
The Right Hon. Sir Robert Peel, M.P., F.R.S.
J. H. Pelly, Governor Hudson's Bay Company, F.H.S.
330 C. R. Pemberton, Esq.
Richard Penn, Esq., F.R.S.
W. Hazledine Pepys, Esq., F.R.S.
T. Erskine Perry, Esq., F.G.S.
Louis Hayes Petit, Esq., F.R.S.
Sir Thomas Phillips, Bart., F.R.S.
Captain Charles Phillips, R.N., F.R.S.
Frederick Pigou, Esq.
John Plowes, Esq.
Rev. C. Plumer.
340 Admiral Sir Charles Morice Pole, Bart., G.C.B., F.R.S.
The Hon. W. Ponsonby, M.P.
Charles Pope, Esq.
Lord Porchester.
Lieutenant Portlock, R.E., F.G.S.

Charles Potts, Esq.
Benjamin Price, Esq.
Captain W. Jones Prowse, R.N.
Captain Lord Prudhoe, R.N., F.R.S.

John Radcliffe, Esq.
350 Crosier Raine, Esq.
C. Reading, Esq.
George Rennie, Esq., F.R.S.
John Rennie, Esq., F.R.S.
Rev. George C. Renouard.
Lieutenant Renwick, R.E.
Dr. Richardson, R.N., F.R.S.
Captain Robe, R.E.
Lieutenant F. H. Robe.
Lieutenant T. Congreve Robe, R.A.
360 Lieutenant C. G. Robinson, R.N.
Rear-Admiral G. Tremayne Rodd, C.B.
P. M. Roget, Esq., M.D., Sec. R.S.
George Rose, Esq.
John Rouse, Esq.
C. E. Rumbold, Esq. M.P., F.S.A.
Lord John Russell, M.P.
His Grace the Duke of Rutland.

Joseph Sabine, Esq., F.R.S.
The Right Hon. Lord St. Helens, G.C.H., F.S.A.
370 Marquis of Salisbury.
Major H. Scott, R.A.
Claude E. Scott, Esq.
Professor Sedgewick, F.R.S., P.G.S.
The Earl of Selkirk.
Lord Selsey, F.R.S.
Nassau William Senior, Esq.
Lieutenant W. L. Sheringham, R.N.
Captain W. H. Shirreff, R.N.
Henry T. Short, Esq.
380 Lord Skelmersdale, F.H.S.
Lieutenant M. A. Slater, R.N.
Marquis of Sligo, F.H.S.
John Smirnove, Esq., F.R.S.
Lieut.-Colonel Sir Charles Smith, C.B., R.E.
George Smith, Esq., F.L.S.
James Smith, Esq.
Joseph Smith, Esq., F.R.S.
Peter Smith, Esq.
William Smith, Esq., M.P., F.R.S.
390 Captain W. H. Smyth, R.N., F.R.S.
Thomas Snodgrass, Esq., F.R.S.
Captain Sotheby, R.N.
William Sotheby, Esq., F.R.S.
Sir James South, F.R.S., P.A.S.
Alexander Young Spearman, Esq.

Ralph Spearman, Esq.
The Right Hon. Earl Spencer, K.G., F.R.S.
Captain the Hon. F. Spencer, C.B., R.N.
A. Spottiswoode, Esq., M.P.
400 R. Spottiswoode, Esq.
Rev. Edward Stanley.
Major-General the Hon. G. A. Chetwynd Stapylton.
Sir George Staunton, Bart., F.R.S.
Daniel Stephenson, Esq.

Earl Talbot, K.P., F.R.S.
Lieutenant-General Sir Herbert Taylor, G.C.H.
John Taylor, Esq.
Richard Taylor, Esq., F.S.A.
Colonel Thatcher, E.I.C.
410 J. Deas Thomson, Esq., F.R.S.
Lord Chief-Justice Tindal.
Charles Tindal, Esq.
Colonel James Tod.
Colonel Trench, M.P.
W. C. Trevelyan, Esq., F.G.S.
Sir Coutts Trotter, Bart.

A. B. Vallé, Esq.
Comte Valsamachi.
Colonel Sir C. Broke Vere, K.C.B.
420 *Col. Sir H. C. Verney, Bart.*, F.G.S.
Lord Vernon, F.R.S.
Captain Vetch, R.E., F.G.S.
N. A. Vigors, Esq., F.R.S.

Horace Waddington, Esq.
James Walker, Esq.
Mr. John Walker.
Mr. John Walker, Jun.
H. G. Ward, Esq.
John Ward, Esq., M.P.
430 John Ward, Esq., F.H.S.
William Ward, Esq., M.P.
Lieutenant Washington, R.N.
Sir Frederick B. Watson, K.C.H., F.R.S.
Ralph Watson, Esq., F.S.A.
J. Weale, Esq.
Thomas Webb, Esq.
His Grace the Duke of Wellington, K.G.
Major Wells, R.E.
John Weyland, Esq., F.R.S.
440 Rev. W. Whewell, F.R.S., Prof. Min. Trin. Col. Camb.
Frederick White, Esq.
The Honourable Richard Bootle Wilbraham, M.P.

William Williams, Esq., F.S.A.
Rev. Dr. Williams, Master of Winchester College.
Charles M. Willich, Esq.
John Wilson, Esq., F.H.S.
John Wilson, Esq.
L. P. Wilson, Esq.
Thomas Wilson, Esq.
450 Alderman Winchester, F.H.S.
William Wingfield, Esq.
Sir Alexander Wood.

Captain W. Woodley, R.N.
John Woolmore, Esq., D.M.T.H.
John Wray, Esq.
Sir Jeffry Wyatville, R.A., F.R.S.
Mr. James Wyld.
Major Wylde, R.A.

The Right Honourable Charles Yorke, F.R.S.
460 James Young, Esq.

4th August, 1830.

FELLOWS IN THE LIST OF 4TH AUGUST, 1830,

LIVING

ON THE 51ST ANNIVERSARY,

1881.

W. F. Ainsworth, Esq.
The Earl of Albemarle (then Major Keppel).
Lieut.-Gen. Sir James E. Alexander, C.B.
John Pelly Atkins, Esq.
George Bentham, Esq.
The Earl of Enniskillen (then Viscount Cole).
Francis H. Dickinson, Esq.
Admiral C. R. Drinkwater Bethune, C.B. (then Captain Drinkwater, R.N.).
Rev. H. Greswell.
Sir Moses Montefiore, *Bart.*
Sir T. Erskine Perry.
General W. T. Renwick, R.E.
Sir Harry Verney, *Bart.*, M.P.
James Wyld, Esq.

CHAPTER VI.

PRESIDENTS AND SECRETARIES

OF THE

ROYAL GEOGRAPHICAL SOCIETY, 1830 TO 1850.

THE new Society commenced its operations under most favourable auspices. King William IV. not only became its Patron, but was also pleased to grant an annual donation of fifty guineas to constitute a premium for the encouragement and promotion of geographical science and discovery. His Majesty desired that the title should be the "Royal Geographical Society."

The African Association was merged in the Geographical Society, and Mr. Bartle Frere, as its representative, became a Member of the Council. The Palestine Association, which had been formed early in the century, also resolved that, as the Geographical Society embraced, in its views, purposes similar to those for which the Palestine Association had been instituted, their funds, papers, and books should be made over to the Society, to be employed as the Council may think fit for the promotion of geographical discovery.

In 1832 a Geographical Society was formed at Bombay, having in view the elucidation of the geography of Western India and the surrounding countries, and mainly supported by the distinguished surveyors of the Indian Navy. The Bombay Society, in a letter from the Secretary dated the 6th of June, 1832, desired to form a junction with that of London, and to be considered a branch of it, not only that it might ensure its own stability, but that it might acquire additional usefulness and efficiency from the patronage and counsels of the European institution. The Bombay branch expressed a wish to receive instructions from the London Society in reference to the general plan of operations which it should adopt. This application met with a cordial response, and the two Societies continued to co-operate and to work together harmoniously.*

---

* The Bombay Society did very good geographical service in its day, and published many valuable memoirs. Its Presidents were:—

1831–38. Captain Sir Charles Malcolm, R.N.
1838–49. Captain Daniel Ross, I.N., F.R.S.
1849–51. Mr. John B. Willoughby, C.S.
1851–52. Commodore Lushington, R.N.

The first President of the Royal Geographical Society was Viscount Goderich, then Secretary of State for the Colonies; and the then Chancellor of the Exchequer, Lord Althorp, became one of the first Council; while other Members of the Reform Ministry joined the Society. It was a friendly neutral ground for both sides of the House, the Duke of Wellington, Sir Robert Peel, and Lord Ellenborough enrolling their names as geographers at the same time. Frederick John Robinson was the second son of Lord Grantham. He was Chancellor of the Exchequer in Lord Liverpool's Administration from 1823 to 1827, was created Viscount Goderich in 1827, and, after the death of Mr. Canning, he was Prime Minister from August 1827 to January 1828. In the Reform Ministry Lord Goderich was Secretary of State for the Colonies and, at the request of Sir John Barrow, he undertook the duties of first President of the Geographical Society from 1830 to 1833.

A goodly company of zealous colleagues rallied round our first President. There were three of the original founders of the Raleigh Club, Sir Arthur de Capell Broke, Colonel Leake, and Captain Mangles; and four members of the Foundation Committee, Sir John Barrow, Sir John Hobhouse, Mr. Robert Brown, and Mr. Mountstuart Elphinstone. Of statesmen there were Lord Althorp and Sir George Murray. Sailors mustered strong. The gallant Sir John Franklin was a Vice-President, and in the Council were Lord Prudhoe, Captain Beaufort, Captain Smyth, Captain Basil Hall—the charming writer— and Captain Mangles.

Captain Francis Beaufort's name will ever be held in veneration by geographers. It appears in the list of our first Council, and in nearly every subsequent list until his death. During his long and honourable career he zealously and staunchly upheld the interests of geography, and maintained the most cordial relations between the Society and the Hydrographic Department of the Admiralty. On the death of poor

---

1853–58. Commodore Sir H. Leake, k.c.b., r.n.
1858–62. Commodore Wellesley, c.b., r.n.
1862–65. Mr. W. E. Frere, c.s.
1865–66. Captain T. Black (*P. & O. Co.*)
1866–67. Mr. Claude Erskine, c.s.
1867–69. Lieut.-General Sir R. Napier, k.c.b.
1869–73. Mr. Justice Gibbs.

The Secretaries were Dr. Heddle, 1831–42; Dr. Buist, 1842–58; and Dr. Kennelly, 1858–73. The Society published 19 volumes of Transactions with maps, and in 1866 Dr. Kennelly completed an index of the first 17 volumes. But the abolition of the Indian Navy was a fatal blow to the Bombay Geographical Society. In January 1873 it came to an end. It was amalgamated with the Bombay Branch of the Asiatic Society, forming a Geographical Section of it, with a special Sub-Committee and Secretary.

Dalrymple in 1808, he was succeeded as Hydrographer by Captain Hurd, who obtained sanction for employing Captain Beaufort to examine the coast of Karamania in the Levant, while Lieut. W. H. Smyth was employed with the Sicilian flotilla. Captain Hurd died in 1823. Sir Edward Parry was Hydrographer from 1825 to 1828, and in the latter year Captain Beaufort succeeded to a post which he held with great benefit to the service and to geography for twenty-six years.

James Horsburgh sat with Beaufort at our first Council Board. Commencing his career as a cabin boy, Horsburgh rose to the command of an Indiaman, and after many years of indefatigable labour in collecting materials, he completed his 'East India Directory,' which passed through many editions and, as newly edited by our Associate Captain Taylor, is still the recognised guide for the navigation of the eastern seas. Horsburgh's superintendence of the publication of charts at the India House commenced in 1810, and continued until his death in 1836. He was an ardent supporter of the Society, and was a benefactor to our library in its first commencement.

Rennell, one of the greatest geographers of this century, died only a few months before our Society was inaugurated. Yet he was represented on the Council by his son-in-law, Admiral Sir J. Tremaine Rodd, c.b., who, with Lady Rodd, had assisted Major Rennell in the preparation of his current charts. Sir John Rodd was a benefactor to our library when in its infancy. He died in 1838. In 1844 Lady Rodd presented the Society with a medallion of her father Major Rennell.

Among men of science and scholars, Lord Goderich was supported by Mr. Baily, Mr. Greenough, Mr. R. W. Hamilton, and Mr. George Long, to whom Roderick Murchison was added in 1833. Mr. Francis Baily was one of our first Trustees, and afterwards a Vice-President; but he was better known as the mainspring of the Astronomical Society, and for his catalogues of stars and Life of Flamsteed. He died in 1845. Greenough and Hamilton became Presidents, and George Long was afterwards a Secretary of the Society. In topography the Council was represented by Mr. John Britton, and by Mr. Brockedon the artist and Alpine explorer.

Such were the men who assisted the first President in the first dawn of our Society. Lord Goderich occupied the Chair from 1830 to 1833; when he was succeeded from 1833 to 1835 by Sir George Murray, the Duke's Quartermaster-General during the Peninsula war, and Secretary of State for the Colonies from 1828 to 1830. Sir George died at the age of seventy-four in 1846.

Sir John Barrow himself, who had been created a Baronet in

1835, was our third President, from 1835 to 1837. To this great man the Society mainly owes its existence, and its early prosperity. He looked upon it as likely to confer a lasting benefit on his country, and to be the efficient means of amassing and disseminating valuable information. He himself was for many years the leading spirit, in this country, in the despatch of expeditions of discovery, and geographers will ever hold his name in reverence. His very numerous geographical articles in the 'Quarterly Review,' during a long series of years, had materially increased the interest taken in geography; and thus the 'Quarterly Review' may be considered as an active agent in leading to the foundation of the Society. Those who have had the privilege of perusing the private correspondence of naval men of that time, especially the letters of the gallant Fitzjames, know that the career of the Secretary of the Admiralty was marked by endless acts of thoughtful kindness, as well as by the industry and ability with which he served his country. After having been Secretary of the Admiralty for forty years, Sir John Barrow retired in 1845, and died full of years and honours in 1849. A portrait of Sir John Barrow hangs in the Council Room of the Society. It is a copy of the picture by Jackson, the original of which is in the collection of Mr. John Murray.

The first Secretary of the Society, who organised the opening work and edited the early volumes of our Journal, was a sailor, Captain Alexander Maconochie, R.N., K.H. This officer entered the navy in 1803, and after seeing active service on the coast of Spain and in the West Indies, became a Lieutenant in 1809. He was a prisoner from that year until 1814, having been obliged to surrender to the Dutch fleet in the Texel, and after the war he served under Sir Alexander Cochrane until he was promoted. At the foundation of the Society, Captain Maconochie became Secretary, an office which he held until 1836. He had been among the foremost promoters of the Society. As Secretary he prepared all the business, had the immediate management of the finance under the Treasurer, superintended the publications, ensured accuracy by a rigid scrutiny, and abstracted the most valuable matter from numerous documents too voluminous to be published entire. For these services, and for his sound judgment, even temper, and untiring zeal, he received the hearty thanks of the Council on his retirement in 1836. He had accepted an appointment in Tasmania, was for some time Secretary to the Government of that colony, and afterwards Superintendent of the penal settlement at Norfolk Island. Captain Maconochie died in 1861. His colleague, as Honorary and Foreign Secretary, was the

Rev. George Cecil Renouard, who held the appointment for sixteen years, from 1830 to 1846. In early life he had been Chaplain to the Embassy at Constantinople, and afterwards to the Factory at Smyrna, and on returning to Cambridge in 1814 he was elected Professor of Arabic. His acquaintance with the geography and languages of the East made his services most valuable to this and other societies, and he gave his time and talents, in unstinting measure, to correct and improve our publications, and especially to promote a uniform system of orthography. Sir Roderick Murchison said that " Mr. Renouard's kindly manners and true modesty endeared him to every one on the Council with whom he acted, and when he spoke on any moot point, he was as logical in his deductions as he was accurate in his facts." As Rector of Swanscombe near Gravesend, he was an excellent parish priest, and he died there on February 15th, 1867, aged 87.

As a successor to Captain Maconochie, our President Sir John Barrow secured for the Society the able and zealous services of another naval officer. John Washington was born in 1800, and entering the navy in 1812, he saw much active service in the waters of the Chesapeake and on the American coasts. He was promoted when serving in the *Forth* on the Pacific Station, and got leave to come home from Valparaiso by crossing the Andes to Mendoza, and thence over the Pampas to Buenos Ayres. Afterwards, while serving in the Mediterranean, Washington explored the interior of Morocco, fixing several positions astronomically. He became a Commander in 1833, and Secretary of the Geographical Society in 1836. In this position he infused vigour into our proceedings, and greatly improved our publications, labouring assiduously with the assistance of only a single clerk. It was Washington who introduced the practice of annually reviewing the progress of geography in the past year. He prepared two such addresses for 1837 and 1838, and it was this initiative which led to the delivery of annual addresses by the Presidents of the Society.

Our fourth President occupied the chair, during his first term of office, from 1837 to 1839. Mr. William Richard Hamilton was born in 1777, and was educated at Harrow and Cambridge, where he acquired thorough classical knowledge. In 1799 he entered the diplomatic service as Private Secretary to Lord Elgin when he went to Constantinople, and in 1801, on the evacuation by the French, he was sent to Egypt to negotiate the terms of peace. He then obtained the cession of several works of Egyptian art, including the famous trilingual stone of Rosetta. In 1802 Lord Elgin obtained the gift of the Parthenon marbles from the Porte. Mr. Hamilton was conveying them to England when the ship was wrecked off Cerigo, and these treasures were submerged, but thanks to the zeal and perseverance of our late President they were rescued from the deep, and have long been among the chief ornaments of the British Museum. In 1809 Mr. Hamilton became Under-Secretary of State for Foreign Affairs, a post which he occupied until 1822, when he was appointed Minister at Naples. In 1825 he retired from public life, and gave himself up to the pursuits of literature and science. He was an early member of the Raleigh Club, was Vice-President of the Society in 1831, on the Council in 1836, and was elected President in 1838. In the first year of his Presidency he set the example of reading an Anniversary Address from the chair, which custom, never since departed from, has been one important means of ensuring the usefulness of our labours, and exciting a general interest in all geographical questions. Previously the Society had been furnished with annual addresses on the progress of geography by the Secretaries, but Mr. Hamilton assumed this duty himself, and his able and admirably conceived discourse of May 1838 is the Inaugural Presidential Address.

After developing the links which connect geography with the other sciences, and with history and statistics, Mr. Hamilton thus proceeds:—" But the real geographer becomes at once an ardent traveller, indifferent whether he plunges into the burning heats of tropical deserts, plains, or swamps, launches his boat on the unknown stream, or endures the hardships of an Arctic climate, amidst perpetual snows and ice, or scales the almost inaccessible heights of Chimborazo or the Himálaya. Buoyed up in his greatest difficulties by the consciousness that he is labouring for the good of his fellow-creatures, he feels delight in the reflection that he is upon ground untrodden by man, that every step he makes will serve to enlarge the sphere of human knowledge, and that he is laying up for himself a store of gratitude and fame." Lord Ripon, in a subsequent Address, said that these stirring words were followed up by such clear and precise analyses of all the prominent geographical researches of the year as to fix a high standard for the discourses of all future Presidents. When those researches had reference to archæology and numismatics, or to any point of ancient history, then it was that Mr. Hamilton shone out as the most powerful comparative geographer, and his hearers felt the true value of the application of his learning.

With the aid of Captain Washington and Mr. Renouard, our accomplished fourth President gave renewed vigour to the Society's operations. He was President for a second term, from 1841 to 1843, and Trustee from 1846 to 1857. He was also a very active Trustee of the British Museum, and managed the affairs of the Dilettanti Club until within a week of his death. Mr. Hamilton died at the great age of 82, in 1859.

Mr. Hamilton was succeeded in the chair of our Society by one of its greatest benefactors, Mr. George Bellas Greenough, who was a Vice-President when the Society was founded, and President from 1839 to 1841. Born in 1778, Mr. Greenough was educated at Eton and Cambridge, and in 1798 went to Göttingen, where the eloquence of Blumenbach attracted him to the study of natural science; and he afterwards acquired the elements of geology and mineralogy under Werner at Freiburg. From 1802 to 1807 he was actively connected with the Royal Institution, and in the latter year he founded the Geological Society and became its first President. His chief geological work was the map of England and Wales, and he also published a ' Critical Examination of the first principles of Geology,' which deservedly attracted much attention at the time. In 1824 Mr. Greenough built a villa in the Regent's Park, where he formed a fine library and a large collection of maps and charts. He was one of the leaders of the first British Association Meeting at York in 1831, and in the same year was elected a Vice-President of our Society, an office which he held until he became President in 1839. His Anniversary Addresses were worthy to follow those of Mr. Hamilton, and they can have no higher praise. After resigning the chair, he was either a Vice-President or Member of the Council until his death in 1854. By his will Mr. Greenough bequeathed his fine collection of geographical books, maps, and charts, to the Society of which he had been so active and useful a member from its foundation until his own death; and he added a sum of 500*l.* to defray the expense of accommodating and arranging the collection. Lord Ellesmere, in his address, concluded his notice by saying that it should be the pride of geographers to record their admiration of the deep thinking philosopher and true geographer, George Bellas Greenough. His Lordship also suggested that a bust of Greenough should be placed near the collections with which he so munificently enriched the Society; and this proposal was promptly adopted. The bust of Greenough, with that of Murchison, stands in the Society's map room.

Mr. W. R. Hamilton succeeded Mr. Greenough, and during this second term of his Presidentship the Society lost the services of its Secretary, Captain Washington. That accomplished surveyor was needed afloat, and he resigned the Secretaryship in 1841. He was appointed to the *Black Eagle*, in which vessel he brought the King of Prussia to England,

and soon afterwards was promoted to post rank. Up to 1847 he was surveying in the *Blazer*, and in 1855 he succeeded Sir Francis Beaufort as Hydrographer to the Admiralty; maintaining the same spirit of activity, action, and order in the surveying service, by following in the footsteps of his revered predecessor. He lost no opportunity presented to him by his official position of rendering essential service to the Society, and of promoting every geographical expedition. He was especially energetic in connection with the search for Sir John Franklin's Expedition, and gave steady and cordial support to Lady Franklin through all her efforts to discover the fate of her husband and his gallant followers. Exhausted by overwork in his office, the Hydrographer died in 1864 at Havre, while seeking rest by travelling abroad.

Captain Washington was succeeded by Colonel Jackson, who was our Secretary from 1841 to 1847. Originally in the East India Company's service, this officer volunteered for the Russian army in 1814, and rose in it to the rank of Colonel of the Staff Corps. When he retired, he received the appointment of Russian Commissioner in London for the Department of Manufactures, and he combined with this duty the Secretaryship of our Society. As a geographer his labours were very useful. He published 'Aide Mémoire du Voyageur' in 1834, which contains many hints and instructions for young travellers; the useful manual, 'What to observe, or the Traveller's Remembrancer;' and also a suggestive paper on 'Picturesque Descriptions.' As Secretary he edited the Journals with ability, and completed an index of the first ten volumes: and he wrote a glossary of geographical terms, a memoir on cartography, and the 'Military Topography of Europe,' edited from the French of Lavallée, which in his hands became almost a new work. He thus devoted many of the best years of his life to advancing our science, and, retiring from the Secretaryship in 1847, he died on March 16th, 1853, in the sixty-third year of his age.

Mr. Hamilton was succeeded in 1843 by Mr. Roderick I. Murchison. It has already been seen that the name of our great President did not appear in the list of our first Council, although he was an active Member of the Foundation Committee. When the Geographical Society was founded, Murchison was just commencing his memorable investigations connected with the Silurian formations. He began this work at Llandeilo in the spring of 1831, and in September he was at Bishopthorpe, active in the foundation of the British Association at York. He continued to work at the geology of South Wales, with ardour and marvellous insight, during the succeeding years. In July 1835 he first proposed the name "Silurian" for the formation, in 1836 he and Sedgwick identified the Devonian rocks with the Old Red Sandstone of Scotland, and in 1838 his great work 'The Silurian System' was published.   In 1839 Lady Murchison bought the house at 16, Belgrave Square, which was for so many years the centre of kindly hospitality for geographers, where young aspirants received help and encouragement, and the old were welcomed with generous appreciation.   From 1840 to 1843 Murchison was hard at work, with his colleagues De Verneuil and Von Keyserling, in Eastern Europe, investigating the geology of Russia and the Ural Mountains, and he had only just returned from this important service, when he accepted the office of President of the Geographical Society for the first time.   But, even in his busiest and most absorbing geological years, he had never been long absent from the work of our Society.   He was on the Council in 1833, Vice-President in 1836, on the Council again in 1838, Vice-President in 1842, and was elected President in May 1843.   His Vice-Presidents were his two predecessors, Mr. Hamilton and Mr. Greenough, with Lord Colchester and Sir John Rennie; and among his Council were Sir John Barrow, Captain Beaufort the Hydrographer, Charles Enderby the great promoter of Antarctic Voyages, Bartle Frere, George Long, Sir Charles Malcolm, and Sir Woodbine Parish.   His Secretaries were Colonel Jackson and Mr. Renouard.

While still deeply immersed in the preparation of his work on Russia, Murchison delivered his first Anniversary Address to our Society on May 27th, 1844.   On that occasion Sir John Franklin and Sir George Back became Vice-Presidents, and Captains Smyth and Washington joined the Council ; while Sir Henry de la Beche, the Director of the Geological Survey, was welcomed by Murchison as a new Fellow of the Society.   The most interesting feature of the new President's first address was the account he gave of the Ural Mountains and the gold produce of Siberia.   In his second address he announced the departure from England of our gallant Vice-President, Sir John Franklin, on the memorable expedition during which he died while "forging the last link of the North-West Passage." Murchison was knighted in 1846, the year after vacating the President's chair at the end of his first term.

The next President was Lord Colchester, who was born in 1798, was educated at Westminster, and went to sea in 1811. He saw active service during the war, both in the Mediterranean and on the coast of North America, and in 1816 went to China in the *Alceste* with Lord Amherst's Mission.   He accompanied the Ambassador in his journey through China, and drew the sketches which illustrated the history of the embassy.   As

Commander he had the *Racehorse* during the Greek war in the Levant, and was posted in 1826. He was in command of the *Volage* on both the east and west coasts of South America, but retired from active service when she was paid-off. Joining our Society in 1836, he was on the Council in 1840, and President from 1845 to 1847. He continued as Vice-President, or as a Member of the Council, with scarcely any intermission, until 1866, the year before his death.

During Lord Colchester's term of office it became necessary, owing to want of funds, to reduce the expenses. The Society's financial embarrassment at this period was caused by excessive expenditure on expeditions as compared with the funds at its command, and was increased by the serious commercial crisis of 1846. The Secretaries, Colonel Jackson and Mr. Renouard, resigned, and it was resolved that there should be two honorary Secretaries, and an Assistant-Secretary on a reduced salary. This new system came into operation when Lord Colchester vacated the chair in 1847. At this time a scheme was submitted to the Council for giving more definite direction to its work. It was in the form of a privately printed pamphlet, " On the Organization of geographical labour," and it received the attention of a Special Committee. But the state of the Society's affairs was not then favourable to the proposal.

In 1847 Mr. William J. Hamilton became President, Mr. George Long and Major Shadwell Clerke the Honorary Secretaries, and Dr. Humble the paid Assistant-Secretary.

Mr. William John Hamilton, the son of the former President Mr. W. R. Hamilton, was born in London on July 5th, 1805. His education was commenced at Charter-house and completed at Göttingen, and in 1827 he entered the diplomatic service as Attaché at Madrid. In 1835 Mr. Hamilton turned his attention to geology and obtained experience in field work with Sir Roderick Murchison. Soon afterwards he undertook an expedition, the main object of which was to investigate the comparative geography of Asia Minor. His ' Researches in Asia Minor, Pontus, and Armenia,' were published in two volumes, in 1842. For his valuable labours he was honoured with the Founder's Medal of our Society in 1843. He was our President from 1847 to 1849, and was twice President of the Geological Society. He was also Conservative Member for Newport from 1841 to 1847, and Chairman of the Great Indian Peninsula Railway Company. He was a most enlightened and zealous supporter of our Society, and continued on the Council until his death on June 27th, 1867. Mr. Hamilton was the father-in-law of one of our best and noblest naval Associates, the late Commodore Goodenough, whose father was also on our Council.

Of the two Secretaries elected in 1847, Mr. George Long was an original Member, and had constantly been a Member of Council or Vice-President. Born at Poulton, in Lancashire, in 1800, he was of Trinity College, Cambridge, and was a Wrangler in 1822. He was afterwards a Professor in the London University, and took an active part in promoting the work of the Society for the diffusion of Useful Knowledge. He was one of the Editors of the 'Penny Cyclopædia,' and the principal contributor to the valuable geographical articles in that work. A profound classical scholar, Mr. Long was the translator of Marcus Aurelius and Epictetus, and he contributed a paper on the Rivers of Susiana to our 'Journal' in 1842. After retiring from the Secretaryship, he was on the Council until 1851; and he died at Portfield, near Chichester, on August 10th, 1879. Major Shadwell Clerke, the Foreign Secretary, was an officer of great talent. He entered the army in 1804, and served with credit and gallantry in the Peninsular War, but he was wounded before Burgos, which resulted in the loss of a limb. He was actuated by a true zeal for geography, and an earnest desire to infuse a love for science into the services. With the latter object in view he ably conducted the 'United Service Journal,' and was one of the founders, with Admiral Smyth, of the United Service Museum. Major Shadwell Clerke was on our Council in 1845-46, Foreign Secretary in 1847-48, and was also Treasurer and Secretary of the Raleigh Club. He died in 1849.

Mr. Hamilton, with the aid of these two zealous and accomplished Secretaries, ably presided over our affairs. But circumstances were, at that time, against success, and the prospects of the Society were not encouraging. Mr. Hamilton himself took a broad and enlightened view of our work. He said in his last Address;—" that it is only by a complete union of scientific truth with popular interest that we can hope to see the science of geography take that hold of the public mind in this country, which shall ensure it the support necessary to secure its efficiency, and to maintain it in a healthful and powerful condition."

It was by a steady adherence to the principle thus laid down by Mr. Hamilton, that the Society's progress was ensured, and that its subsequent prosperity became so great. The work of retrenchment, preparatory to very energetic measures to increase our numbers and efficiency, was commenced by the next President, Admiral Smyth, whose bold and yet prudent management formed the turning-point of the Society's history.

CHAPTER VII.

PRESIDENTS AND SECRETARIES

OF THE

ROYAL GEOGRAPHICAL SOCIETY,

1851 TO 1881.

ADMIRAL W. H. SMYTH, C.B., who was President from 1849 to 1851, was the restorer of the prosperity of the Society. He was descended from Captain John Smith, whose valour and genius were so instrumental in the colonisation of Virginia. His father, Mr. Joseph Smyth, had estates in New Jersey, which were confiscated when the American Revolution succeeded, owing to his staunch loyalty to the old country. His only son, born on January 21st, 1788, entered the navy in 1805, and saw active war service in the China and Indian seas. In 1810 he was in command of a large gunboat in the defence of Cadiz, and was often engaged and under heavy fire from the French forts. As a reward for his excellent services at Cadiz, and for a valuable survey he had made of the Isla de Leon and adjacent coast, he was promoted to the rank of Lieutenant in 1813, and was sent to command a flotilla employed in the defence of Sicily. He executed some most valuable surveys, entirely through his own resources, for which he was made Commander in 1815. His 'Atlas of Sicily,' with a memoir, was published soon afterwards. From this time he was, for several years, actively engaged on surveys in the Mediterranean and Adriatic, first in the *Aid*, and from 1821 in the *Adventure*. His labours raised him to the first rank among maritime surveyors, and Sir Francis Beaufort, the Hydrographer, wrote to him : " The more I see of your Mediterranean Surveys, the more I admire the extent of your labours, the perseverance of your researches, the acuteness of your details, and the taste with which you have executed the charts." Smyth was promoted to post rank in 1824, and paid-off the *Adventure* in November of the same year. As an astronomer and meteorologist he was an untiring observer to the close of his life. He erected an observatory at Bedford, and from 1828 to 1842 a meteorological register was kept there and at Cardiff, which was published monthly in the ' United Service Journal.' Admiral Smyth's equatorial refractor was one of the first constructed in this country, and with it he made a series of observations of the highest value. His astronomical instruments were afterwards transferred to Dr. Lee's observatory at Hartwell, and in 1844 Admiral Smyth published his 'Cycle of Celestial Objects.' As an astronomer this distinguished officer stood in the first rank, and he was also an accomplished antiquary and numismatist. He translated and edited the 'History of the New World,' by Girolamo Benzoni, in 1857, for the Hakluyt Society. But it is for his great attainments as a geographer and hydrographer that our Society cherishes his memory. We have seen that he was one of our Founders. He was constantly on our Council from 1830, and Vice-President in 1845. He was President of the Society from 1849 to 1850, and Vice-President again from 1851 to 1855. In 1853 he became one of our Gold Medallists for his valuable and very popular work on the Mediterranean, as well as for his surveys. He died, at the age of 77, in September 1865, and his portrait hangs in the Society's Council Room. Admiral Smyth's eldest son, Mr. Warington Smyth, served on our Council from 1871 to 1874.

The Honorary Secretaries, during Admiral Smyth's Presidency, were Mr. John Hogg and Mr. Trithen. Mr. Hogg of Norton House, near Stockton-upon-Tees, was a zealous antiquary and comparative geographer, who served on our Council for several years, and was one of the Secretaries from 1849 to 1851. He contributed several papers, chiefly on scriptural geography, and always continued to take an interest in our work until his death on September 16th, 1869. Mr. Trithen was an Oriental scholar, and, after serving for a short time as our Secretary, became Professor of Modern Languages at Oxford, where he died in 1855.

But the official from whom Admiral Smyth received the most active assistance was Dr. Norton Shaw, who was appointed Assistant-Secretary in 1849. His activity and zeal were chiefly exerted in procuring numerous additions to the list of Fellows. Norton Shaw was the son of an officer in the Danish service, and was born in one of the Danish West India Islands. He adopted the medical profession, and, before becoming our Assistant-Secretary, he had served as a surgeon under one of the great Companies of ocean steamers. Dr. Norton Shaw infused new life into the Society's proceedings, and through his energetic management the roll of our Fellows first assumed that progressive enlargement which continued long after his retirement. He was Assistant-Secretary for fourteen years, and soon after he resigned in 1863 Lord Stanley appointed him British Consul at Ste. Croix, where he died in 1868.

With such efficient aid, Admiral Smyth applied himself vigorously and boldly to the work of restoring the Society's affairs to a prosperous condition. Arrears were called in, and expenditure was reduced until it did not exceed the actual income. Very successful efforts were then made to increase the sterling value of the work, and the interest of the evening meetings, and the result was a considerable rise in the opinion, both at home and abroad, of the merit of the Society, and a rapid and unchecked increase in its numbers. In 1851 Admiral Smyth was able to announce that the Society was fairly afloat again, and his two spirit-stirring Addresses contributed, in no small degree, to this end. But no higher tribute could be offered to the value of Admiral Smyth's services than was done in the generous acknowledgment of his successor. Sir Roderick Murchison said :—" I found our geographical vessel had been so ably piloted through the shoals with which she had been surrounded, and that her crew was in so healthful and sound a condition, that it would be easy for me to steer her onwards with the same genial trade-wind in which her good commander had transferred her to me. The present flourishing condition of the Society is due to the skill and moral courage with which Admiral Smyth conducted your affairs, supported by an efficient Council, and by our zealous Assistant-Secretary Dr. Norton Shaw."

Admiral Smyth was succeeded by Sir Roderick Murchison, who had been knighted in 1846, and was President from 1851 to 1853. The Honorary Secretaries, during this period, were Colonel Philip Yorke and Dr. Hodgkin. Colonel Yorke, the son of the Hon. and Rev. Philip Yorke, Rector of Great Horkesley and Prebendary of Ely, was an officer in the Guards, and always took a warm interest in our work. He was on the Council from 1847 to 1849, Secretary in 1851, and Vice-President in 1853. Colonel Yorke died childless in 1874. Dr. Thomas Hodgkin, a Member of the Society of Friends, was born in 1798, and adopted the medical profession. He was Curator of the Museum at Guy's Hospital, and well known as a very active philanthropist. Dr. Hodgkin was one of our Honorary Secretaries from 1851 to 1862, and Foreign Secretary from 1862 to 1865. He accompanied Sir Moses Montefiore on a mission to Morocco, for the purpose of obtaining concessions in favour of the Jewish population, and he undertook two journeys to the Holy Land on philanthropic errands. Whilst on the second of these he was seized with the illness which terminated his useful life at Jaffa on April 5th, 1866.

During his second term of office, Sir Roderick was supported by a very strong geographical Council. His Vice-Presidents were the Earl of Ellesmere, Admiral Smyth, Sir Woodbine Parish, and Sir George Back. Among the most active supporters of the Society was Sir Woodbine Parish, who served almost continuously as Vice-President or Member of Council, from 1836 to 1853. He was for many years the regular referee on all subjects relating to South America. In the Council were four former Presidents besides Admiral Smyth; there were the Hydrographer Sir Francis Beaufort, Captain FitzRoy, the sailor Duke of Northumberland (formerly Lord Prudhoe), Colonel Sykes, Sir Gardner Wilkinson, Mr. Murray of the Foreign Office, Mr. Renouard and Mr. Hogg, the former Secretaries, Lieut. Raper, R.N., the author of the standard work on navigation, and John Arrowsmith the cartographer. Another great acquisition to the Council was Mr. A. G. Findlay. He served on it, almost continuously, from 1857 to 1874, and his assistance was highly valued by his colleagues, for his sound hydrographical knowledge.

Hitherto one branch of geographical work, which had been considered essential in the days of Hakluyt and of Purchas, and is even more important now to the comparative geographer, had not been provided for. While current work was collected and published, no progress had been made in the efficient editing of earlier labours in the geographical field. But in 1847 the HAKLUYT SOCIETY was formed for the purpose of printing rare and unpublished voyages and travels. This is a legitimate part of the work of geographers. For "the narratives of travellers and navigators make us acquainted with the earth, its inhabitants and productions; they exhibit the growth of intercourse among mankind, with its effects on civilization, and, while instructing, they at the same time awaken attention by recounting the toils and adventures of those who first explored unknown and distant regions." Sir Roderick at once perceived the importance of these objects, he became President of the Hakluyt Society at its foundation, and continued to hold that office until his lamented death, looking upon the Hakluyt as an auxiliary to the Geographical Society. In 1847 and 1848 the Secretary was Mr. Desborough Cooley, but in 1849 he was succeeded by Mr. R. H. Major of the Map Department in the British Museum, and by 1850 the Society was in that flourishing state in which it has ever since continued, performing work which is a needful supplement to that of the Royal Geographical Society.

Another important service to our science was done by Sir Roderick at this time. The papers on geographical subjects sent to the British Association had, since its foundation in 1831, been considered in the Geological Section. But in 1850 our President obtained a separate Geographical Section for us—Section E, and in 1851 the Geographical Section of the British Association assembled for the first time at Ipswich. The annual organization of this Section, after our own Session has come to a close, and its supply with original papers or reviews of work done, has ever since been an interesting and useful branch of the business of our Society.

Sir Roderick Murchison's Anniversary Addresses, during his second term, were distinguished for those painstaking analyses of the work of travellers, and generous recognitions of their merits, which have invested the whole series of his geographical discourses with permanent value. He also commenced those brief but lucid essays on some special point which subsequently formed an admirable feature of his Addresses. In 1852 and 1853 he discoursed on the great features of the African Continent, and on the physical geography of the ocean. Sir Roderick extended his private hospitality, in the most liberal manner, to all the members of the Society, and frequently afforded them the opportunity of meeting the most distinguished men of the day at his receptions in Belgrave Square. There can be no doubt that these *soirées* lent great support to the vigorous efforts of Dr. Norton Shaw in increasing the number of Fellows. This stimulating influence reached its highest point when the assemblies were held in the great art galleries of Lord Ellesmere and Lord Ashburton.

The next President, who occupied the chair from 1853 to 1855, was, from his position and his love for geography, most admirably fitted for the post. Lord Francis Egerton was born on January 1st, 1800, and, as second son of the first Duke of Sutherland, became heir to the Duke of Bridgewater and was created Earl of Ellesmere in 1846. Educated at Eton and distinguished at Oxford, he soon took a high place in the House of Commons, and was Secretary for Ireland in the Duke of Wellington's administration (1828–30). But Lord Ellesmere, during the course of his useful and well-spent life, showed a greater love for literature and the arts than for politics. Between 1834 and 1854 he contributed fifteen articles to the ' Quarterly Review,' and about half related to geographical research. In these charming essays he has discussed the manners and usages of the Japanese as told by the old Dutch writers, the chivalrous expedition of Rajah Brooke, and the researches of our Arctic and Antarctic explorers. Master of several languages, Lord Ellesmere was a poet by nature, and was thus able to put before his countrymen the thoughts of Goethe and of Schiller. Above all he was full of sympathy for the efforts of others, and, on several occasions, sustained with his purse men of genius who were labouring under difficulties, and who but for his timely aid could never have produced works which have taken a high place in science and letters.

In the first year of Lord Ellesmere's Presidency, that distinguished Surveyor, Captain Francis Price Blackwood was Honorary Secretary, with Dr. Hodgkin. In 1841 Captain Blackwood had been appointed to the *Fly*, to assign the true positions and exact limits to the Great Barrier Reef, which stretches along the north-eastern shore of Australia. In the four years that he was thus employed, more than a thousand miles were surveyed and charted, and a beacon 70 feet in height was raised on Raine's Islet as a guide for passing through the Barrier Reef. In 1851 he went to Helsingborg, to observe the eclipse of the sun, and carefully examined the extraordinary projections of flame from the sun's limb. Captain Blackwood died in 1854, and was succeeded, as Honorary Secretary, by Sir Walter Trevelyan, one of our oldest and most zealous members, who had been on the Council since 1843. After passing through Harrow and Cambridge, Sir Walter studied at Edinburgh, and became an excellent botanist and sound geologist; and he was besides an accomplished antiquary. In 1821 he visited the Faroe Islands, and was the author of an excellent work, to which his name is not attached, entitled 'Greenland, Iceland, and the Faroe Islands.' Sir Walter Trevelyan was Honorary Secretary from 1854 to 1857, Vice-President in 1857, and one of our Trustees from 1860 until his death, which took place at Wallington, his seat in Northumberland, on March 23rd, 1879, when he was in his eighty-second year.

Thus ably supported, Lord Ellesmere's term of office saw the Society rapidly increasing in prosperity, and in 1854 it was moved to more spacious and convenient premises in Whitehall Place. Our noble President also obtained the annual Government grant of 500*l.* for the map room. He thus put the matter to the Chancellor of the Exchequer:—" The objects of our Society are of a nature which attracts to its operations men not only of first-rate, but of very varied eminence in all departments of science and of the public service. We can command for our Council and management the services not only of men devoted to our special scientific pursuit, but of others also who are familiar with the conduct of business in every shape. We can thus offer a guarantee for redeeming our obligation to the public. Trust us and you will have no reason to repent of your confidence." The propriety and usefulness of the grant was further guaranteed by the powerful support of Mr. Joseph Hume. The library and maps were classified and arranged in the new premises by Mr. Trelawney Saunders, who was then the Curator. He drew up an account of the method adopted, which is preserved in our archives.

It was a source of great regret that, owing to the rule that a

President can only hold office continuously for two years, the Fellows were obliged to lose the services of Lord Ellesmere. In resigning his office, he gracefully insisted upon the hospitable privilege of still receiving his colleagues at Bridgewater House. " There are some functions," he said, " which I should be reluctant altogether to resign; and I have been better able than most men, from mere accidents of residence, to collect together, with the least inconvenience to the greatest number, the Members of the Society. If I am not wrong in supposing that such opportunities of occasional intercourse, to use an expression of Lord Stowell, 'lubricate the wheels of science,' I may hope to retain, as a simple Member of this Society, the honour, the privilege, and I must add the singular pleasure to myself, of promoting such intercourse as I have enjoyed as your President."

Never has the Society had a warmer friend than Lord Ellesmere, or a President who was, from his varied accomplishments and popularity, better fitted to preside over its interests. He died, at the age of fifty-seven, on February 18th, 1857.

He was succeeded by Admiral Beechey, our Arctic President, the son of the eminent artist Sir William Beechey. Born in February 1796, young Beechey was in Commodore Schomberg's brilliant action off the Isle of France in 1811, and in the *Vengeur* at the attack on New Orleans. In 1818 he was Lieutenant of the *Trent* under Franklin, in the Spitzbergen Expedition, of which he published a charming account in after years. No narrative had been given to the public when the expedition returned, and Beechey, remembering old Hakluyt's imputation on some of our early writers who, he says, " should have used more care in preserving the memory of the worthy acts of our nation," made up for the omission in 1843. In 1819-20 Beechey was first Lieutenant of the *Hecla* in Parry's first voyage, when he wintered at Melville Island. In 1821 he was with Smyth in the *Adventure,* surveying the north coast of Africa, and he went overland eastward from Tripoli as far as Derna, in July 1822. During the three and a half succeeding years, Captain Beechey had command of the *Blossom,* engaged on a surveying and exploring voyage in the Pacific and up Behring Strait, where he extended the knowledge of the north coast of America to Cape Barrow. His ' Narrative of the Voyage of the *Blossom,*' was published in 1831. From 1837 to 1844 he was engaged on the survey of the coast of Ireland, and finally succeeded to the important post of Superintendent of the Marine Branch of the Board of Trade. In 1854 he became a Rear-Admiral, and succeeded Lord Ellesmere as President of the Society in 1856. Suffering from ill-health, he still devoted his energies to the advancement of geography, and was transacting the Society's business up to the last week of his life. He died on November 29th, 1856.

Sir Roderick Murchison filled the post which was vacated by Admiral Beechey's death for one year, and was then elected President for the regular term of two years, from 1857 to 1859. At this time Mr. Francis Galton succeeded Sir Walter Trevelyan as Honorary Secretary. Mr. Galton, the youngest son of Mr. S. T. Galton of Duddeston near Birmingham, and grandson of Dr. Erasmus Darwin, was born in 1822, and graduated at Trinity College, Cambridge, in 1844. In 1850, at his own cost, Mr. Galton fitted out an expedition to explore the interior of Southern Africa, through the country of the Damaras, and the Ovampo. In a journey of upwards of 2000 miles he fixed several positions astronomically, and for this service he was honoured with the Founder's Medal in 1853. In 1860 Mr. Galton published 'The Art of Travel, or Shifts and Contrivances available in Wild Countries,' which went through several editions; and he also edited a volume entitled ' Vacation Tourists' in 1862 and some succeeding years. He first joined the Council in 1854, was Secretary from 1857 to 1863, Foreign Secretary from 1865 to 1866, and, though occupied with other scientific pursuits, has ever since worked actively for the Society either as a Member of the Council or Vice-President.

During the whole period of the Society's existence, from 1830 to 1854, the old Raleigh Traveller's Club continued to perform its useful and convivial share of geographical work. Sir Roderick Murchison always strove to make the connection between the Club and the Society closer and more intimate. In 1834 the Raleigh Club gave a great dinner to welcome back Sir John Ross and his illustrious nephew from the Arctic Regions, and in 1838 a similar reception was given to the officers of the Euphrates Expedition. Returning travellers ever received a hearty reception at the Raleigh, and in June 1838 Sir Roderick carried a resolution that the dinners should always take place on the same days as the meetings of the Society. He also urged all its Members to enrol themselves as Fellows of the Society. At last it was thought desirable to make the connection still closer. On the 1st of May, 1854, at a special meeting of the Raleigh Club, four resolutions were carried by Sir Roderick: that the Raleigh Club should be dissolved, in order that a new Club might be formed in closer connection with the Society; that the new Club should be called the GEOGRAPHICAL CLUB, composed of Members of the Raleigh Club and Fellows of the Geographical Society; that the first dinner should be on June 12th, 1854, and that Sir

Roderick Murchison should be President; an office which he held during the rest of his life. Ever since, the dinners of the Geographical Club, with the President in the chair, have taken place previous to the meetings of the Society, to which the Members have adjourned. Here geographers and explorers of all nations have been welcomed and entertained, and our beloved President, Sir Roderick Murchison, presided at 206 out of the 223 Geographical Club dinners which took place between 1854 and 1870. The annually increasing number of Fellows attending the evening meetings led to the formation of a second dining Club connected with the Society, called the KOSMOS CLUB. It was founded in 1858 by Dr. Norton Shaw, and continues to flourish under the auspices of its present Secretary Mr. Bates.

In 1859 Earl de Grey and Ripon, the son of our first President, was elected to the same post, but he was obliged to vacate the chair on accepting office in the following year, and was succeeded by Lord Ashburton, from 1860 to 1862.

It was in 1859 that the Royal Geographical Society received a Charter of Incorporation, and became a body politic and corporate, with perpetual succession, and a common seal. In this Charter the Council or governing body is declared to consist of a President, Vice-Presidents, a Treasurer, Trustees, Secretaries, and not more than twenty-one other Fellows; and the Council is to have the sole management of the income and funds of the Society, and the appointment of officers and attendants. The Charter is dated February 8th, in the twenty-second year of Queen Victoria.

In May 1862, on the retirement of Lord Ashburton, Sir Roderick Murchison was elected President for the fourth time, and he continued to occupy the chair during the eight succeeding years. Sir George Everest, the former Superintendent of the Great Trigonometrical Survey of India, Admiral Collinson, the talented surveyor and Arctic Explorer, the veteran Sir George Back, John Crawfurd, the learned ethnologist and geographer, Sir Henry Rawlinson, and Viscount Strangford supported him as Vice-Presidents; while he was aided on the Council by such surveyors as Sir Henry James and Sir Andrew Waugh, by such Arctic Explorers as M'Clintock and Sherard Osborn, by Galton, Baker and Grant among African travellers, and by our most eminent cartographers, Arrowsmith, Findlay, and John Walker.

It was decided in 1862 that there should be two Honorary Secretaries, besides the Foreign Secretary; and Mr. Francis Galton and Mr. William Spottiswoode (now President of the Royal Society) were elected. In the following year Mr. Galton

retired, and Mr. Spottiswoode and Mr. Clements Markham
became the Honorary Secretaries. Mr. Clements Markham
succeeded Mr. Major as Secretary of the Hakluyt Society in
1858, and has continued to hold that post also. In 1865 he
was elected Treasurer of the Geographical Club. In 1864 and
1865 Mr. Clements Markham and Mr. Laurence Oliphant were
the two Secretaries of the Geographical Society, and in 1866
Mr. Oliphant was replaced by Mr. R. H. Major. After the
retirement of Dr. Norton Shaw in 1863, Mr. Greenfield was
Assistant-Secretary for one year, and in 1864 he was succeeded
by Mr. Henry Walter Bates, the well-known author of that
charming work, 'The Naturalist on the River Amazons.' The
Secretariat arrangements have since remained unchanged. Mr.
Clements Markham and Mr. Major have, during all the succeeding years, been the Honorary Secretaries, and Mr. Bates the
Assistant-Secretary and Editor of the Society's publications.

Sir Roderick Murchison was created a K.C.B. in 1863, and
a Baronet in 1866; and from other Sovereigns he also received well-earned honours. During the long period that he
presided over the Society, Sir Roderick saw an extraordinary
advance made in geographical discovery in all parts of the
world, and his encouragement and active assistance were no
slight elements in the success which attended the efforts of
many explorers. Ever steadfast in forwarding the searches for
our Vice-President Sir John Franklin, and his brave comrades,
Murchison stood by Lady Franklin when the Government
abandoned her, and was her warmest friend and supporter when
she resolved to despatch M'Clintock's expedition. As regards
African explorers, Sir Roderick, as is well known, became
the personal friend of Dr. Livingstone, and the energetic
supporter of Burton, Speke, Grant and Baker. Livingstone
spoke of him as "the best friend I ever had—true, warm, and
abiding." Almost the last work of our beloved President was
the earnest endeavour to obtain a resumption of Arctic discovery, which was so warmly advocated by Sherard Osborn.
He held that—"independent of the great geographical problem
to be solved, the navy lacked something to occupy its energies
in time of peace;" and he sighed for the good days of adventure,
of Raleigh and Drake, Hudson and Baffin.

The character of Murchison was admirably portrayed by his
successor, who served for so many years on the same Council with
him. "Industry and energy, a clear head, a strong will, and
great tenacity of purpose were among his leading character-
istics; while his warm feelings, his thorough honesty, his kindness of manner, his entire absence of jealousy, his geniality, fine
temper, tact and firmness, peculiarly fitted him to preside over

public bodies, and to lead his followers to good and useful ends. Many a young traveller has been sustained under his hardships by Sir Roderick's hopeful counsels. Sir Roderick indeed never deserted a friend in need. At one time he might be seen urging the Government to send out expeditions to search for Franklin; at another he would be energetically defending Governor Eyre, an old Medallist of the Society, from what he regarded as persecution. When Speke and Grant were supposed to be in difficulties in Africa, he was active in organising relief. He was ever a steady supporter of Sir Samuel Baker; and with Livingstone his name is entirely identified."

One well-known face was missing from our meetings before we sustained the great loss of our revered President. Sir Roderick lived to record the merits of John Crawfurd, the great traveller and scholar. Born on the Island of Islay in 1783, Mr. Crawfurd was in his 85th year when he was unexpectedly carried off. In the East India Company's service, he was in the campaign with Lord Lake, but was soon afterwards transferred to Penang, where he commenced those studies of the Malay languages and people which enabled him eventually to compose his Malay grammar and dictionary. In 1811 he accompanied Lord Minto in his expedition to Java. Here he remained for nearly six years, amassing ethnological and geographical materials; the results of his researches appearing in 1820, in his 'History of the Indian Archipelago.' In 1821 he was sent on a mission to Siam and Cochin China, and he acted as Governor of Singapore from 1823 to 1826. In the latter year he went to the capital of Burma on an important mission, and on his return to England he took a somewhat leading part in the advocacy of free trade. Afterwards he devoted his energies to the study of ethnology, and was the life and soul of the Ethnological Society for many years, writing no less than thirty-eight memoirs for its journal. He first came upon the Council of our Society in 1857, and continued to serve upon it, and to be a constant attendant of our meetings, until his death in 1867. He scarcely ever failed to take part in our discussions, and while stoutly maintaining his own views, he always showed forbearance and courtesy to others.

Sir Roderick deeply felt the loss of his dear old friend John Crawfurd. He was himself struck down with paralysis in the end of 1870, and he died full of years and honours on October 22nd, 1871. His remains were followed to the grave by his successor Sir Henry Rawlinson, by the Secretaries Mr. Clements Markham and Mr. Major, by the Assistant-Secretary Mr. Bates, and by Admiral Collinson, Admiral Richards, Colonel Grant, and Mr. John Murray. He bequeathed 100*l.* to the Society he had served so well; and his bust now stands in the Map Room. There is also a portrait of Sir Roderick in the Society's Council Room.

In each of his Anniversary Addresses Sir Roderick Murchison usually dwelt upon one special point relating to discovery or to a question of physical geography, which formed a complete essay in itself. In 1853 his theme was physical geography; in 1857, earthquakes; in 1863, the sources of the Nile; in 1864, the glaciers of the Himálayas and New Zealand compared with those of Europe, and on the power of glaciers in modifying the surface of the earth, and the agency of floating icebergs; in 1865, on the importance of Arctic research; in 1867, on the Aralo-Caspian basin; in 1868, on the dependence of geography on geology; in 1869, on a comparison between the former and present physical changes of the surface of the earth; and, in 1871, on the connection of geographical with geological science.

Sir Roderick Murchison was succeeded as President of the Geographical Society and of the Club by Sir Henry Rawlinson, and as President of the Hakluyt Society by Sir David Dundas. Since 1871 the President of the Society for the time being has always been President of the Geographical Club. Henry Creswicke Rawlinson was born in 1810, and served in the Bombay army from 1827 until 1833. From the latter year until 1839 he was actively employed in Persia. During that period he explored, with great zeal, perseverance, and industry, the provinces of Luristan, Khuzistan, and Azerbaijan, and the mountain ranges which divide the basin of the Tigris from the elevated plains of Central Persia. He brought great learning and a vast extent of historical research to bear on his geographical enquiries, and identified rivers and towns by a comparison of their ancient and modern names. For these great services to geography Major Rawlinson received the Founder's Medal in 1839. In 1840 he was appointed Political Agent at Kandahar, and he held the southern capital of the Afghans in safety, throughout all the troubles that ensued, eventually returning to India by way of Kabul and the Kaïbar Pass. In 1844 he became Political Agent in Turkish Arabia, and in 1851 Consul-General, resigning his appointment in 1855, when he returned home, and became a Director of the East India Company and K.C.B. He had first joined our Council in 1850, and was almost constantly Vice-President until Sir Roderick's death in 1871. During 1858–59 he was Envoy in Persia, and has since 1868 been a Member of the Council of India. Sir Henry Rawlinson was President from 1871 to 1873, again from 1874 to 1876, and has since been Vice-President.

Sir Henry Bartle Frere succeeded Sir Henry Rawlinson as President in 1873. He is a nephew of Mr. Bartle Frere, one of the Founders of our Society, and also of the Right Hon. John Hookham Frere. Born in 1815, and entering the Indian Civil Service in 1833, he became Resident in Sind in 1856, a K.C.B. in 1859, and was Governor of Bombay from 1862 to 1867. Always taking an instructed and warm interest in geographical pursuits Sir Bartle Frere has contributed papers to our Journal, and has done valuable service to the Society in many other ways. He had joined our Council soon after his return to this country, and in November 1872 a farewell dinner, with the President Sir Henry Rawlinson in the chair, was given to him on his departure to Zanzibar on an important diplomatic mission. It was the largest gathering of the Geographical Club that had ever taken place up to that time. On that occasion our President said that Sir Bartle Frere's administration of Sind, during the Sepoy mutiny, evinced the very highest qualities of statesmanship, and that his great administrative success was achieved under every possible disadvantage and when, in other parts of India, disorder and rapine reigned supreme. It was under such circumstances that Sir Bartle succeeded in converting the lawless marauders of Sind into a peaceful and industrious peasantry. His subsequent government of Bombay is still remembered in the island with feelings of the utmost gratitude, and no Indian statesman was ever more beloved by every class of the native population. On his return from Zanzibar Sir Bartle Frere was elected President of the Society, in May 1873. He was obliged to resign in the following year in order to accompany the Prince of Wales to India, and soon after his return he went out as Governor of the Cape and High Commissioner in the end of 1875. While filling that responsible post, during a most anxious and difficult period, he never lost sight of the interests of our Society, and was ever ready to extend the most cordial assistance and encouragement to explorers of all nations. Leaving the Cape, to the deep regret of the people he had so ably governed, he returned to England in the end of 1880 to be warmly welcomed by his numerous friends and well-wishers at home. His great services to the State had obtained for him the Grand Cross of the Bath, the Grand Commandery of the Star of India, a Baronetcy, and a seat in the Privy Council.

Sir Rutherford Alcock, K.C.B., succeeded Sir Henry Rawlinson at the end of his second term of office in 1876. Sir Rutherford's knowledge of China and Japan, where he had served in various diplomatic posts from 1844 to 1871 when as Envoy Extraordinary and Minister Plenipotentiary at Peking he finally retired from active service, made him a great acquisition to our Council. He held the office of President from 1876 to 1878, and has since actively aided in the Society's work as Vice-President and as Chairman of the African Exploration Fund Committee.

The Earl of Dufferin was elected President in 1878, before he had returned from Canada, and the author of the charming "Letters from High Latitudes," the accomplished statesman and geographer, was very warmly welcomed when he first took the chair in the following November. But his acceptance of the appointment of Ambassador to Russia obliged him to resign shortly afterwards, and he was succeeded in May 1879 by the Earl of Northbrook. It was a great advantage to the Society that, while we were receiving so much new geographical information from the little-known countries beyond our north-western frontier, the affairs of the Society should have been presided over by a statesman who had so recently been Viceroy of India. Resigning, owing to his acceptance of the office of First Lord of the Admiralty, Lord Northbrook was succeeded as President, in May 1880, by Lord Aberdare.

CHAPTER VIII.

EXPEDITIONS PROMOTED BY THE ROYAL GEOGRAPHICAL SOCIETY

AND

GRANTS OF THE ROYAL AWARDS,

1830 TO 1855.

THE measures adopted by the Royal Geographical Society for promoting and encouraging discovery and research have been of four kinds. Awards have been presented to eminent explorers and geographers, in the form of gold medals, grants of money, gold watches, or instruments. Aid has been given to travellers. The Government has been urged, by the Council, to undertake important discoveries by the despatch of expeditions; and, on very rare occasions, the Society has itself undertaken the despatch and conduct of an expedition.

The Royal Award of 50 guineas was, during the reign of King William, presented in money or as a single medal. Such recognitions have always been highly valued by discoverers and surveyors, and have formed a strong incentive to exertion. They were not wholly wanting in former days, and even, in the dawn of English geography, the Sovereign bestowed honorable decorations on those who nobly and successfully strove to increase our knowledge of the earth's surface by land and sea. Queen Elizabeth presented to Sir Humphrey Gilbert a jewel consisting of a small anchor of beaten gold with a large pearl on the peak, which he evermore wore on his breast. Sir Francis Drake received a medal suspended from his neck by a ribband. The Royal Society granted its Copley Medal to geographers on five occasions. Captain Cook received it in 1776, and a medal was also specially struck in his honour. The Copley Medal was granted to Major Roy in 1785 for his measurement of the Hounslow base, to Major Rennell in 1791, and to Captain Sabine and Lieut. Foster, R.N., in 1821 and 1827 for Arctic work.

The Society, on its first establishment, and during its early days in King William's reign, found that explorers were actively at work in various parts of the world. The faithful Lander was completing the discoveries of Clapperton on the Niger, Enderby was despatching vessels to the Antarctic Regions, Ross was still absent in the far north, and Back was at work on his errand of rescue, Burnes was making his remarkable journey to Bokhara,

Chesney was surveying on the Euphrates, and FitzRoy was executing his valuable surveys along the coasts of South America.
These were the first seven recipients, from our Society, of the
award granted by King William for geographical discovery and
research.

In 1832 the sum of fifty guineas was conferred on Mr.
Richard Lander, in acknowledgment of his services in determining the course and termination of the Quorra or Niger. A
portrait of this intrepid explorer, the faithful companion of
Clapperton, hangs in the Society's Council Room. The second
Award was granted for Antarctic service. Mr. John Biscoe,
R.N., left England in the brig *Tula* in 1830, despatched by
Messrs. Enderby ; and he added one more to the many examples
previously set by British seamen of patient and untiring perseverance amidst the most discouraging difficulties. He was the
discoverer of Graham's Land and Enderby's Land. Mr. Biscoe
died in 1848. Sir John Ross received the third Award for his
discovery of Boothia Felix and King William Land, and for his
famous sojourn, during no less than four winters, in the Arctic
Regions. The remarkable and most important journey of Sir
Alexander Burnes from Kabul to Bokhara and back through
Persia, secured for that accomplished but unfortunate officer
the fourth Award granted by the Society. His portrait hangs
in the Society's Council Room. The fifth, in the form of a
medal, was granted to Sir George Back for his memorable
journey for the rescue of Ross, and discovery of the Great Fish
River. Captain FitzRoy for his South American surveys and exploration of Patagonia, and Colonel Chesney for his Euphrates
Expedition won, respectively, the sixth and seventh Awards.

The Society, in its early years, did not confine its operations
to the annual grant of the Royal Award. Expeditions were
despatched, with its aid or under its auspices, to Africa, South
America, Asia, and Australia ; and active encouragement was
extended to explorers. Captain Alexander of the 42nd High-
landers (the present General Sir James Alexander of Westerton,
co. Stirling) undertook an expedition north of the Orange River.
Leaving Cape Town in September 1836, he advanced, through
the then unknown country of the Namaquas, as far north as
Walfisch Bay, and gave an interesting account of that sterile
region. The Council obtained Government aid for Captain
Alexander, subscribed towards his expenses, and took a warm
interest in his proceedings. He was knighted for his services
in Africa ; and afterwards commanded the 14th Regiment at
the siege of Sebastopol.

The expedition of Schomburgk to Guiana was supported by
our funds, and was still more closely connected with our

Society. Robert Hermann Schomburgk was a Prussian scientific traveller who was first brought into notice by his careful examination of the West Indian Island of Anegada, and his delineation of the rocks and reefs which surround it. In 1834 his services were engaged by the Society, to discover the interior of British Guiana, and to connect the positions astronomically fixed in that region, with those of Humboldt on the Upper Orinoco. It was intended that the work should occupy three years, and the Society undertook to contribute 900*l.* towards the expenses. In pursuance of his instructions Schomburgk left Demerara in September 1835 and, ascending the Essequibo, reached the s.w. extremity of British Guiana. Thence he ascended the Ripanuny, and in 1836 he sent home most interesting accounts of the physical aspects of the region, its vegetation and scenery. In 1837 he ascended the Berbice, and in the following year he reached the Carumá Mountains and the Rio Branco. Schomburgk was engaged on these arduous journeys during five years, and worthily followed in the footsteps of the illustrious Humboldt, while making a portion of his great predecessor's work more complete. During his researches, he discovered and sent home the magnificent *Victoria Regia,* constructed an admirable map, and illustrated his discoveries by large and valuable collections. In 1840 he received the Gold Medal of the Society, and in 1843 he was knighted. Sir Robert Schomburgk edited Sir Walter Raleigh's ‘Discovery of the Empire of Guiana’ in 1848, for the Hakluyt Society. During the latter years of his life he was Consul-General in Siam, and very soon after his retirement, he died on March 11th, 1865.

Another expedition was fostered by our Society, in conjunction with the Society for the promotion of Christian Knowledge. Its object was to make acquaintances with the Nestorian Christians, and the mountainous country they inhabit, and it was entrusted to Mr. Ainsworth, formerly naturalist to the Euphrates Expedition, and Mr. Rassam of Mosul. Each Society granted a sum of 500*l.* towards the expenses; and joint instructions were carefully prepared. Leaving England in 1838, the travellers explored part of Asia Minor, and reached Mosul in 1839, proceeding thence into Kurdistan, and as far as Urumiyah. The expedition closed its labours in 1840, and although the work was not carried out to the extent anticipated, yet a great deal of geographical information was collected along the line of route.

In 1837 the Council took an active part in promoting an expedition for geographical discovery in Australia. A deputation, composed of the President, Mr. Murchison, and the Hydrographer, waited upon the Secretary of State for the Colonies, pointing out the advantages likely to accrue from exploring

Australia, and also recommending a nautical survey. The deputation was very favourably received, and a grant was obtained of 1000*l.* for the expenses of a land expedition under Lieuts. Grey, of the 83rd (now Sir George Grey, K.C.B.) and Lushington, to start from Swan River. At the same time a survey of the coast was ordered in H.M.S. *Beagle*, commanded by Captain Wickham. Thus was Australian exploration commenced under the Society's auspices.

The Council, from the first foundation of the Society, gave its attention to the important subject of Arctic discovery. Our first efforts were to throw more light on the geography of the northern shores of America. The highest Arctic authorities were invited to furnish the Council with their views on the subject, and valuable minutes were received from Sir John Barrow, Sir John Franklin, Sir John Ross, Dr. Richardson, and Captain Beaufort. A committee was then appointed to examine the various plans. The Hydrographer entreated the Council to take every means they possessed of persuading the Government to fit out an expedition, and accordingly a deputation consisting of Lord Ripon, Sir John Franklin, and Captain Back, laid the case before His Majesty's Government in 1836. The authorities were pleased to attend favourably to the representatives of the Council, and Captain Back was appointed to H.M.S. *Terror*, to proceed with her to the western shore of Sir Thomas Roe's Welcome, to winter there, and thence to complete the exploration of the American coast in the spring.

It is well known that the object of the expedition was frustrated, owing to the impossibility of penetrating through the ice in Frozen Strait. But the failure by Sir George Back has proved better than many a success achieved by less gifted men. The exploration of the patches of coast connecting the discoveries of former explorers was work which could be done at a future time, and for which geographers could wait. But the narrative of the voyage of the *Terror*, of the hair-breadth escapes, the masterly conduct of the officers, and gallantry of the men, is a distinct gain to our country's literature. It is an Arctic classic—a treasure worth more than many leagues of new coast line.

On the accession of Queen Victoria, Her Majesty was pleased to announce her gracious intention of continuing the grant of fifty guineas which was commenced by her uncle. It was then decided that in future two gold medals should be annually awarded, each of the value of twenty-five guineas, to be called the Founder's and the Patron's Medal. At this time Mr. W. R. Hamilton, in his Anniversary Address, made some interesting remarks on the subject of our medals. He suggested that we ought to expend the means at our disposal in having the portrait of the receiver engraved upon the die. " We should present him with one impression in silver, and strike off at least a hundred others in bronze for circulation among the various public museums at home and abroad, and for the supply of private collections. By such an arrangement the honour, name, and success of the receiver would not only be made known throughout Europe, but would be perpetuated, together with the delineation of his features, to the latest posterity." Mr. Hamilton referred, as an instance in point, to the bronze medal of Capt. Cook, which was struck, with his portrait, by the Royal Society, as a testimony of admiration for his great services to geography. Mr. Hamilton added, " But I fear this is a unique instance of the kind in this country." The President mentioned an additional argument in favour of his suggestion, namely the encouragement it would give to a department of the fine arts which had long been neglected by our countrymen. It was eventually decided by the Council that two medals of equal value and equal honour might annually be presented to the two gentlemen who might be judged to have rendered the most distinguished services to the cause of geography. The Founder's Medal bears the portrait of King William IV., and the Patron's Medal that of Her Majesty Queen Victoria.

From the return of Schomburgk and Ainsworth until after the restoration of the Society's prosperity by Admiral Smyth, the Council was able to do little more than recognise the merits of travellers by granting the Royal Awards. £100 was granted to Dr. Beke in 1842, and in 1846 the Council obtained grants of small sums from the Government and the East India Company for Mr. Brockman, who was about to attempt a journey into the interior of Hadramaut. Otherwise it was only through the bestowal of our Gold Medals that the Society was able to encourage and promote geographical discovery during more than fifteen years.

Still, even in our least prosperous period, we continued to encourage exploration, and to do good service by disseminating geographical knowledge through our publications. For work in Asia our Gold Medal was conferred on Sir Henry Rawlinson * in 1840, and on Lieut. John Wood of the India Navy in 1841, for discovering the source of the Oxus. Lieut. Symonds, R.E., received it in 1843 for his survey in Palestine, and for ascertaining the difference of level between the Dead Sea and the Mediterranean; our former President, Mr. W. J. Hamilton, in 1844, for his exploration of Asia Minor; Mr. Layard, in 1849,

---

* See p. 54.

for his Nineveh excavations; and Baron von Hügel for his enterprising journey into Kashmir in the same year. In 1852 Captain Henry Strachey received the Gold Medal for his extensive surveys in Western Tibet, and the sum of 25*l.* was granted to Dr. Wallin of Helsingfors, for his remarkable journey across Arabia. On this, and some other occasions, the amount of the Royal Award was distributed in money, when, in the opinion of the Council, travellers had established for themselves strong claims to participate in the fund, although their services had not been of sufficient importance to justify the award of the medal, which is the highest honour at the disposal of the Society.

In Africa the principal work of this period was performed in Abyssinia. Dr. Rüppell, of Frankfort, received the Gold Medal in 1839 for his labours in that country, during which he made a large natural history collection and presented it to the museum of his native country; and in 1845 the same honour was conferred upon Dr. Beke for his important geographical researches in the Abyssinian kingdom of Shoa, and in the province of Godjam, which he traversed in all directions, visiting the source of the Abai, Bruce's famous fountain of the Nile. Mr. Francis Galton earned the Gold Medal in 1853 for having, as already mentioned, fitted out an expedition to explore the interior of South Africa at his own cost, and for having successfully conducted it through the country of the Damaras and the Ovampo, a journey of upwards of 2000 miles. It was his merit also to have constantly and accurately observed for latitude and longitude. His companion, Mr. Anderssen, who afterwards continued the work of exploring as far as Lake N'gami, was presented with a portable box of surveying instruments, in 1855.

The action taken by the Council, in encouraging the undertakings of Lieuts. Grey and Lushington, was the stimulus to further important geographical labours in Australia. Mr. Edward John Eyre was the first Gold Medallist who received that honour for Australian discoveries. Son of the Rev. Anthony Eyre, the Vicar of Stillingfleet, near York, our Medallist was born in 1815, went out to Sydney in 1833, and bought a sheep farm on the Lower Murray. After several shorter expeditions, Mr. Eyre undertook a journey in 1840 to ascertain whether there were fertile lands in the interior, beyond a salt marsh called Lake Torrens. He endured the most terrible privations, largely added to our geographical knowledge, and well earned the Society's highest honour. From 1846 Mr. Eyre was employed by the Colonial Office as Lieut.-Governor in New Zealand under Sir George Grey until 1852, as Governor of St. Vincent and Antigua, and finally of Jamaica from 1862 to 1865.

When Mr. Eyre was suffering persecution for his prompt suppression of a negro revolt, he was generously befriended by our President Sir Roderick Murchison, who knew that our gallant Medallist, who had for years been the humane friend of the aborigines of Australia, was not the man to err on the side of unnecessary severity. In 1845 Count Strzelecki received the Founder's Medal for his discovery of the extensive tract of New South Wales named Gipps's Land, and for his physical description of New South Wales, comprehending the fruits of five years of continual labour, during a tour of 7000 miles on foot. Count Strzelecki, was afterwards a Member of our Council from 1855 to 1862. He was created a K.C.M.G., and died in December 1873. In 1846 two other Australian explorers received our Medals, Charles Sturt and Ludwig Leichhardt. Captain Sturt had explored the rivers Darling and Murray, and afterwards undertook a journey in 1844, with the object of traversing the whole extent of the continent from Adelaide to the Gulf of Carpentaria. He succeeded in penetrating to within 200 miles of the centre of the continent, when the illness of one of his party compelled him to retrace his steps. For these services to geography, for his energy and courage, combined with prudence and sound judgment, the Gold Medal was granted to Captain Sturt. This admirable traveller, the grandson of Mr. Humphrey Sturt of Critchill in Dorsetshire, was born in 1796 and, entering the army, accompanied the 39th to Sydney in 1827. His great services, though recognised by our Society, were entirely neglected by the Government for a quarter of a century. Justice, as is so often the case, came too late. In May 1869 he received notice that he was to be created a Knight Commander of St. Michael and St. George, but he died on June 16th before the tardily bestowed honour was gazetted. Dr. Leichhardt received our Gold Medal in 1847 for his journey of 1800 miles from Morton Bay to Port Essington, by which he opened to Australian settlers new and extensive fields of enterprise, and connected the remote settlements of New South Wales with a secure port on the confines of the Indian Ocean. He afterwards perished while conducting another expedition over the waterless deserts of the interior in 1850. In 1851 the Council awarded 25*l.* to Mr. Thomas Brunner, for a very enterprising journey among the Alps and along the western shore of the Middle Island of New Zealand, which, in those early days of colonization, was an undertaking of some risk and difficulty.

Sir James Brooke, the Rajah of Sarawak and Governor of Labuan, worthily received our Gold Medal in 1848. The object to which he determined to devote his energies and means, from an early period of his life, was the civilization of the Malay race. He sailed from England on his gallant and hazardous adventure in October 1838, in his yacht *Royalist*, and on August 1st, 1839, dropped anchor off the coast of Borneo. Details of the skilful and gallant operations which led to the cession of Sarawak to Rajah Brooke are given in the interesting volumes of Admiral Sir H. Keppel, and Sir Rodney Mundy. Great advantages to geographical science, especially in the survey of coasts and rivers, resulted from the introduction of civilization and commerce amongst the Malays and Dyaks of Borneo, and he who originated and ably carried out these plans was well entitled to the Medal of our Society. The last year of his residence in Sarawak was 1857, and he died at his seat in the south of Devonshire, on June 11th, 1868.

For his valuable services in Guiana it has already been recorded that Sir Robert Schomburgk received the Medal in 1840, and in 1850 Colonel Fremont was awarded the same honour for his conduct of an exploring expedition to the Rocky Mountains and North California, from 1842 to 1846.

After the return of Sir George Back in 1838, the attention of Arctic explorers was mainly turned to the completion of the delineation of the northern coast of America. In the summer of 1837 Mr. Thomas Simpson, accompanied by Mr. Dease, had already started from the Great Slave Lake, under instructions from the Hudson's Bay Company. By tracing the coast from Franklin's furthest to Cape Barrow they succeeded in connecting the work of Franklin and Beechey; and completed our knowledge from the Coppermine River to Behring Strait. In 1839 Simpson turned eastward from the Coppermine, passed Cape Turnagain of Franklin, and advanced as far as Castor and Pollux river, thus connecting the work of Back and Franklin. Simpson also discovered the south coast of King William Island and built a cairn at Cape Herschel. When, in 1848, this cairn was reached by a band of dying heroes from the north, the North-West Passage was discovered. For these services Simpson received our Gold Medal in 1839.

The work of delineating the Arctic shores of America was completed by Dr. John Rae, who was appointed to the command of an expedition by Sir George Simpson, the Governor of the Hudson's Bay Company, in 1846. Starting in boats from York Factory in Hudson's Bay, Dr. Rae wintered at Repulse Bay, in a stone hut, without fuel of any kind to give warmth; he and his party maintaining themselves on deer, a large proportion of which were shot by himself. During the spring of 1847 he explored on foot the shores of a great gulf, having 700 miles of coast line, connected the work of Parry with that of

Ross, and proved that Boothia was part of the American Continent.

In 1848 Rae accompanied Sir John Richardson on an expedition down the McKenzie River, which examined the Arctic shores eastward to the Coppermine River, in search of Sir John Franklin's party. In 1849 he continued the search in a boat *viâ* the Coppermine River, but found the coast impenetrably blocked with ice. In 1850, at the request of Government, he undertook a further search for the missing explorers, and by a long sledge journey (the daily distance of which averaged more than twenty-four miles) in the spring of 1851, and a boat voyage the same summer, the south shores of Wollaston and Victoria Lands were closely examined, their continuity proved, and Victoria Strait seen, named, and ascended from the south, to a higher latitude than the position where Franklin's ships were abandoned in 1848.

These discoveries earned for Dr. Rae the well-merited honour which was conferred on him in 1852 by the award of the Society's Founder's Gold Medal.

In 1854, after passing a second winter at Repulse Bay, he connected the work of Simpson and Ross, west of Boothia, established the insularity of King William Land, and brought home the first information of the fate of the Franklin Expedition, for which he and his party of seven men received the Government reward of 10,000*l.*

The Gold Medal was bestowed on Professor Middendorff in 1846, for his remarkable travels in northern Siberia, and for having reached the great headland of Taimyr. He also threw light on the boreal range of vegetation, and on the question of the frozen soil and sub-soil of Siberia. In 1853 Captain Inglefield, R.N., received our Gold Medal for his voyage in Baffin Bay.

Although, in his first volume, Sir James Ross quite correctly attributes the despatch of his memorable Antarctic Expedition to the action of the British Association in 1838, still the initiation of the idea of such an expedition was due to the Secretary of our Society. An important suggestion for this Antarctic voyage was addressed by Captain Washington to the President and Council of the Royal Geographical Society, and although it was not printed by us, it was recorded in the Bulletin of the French Geographical Society, and is referred to by M. d'Avezac in his eloquent obituary sketch of Washington. Sir James C. Ross had more experience of Arctic service than any other officer that ever lived. He endured nine Arctic winters, and passed sixteen navigable seasons in the Arctic regions. He was, without comparison, the fittest man for the command of the

F

expedition which first crossed the Antarctic Circle on January 1st, 1841. In one short month he made one of the greatest geographical discoveries of modern times, amid regions of perpetual ice ; including a long range of high lands, named Victoria, the great volcano, 12,400 feet above the sea, called Mount Erebus, and the marvellous range of ice cliffs. Ross attained a latitude of 78° 11', thus approaching the South Pole more nearly, by hundreds of miles, than any of his predecessors. For this great service to geography, the Founder's Medal was granted to Sir James Ross in 1842.

In 1848 the Founder's Medal was conferred on Captain Wilkes, of the United States Navy, for his services in command of the scientific exploring expedition, from 1838 to 1842.

On the return of Sir James Ross, attention was once more turned to Arctic discovery. The despatch of Sir John Franklin's Expedition in 1845 was due to the representations of our Founder and former President, Sir John Barrow, who was then Secretary to the Admiralty. Sir John Franklin was at that time our Vice-President, and he had from the first been a frequent diner at the Raleigh Club, and a constant supporter of our interests. The Society therefore took a special interest in his expedition, the object of which was to add so largely to geographical knowledge. Never was an abler or a more gallant set of men assembled together under a more capable leader. The second in command was Captain Crozier, who had served with Parry and James Ross in Arctic and Antarctic voyages; while foremost among their subordinates was our brave and accomplished Associate, Captain Fitzjames. During the first year the *Erebus* and *Terror* performed one of the most remarkable Arctic voyages on record, by sailing up Wellington Channel to 77° N., circumnavigating Cornwallis Island, and returning to winter at Beechey Isle. In the second year Sir John Franklin followed his instructions by pushing his way southwards towards the coast of America, knowing, from previous experience, that if he could once reach it, the passage along the navigable lane which exists there every summer, would be comparatively easy. If he had been aware of the insularity of King William Land, and had hugged the Boothian coast, he would have succeeded. As it was his attempt was the best ever made; it was ably conceived and most gallantly carried out in accordance with existing knowledge. Franklin nobly died in the execution of his duty. His brave followers lived on, to perish it is true, in the same glorious cause, but not until some of them, by reaching Simpson's Cairn, at Point Herschel, had discovered the North-West Passage.

While most frequently conferring its honours on explorers

and discoverers, the Council of our Society did not overlook the less conspicuous, but not less useful labours of the scholar and the cartographer. The first recipient of the Gold Medal for literary work was Lieut. Henry Raper, R.N. The son of Admiral Raper, who was well known in his day as a great improver of maritime signals ; this officer was born in 1799, and entered the navy at the age of twelve, on board his father's ship, the *Mars.* He was shipwrecked in the Strait of Gaspar in 1817, and suffered great hardships and privations on the rocky islet called Pulo Leat, until he was rescued by a vessel from Batavia. Afterwards, at his father's express wish, young Raper joined the *Adventure* surveying ship in the Mediterranean, under Captain Smyth, where he had charge of the chronometers. His last active service was in 1824, after which time he devoted himself to the cultivation of the scientific departments of the navy, and in 1840 he published his 'Practice of Navigation,' a book of sterling merit, for which he was awarded our Gold Medal in 1841. Lieut. Raper served for several years on our Council, and was also Secretary to the Astronomical Society. He died at Torquay in January 1859. In 1842 the Gold Medal was awarded to Dr. Edward Robinson, the Professor of Biblical Literature at New York, for his biblical researches as connected with geography ; and in 1844 a similar honour was conferred on Professor Adolph Erman for his services in physical geography, meteorology, and terrestrial magnetism. The great German geographer, Carl Ritter, received the Patron's Medal in 1845. Ritter was the first who laid down and admirably carried out the principle that, in order to form clearer and more instructive ideas of geography, it was above all essential to study the configuration of the great masses of land. He was a perfect master of condensed description. His vast erudition and extreme accuracy enabled him to furnish, in his compendious works, as much knowledge as if his readers had laboured through all the original sources of his information. Humboldt truly pronounced Carl Ritter to have been the first geographer of the age.

In these ways : at first, and so long as the funds admitted of it, by assisting expeditions with money grants, and afterwards by conferring rewards, the Society strenuously endeavoured to advance the cause of geography during the first quarter of a century of its existence. The Royal Awards became the goals which aroused the ambition of young explorers, and urged them on to renewed efforts. The greatest honours that the Society could confer, they have always been very highly prized, and have been strong incentives to brave and even desperate enterprises in the cause of discovery. It was not, however, through these rewards alone that the Society made its influence felt for good. Of not less service were the publications which secured a permanent place of record for geographical achievements, and the library and map room through which the means of information was secured for our countrymen. The Society formed that home for geography the want of which had been more and more sorely felt during the previous half century.

It is interesting to note how influential the education acquired by travel and geographical research has been in training men who have afterwards become eminent in science. Among the great scientific worthies who have travelled or made exploring voyages in far distant regions, the names of Banks, Robert Brown, Sabine, Hooker, Darwin, Huxley and Wallace may be mentioned, and these by no means exhaust the list.

CHAPTER IX.

EXPEDITIONS PROMOTED BY THE ROYAL GEOGRAPHICAL SOCIETY

AND

GRANTS OF THE ROYAL AWARDS,

1855 TO 1880.

WHEN the prosperity of the Society rapidly began to increase under the fostering care of Admiral Smyth and Sir Roderick Murchison, it was not long before active aid to labourers in the field began again to combine with rewards for work achieved, in the furtherance of the cause of geography. As the funds of the Society increased, the encouragement and power to assist explorers increased also, but such aid mainly took the direction of African discovery.

In briefly recording the Society's work, it will be convenient to treat of each continent or great division of the globe separately, beginning with Asia, and then taking in order Africa, Australia, America, and finally the Arctic Regions.

So far as English labours are concerned, the most important Asiatic exploration has been undertaken from India, and generally under the orders of the Survey Department. It was therefore a well merited recognition of the value of the Indian Surveys when, in 1857, the Patron's Gold Medal was awarded to Sir Andrew Scott Waugh. The grant was made for his able extensions of the Great Trigonometrical Survey, and especially for his work in fixing 79 Himálayan peaks, one of which— Mount Everest (29,002 ft.)—is the loftiest mountain in the world. After his retirement in 1861 Sir Andrew Waugh was many years a Member of our Council, and a Vice-President, actively assisting us, almost until his lamented death in February 1878. In 1865 another eminent Indian Surveyor, Captain T. G. Montgomerie, received the same honour for his survey of Kashmir, and of the mighty mass of mountains up to the Tibetan frontier, from 1855 to 1865. Observations were taken from peaks over 20,000 feet above the sea, and the accuracy of this most difficult and laborious survey was such that in a circuit of 890 miles, only a discrepancy of $\frac{8}{10}$ of a second in latitude and of $\frac{1}{10}$ in longitude was found. But the work for which Montgomerie is best known among geographers is that comprised in his system of employing carefully trained native observers to make discoveries in the unknown regions beyond the northern frontiers of British India. Colonel Montgomerie died prematurely on the 31st of January, 1878, but both before and since his death the Society has recognised the useful labours of his trained subordinates.

In 1875 a gold watch was presented to Mr. W. H. Johnson, of the Indian Survey Department, for his journey in 1865 across the Kuen-Lun Mountains to Ilchi in Khotan. Another gold watch had been granted, in 1866, to Mulla Abdul Medjid, for the service he had rendered to geographical science by his adventurous journey from Peshawur to Kokand, along the upper valley of the Oxus, and across the Pamír Steppes. In 1868 the Pundit Nain Sing, another of Montgomerie's trained explorers, received a gold watch for his route survey from Lake Mansarowar to Lhasa, the capital of Tibet; and in 1877 he had conferred upon him the Society's Gold Medal for his important journey across the vast lacustrine plateau of Tibet, and thence by a new route into Assam.

But our rewards for Trans-Himálayan exploration have not been confined to Government surveyors. In 1875 the eminent botanist, Dr. Thomas Thomson, the companion of Sir Joseph Hooker in the Eastern Himálayas, and the first who reached the Karakorum Pass in the west, received the Founder's Gold Medal for work done nearly thirty years before. Mr. Hayward and Mr. Shaw both received our Medals for their adventurous and interesting journeys into Eastern Turkistan. In the case of Mr. Hayward the Society granted the explorer a sum of 600*l.*, and received a report and map of his journey across the Kuen-Lun to Yarkand and Kashgar. In 1870 he was honoured with the Founder's Gold Medal, but his useful career was brought to an untimely end in the same year. Mr. Shaw was more fortunate. He visited Yarkand and Kashgar in 1869, and was again at Yarkand with the first Mission of Sir Douglas Forsyth, executing a valuable survey of the country between the high table lands at the head of the Karakash River and the valley of the Upper Shayok, and taking numerous accurate observations for latitude and longitude and variation of the compass. He well merited the Patron's Medal which was conferred upon him in 1872. Mr. Shaw was afterwards Resident at Leh, where he continued his geographical researches, and his lamented death in 1879 was a serious loss to our science. His ' Journey to Kashgar ' continues to be one of the most popular books in our library.

Lastly, as concerns the Trans-Himálayan Region, a very eminent Surveyor received our Gold Medal in 1878. Captain Henry Trotter, R.E., of the Great Trigonometrical Survey, accompanied the mission of Sir Douglas Forsyth to Kashgar as geographer. He made a boat voyage on the Pangong Lake in October 1873, described the routes between Ladak and Turkistan, and his excursions in the neighbourhood of Kashgar as far as the Artysh district ; and made an important journey over the Pamír Steppe into Wakhan, during March and April 1874. He visited the Victoria Lake, which is Wood's source of the Oxus, and succeeded in connecting the Indian Surveys with those of Russia, at the same time throwing a flood of light on the geography of the Pamír and Eastern Turkistan.

Four explorers in the Chinese Empire have earned the Royal Award. In 1862 Captain Thomas Blakiston received the Patron's Medal for his survey of the Yang-tsze-kiang for 900 miles beyond the farthest point previously reached by Englishmen. Mr. Ney Elias, in 1873, earned the Founder's Medal for his enterprise and ability in surveying the new course of the Yellow River in 1868, and for his remarkable journey through Western Mongolia, by Uliassutai and Kobdo, during which he took a large series of observations for fixing positions and altitudes. In presenting the Medal to Mr. Ney Elias, Sir Henry Rawlinson recorded his opinion that the young explorer had performed one of the most extraordinary journeys of modern times. Baron F. von Richthofen travelled in various parts of China from 1868 to 1872, mapping the country and making a systematic examination of the physical geography and geology of twelve of its provinces. Colonel Yule said of Baron von Richthofen that in his person were combined the great traveller, the great physical geographer, and the accomplished writer, in a degree unknown since Humboldt's best days. For his great merits as a traveller Baron von Richthofen was awarded the Founder's Medal in 1878. In the following year the same Medal was given to Captain W. J. Gill, R.E., for his important geographical work in Western China and Tibet during 1877, and for his traverse survey and very complete maps of his route.

Lieutenant Francis Garnier, of the French Navy, earned the Patron's Medal in 1870, for his exploring expedition from Cambodia to the Yang-tsze-kiang, during which he made valuable surveys, visited Talifu, and brought his party in safety to Hankow, travelling over 5400 miles. This distinguished young traveller was murdered by the Chinese rebels of Tonquin on the 20th of December, 1873, when only in his 34th year.

Two eminent Russian explorers have received our Gold Medals for geographical work on the Asiatic continent. Admiral Alexis Boutakoff was the first to launch and navigate ships on the Sea of Aral, and he made a valuable survey of the chief mouths of the Oxus, for which he received the Founder's Medal in 1867. Colonel Prejevalsky, our other Russian Medallist, made successive expeditions, from 1870 to 1873, into Mongolia and to the high plateau of Northern Tibet, and in 1876 and 1877 he penetrated from Kulja to Lob Nor. For these great services to geography our Patron's Medal was conferred upon him in 1879. Another adventurous traveller in Central Asia, the Magyar, Dr. Arminius Vambéry, was awarded the sum of 40*l.* in 1865, for the self-reliance, courage, and perseverance with which he penetrated to Khiva and thence, through the deserts of the Oxus, to Bokhara and Samarkand, in the disguise of a Dervish. Lastly, Mr. W. Gifford Palgrave was, in 1863, granted a sum of 25*l.* for his very daring and remarkable journey in and across Arabia. As regards assistance given by the Society, the grant of 34*l.* for instruments to the Rev. F. W. Holland, to aid him in his valuable Sinai exploration in 1868, and of 50*l.* towards the survey of the Sinai Peninsula by Captains Wilson and Palmer, in 1869, must be mentioned. This by no means exhausts the list of travellers and surveyors on the Asiatic continent who have been helped on their way and cordially welcomed on their return by the Council of our Society. It is only the roll of the most deserving or the most fortunate, who have been carefully selected for special honour.

Turning from Asia to the African Continent, the Society's great activity and liberal expenditure during the last quarter of a century have been two very important factors in the solution of geographical problems which have occupied the thoughts and defied the efforts of former generations for many centuries. It is over thirty years ago since, in 1850, Admiral Smyth presented a chronometer watch to "the Rev. David Livingstone of Kolobeng," for his successful exploration of South Africa; and since then our Gold Medals have been presented to explorers of Africa no less than eleven times, a fact which indicates the constant efforts that have been made to increase our knowledge of the vast unknown portions of that Continent.

The Society showed its high appreciation of the labours of the greatest of modern African travellers from the very first. David Livingstone was born at Blantyre in 1813, and after studying at Glasgow University, he went out to South Africa as a Missionary in 1840, settling at Kolobeng in the far interior in 1847. His first great journey, undertaken with the aid of General Sir Thomas Steele, Mr. M. C. Oswell, and Mr. Murray, was commenced in June 1849, with the object of discovering Lake N'gami, which he reached in August of the same year. Sir T. Steele sent the account of this journey to our Society, and it was at once resolved to recognise its importance by the award of a chronometer watch to the intrepid explorer. In 1851 Livingstone, accompanied by his wife and

Mr. Oswell, undertook another journey, and reached the Zambesi river. In 1852 he was in Cape Town, receiving instruction from Sir Thomas Maclear, the Astronomer Royal of the Colony. He then set out on his most famous expedition, reaching Linjante, the capital of the Makololo in May 1853, and São Paulo de Loanda on May 21st, 1854. Returning to Linjante he visited the Victoria Falls of the Zambesi, and reached Quilimane, after having marched across the Continent of Africa, on May 26th, 1856.

This famous journey, including great discoveries, secured for Livingstone our Founder's Medal in 1855, while it excited the interest of the whole civilized world. On reaching England he received a most enthusiastic welcome at our Meeting on December 15th, 1856, and during the next few months he was engaged on his narrative entitled 'Missionary Travels,' 45,000 copies of which were sold. The Government, struck by the importance of his discoveries, placed at Dr. Livingstone's disposal those means and materials which formed the Zambesi Expedition. Sir Roderick Murchison, the great traveller's steadfast and unfailing friend, organised what was called the Livingstone Festival, a farewell dinner, at which 350 guests assembled on February 13th, 1858. In March Livingstone started for the Zambesi, accompanied by his brother Charles Livingstone, by Dr. Kirk, Mr. Thornton as geologist, Captain Bedingfield, R.N., and Mr. Baines the zealous traveller and artist. Livingstone, during this expedition, traced the course of the river Shiré, and in September 1860 he discovered the beautiful Lake Nyassa and the smaller Lake Shirwa. But except as regards the geographical discoveries, this expedition was not successful. In 1862 Livingstone's wife died of fever at Shupanga. The "Universities Mission," which had come out with high hopes owing to Livingstone's representations, lost its leader, Bishop Mackenzie, and the work was eventually abandoned. Dr. Livingstone returned to England in 1864.

The years which include the discoveries of Livingstone saw much valuable work achieved in other parts of Africa. Dr. Henry Barth, a native of Hamburg, born in 1821, was an accomplished classical scholar as well as a great traveller. First associated with Richardson, Overweg, and Vogel, and afterwards by himself, he made numerous excursions around lake Chad, discovered the great river Benué, and succeeded in completing a hazardous and adventurous journey to Timbuktu. For these services he received our Gold Medal in 1856, and in the following year he completed a work which Sir Roderick Murchison pronounced to be the masterpiece of all his labours, entitled 'Travels in North and Central Africa,' in five volumes. This work was published under the auspices and by the assistance of our Government, and Her Majesty conferred on him a Companionship of the Bath. Dr. Barth had undertaken to edit Leo Africanus for the Hakluyt Society, thus filling up a serious desideratum in our geographical literature, but this was prevented by his untimely death at the early age of 44, in 1866.

Corporal Church of the Sappers and Miners was granted a gold watch and chain by our Council in 1856, for his meritorious and intelligent services while employed upon the African expedition under Dr. Vogel, and especially for his diligence in conducting a long series of meteorological observations at Kuka.

The exploration of the African equatorial lakes, commenced by that intrepid traveller and accomplished scholar, Captain R. F. Burton, forms an era in the history of discovery. The Council, in 1853, had secured the services of Captain Burton to explore the interior of Arabia, and assisted him with a grant of money. The result was his memorable journey from Yambu to Medina and Mecca. In the following year he attempted to explore Eastern Africa from Berbera to Zanzibar, with Lieutenants Speke and Stroyan, and he himself succeeded in reaching Harar, a place never before visited by Europeans. But further progress was prevented by an attack of the Somalis, in which Stroyan was killed, and both Burton and Speke were severely wounded. These preliminary services had shown Burton to be an able and resolute explorer as well as an accomplished orientalist. He was therefore selected to conduct an expedition from Zanzibar, under the Society's auspices, and with assistance both from the Foreign Office and the East India Company. A Treasury grant of 1000*l.* was also obtained. In June 1857 Captain Burton, accompanied by Captain Speke, started from Zanzibar and succeeded in reaching the great Lake Tanganyika, about 700 miles from the coast. Careful and complete itineraries, and astronomical observations by Captain Speke, were made in spite of severe hardships, privations, and sickness. On their return Speke made a journey northwards from Unyanyembe, and discovered the southern shore of a vast inland fresh-water lake, which was named Victoria Nyanza. Burton generously gave all the credit of the topographical work to his companion, he himself undertaking the history and ethnography, with accounts of the languages and peculiarities of the people. Captain Burton's exhaustive memoir of the Lake Regions of Central Equatorial Africa, occupies the whole of the 29th volume of our 'Transactions.' It contains a complete description of the physical geography, the fauna and flora, the inhabitants and history of the countries along his line of route.

He worthily earned our highest honour, which was conferred upon him in 1859.

In 1860 another expedition was despatched under the Society's auspices, commanded by Captain Speke, to land at Zanzibar and explore the Victoria Nyanza, which was believed to be a main source of the Nile. A Treasury grant of 2500*l.* was obtained to aid in defraying the expenses. On this occasion Captain Speke was accompanied by Captain Grant. Leaving Zanzibar in October 1860, the travellers reached Unyanyembe in 1861, and during that and the following year they marched northward to the Victoria Nyanza, skirted its western shore, and reached the kingdom of Uganda. Following the Nile for 120 miles north of the lake, Speke and Grant were then obliged to leave the stream, but again struck it some 70 miles lower down, and at length reached Gondokoro on February 15th, 1863, where they were met and assisted by Samuel Baker. The travellers descended the Nile and received a very hearty welcome on their return to England. Speke had been granted the Gold Medal of our Society, and further honours were in store for him from his Sovereign, when a melancholy accident terminated his life in August 1864. His companion, Captain Grant, received our Gold Medal in 1864, and was created a Companion of the Bath, and the honour of knighthood was conferred on Sir Samuel Baker, who had so opportunely aided the explorers at Gondokoro. In 1864 Baron von der Decken, who had made two surveys of the lofty mountain of Kilimanjaro, received the Founder's Medal, and this gallant young explorer would have done further valuable service had not his career been cut short prematurely in 1866, when attempting to ascend the river Juba in a steamer. He had only reached his 33rd year.

Before he succoured Speke and Grant, Sir Samuel Baker had made discoveries in the basin of the Atbara, and afterwards, advancing up the White Nile, he discovered the second great water-basin, to which he assigned the name of " Albert Nyanza." Sir Roderick Murchison had presented our highest honour to him through his brother, in 1865 ; and on hearing of his great success, our President declared that nothing which had happened since the foundation of the Society had given him greater satisfaction than that this devoted and high-minded traveller should have thus proved himself to be truly worthy of the Medal. It was actually granted for the chivalrous spirit he displayed in rushing to the rescue of Speke and Grant. In 1871 Sir Samuel Baker, in the service of the Khedive of Egypt, again visited the scenes of his former discoveries, with the object of rooting out the slave-traders and kidnappers. In the

performance of this great service he explored the kingdom of
Unyoro, and collected much valuable information respecting
the equatorial lake region. His devoted wife accompanied him
in all his journeys, and the hero and heroine of a noble and
most arduous achievement received a cordial and heartfelt
welcome on their return. A dinner was given in honour of
Sir Samuel and Lady Baker by the Geographical Club on
December 8th, 1873.

The Society, ever anxious to encourage the efforts of individual explorers, presented a sum of 100*l.* to M. Du Chaillu in
1866, for his efforts to penetrate into the interior from the West
Coast of Africa, during which he made good astronomical observations, and also to reimburse him for the loss of his instruments.
Assistance was also given to M. Gerhard Rohlfs of Bremen, in
the shape of a grant of 100*l.* to enable him to continue his
journeys which, during five years, commencing in 1861, he
made in the northern part of the African Continent. His
expedition in Morocco in 1863 and 1864, included the passage
of the Atlas southward to the oasis of Tuat; and afterwards he
went from Tripoli to Kuka on the shores of lake Chad, and
southwards by the Benué and Niger, and across the Yoriba
country to Lagos, in the Gulf of Guinea. For these remarkable
journeys M. Gerhard Rohlfs received the Patron's Medal in
1868.

Dr. Livingstone returned from his Zambesi Expedition with
feelings of disappointment. It was then that Sir Roderick
Murchison proposed to him the great work of defining the true
watershed of Inner Southern Africa. He gladly undertook
this hard achievement, the Society granting 500*l.* towards his
expenses, and obtaining for him the title and position of a
Consul, the Government adding another 500*l.* Livingstone left
England in August 1865, spent the following winter in Bombay
and in Zanzibar, and finally advanced into the interior from
the mouth of the Rovuma in April 1866. Travelling thence to
Ujiji on lake Tanganyika, he discovered lake Bangweolo and
the magnificent river Lualaba on his way. Afterwards he penetrated into the Manyuema country, enduring most terrible privations and, after having been lost to the outer world for years,
he was at length found and succoured by Mr. Stanley at Ujiji.
Mr. Stanley finally parted with Livingstone at Unyanyembe in
March 1872, and in the following August the dauntless veteran
resumed his explorations. He died near the shores of Lake
Bangweolo on May 4th, 1873. His faithful servants, Chuma
and Susi, conveyed their beloved master's body, with his
journals and other property, during an eight months' march, to
Zanzibar. The remains arrived in England on April 15th,

1874, and were in the Society's Map Room until they were deposited in their last resting-place in the nave of Westminster Abbey. As an explorer, Livingstone trod some 29,000 miles of African soil, and laid open nearly one million square miles of new country. Sir Bartle Frere, who was our President when the great traveller died, thus concluded his sympathetic and careful sketch of Livingstone's career:—" As a whole, the work of his life will surely be held up in ages to come as one of singular nobleness of design, and of unflinching energy and self-sacrifice in execution. It will be long ere any one man will be able to open so large an extent of unknown land to civilized mankind. Yet longer, perhaps, ere we find a brighter example of a life of such continued and useful self-devotion to a noble cause."

Livingstone's long absence caused great anxiety to his friends, and especially to the Council of our Society, which was unceasing in its efforts for his succour, and liberal, beyond all precedent, in the expenditure of funds with that object—not only of money voted from the Society's own resources, but of still larger sums mainly subscribed by the Council and Fellows. These efforts for the relief of the great traveller form a very noble episode in the history of the Geographical Society. They were commenced, owing to a false report of Livingstone's death, with a searching boat expedition, under the command of Mr. Young, R.N., which our Council induced the Government to despatch in 1866, and to which we contributed 160*l.* Mr. Young proceeded to the Zambesi, went up the Shiré to lake Nyassa, navigated that inland sea, and satisfactorily disposed of the story, having performed the duty with skill, promptitude, and success. In 1870, at the recommendation of our Council, the Government sent out 1000*l.* to Zanzibar to furnish Livingstone with fresh supplies, to which a further sum was added by the great traveller's friend, Mr. James Young. Meanwhile Mr. Stanley, correspondent of the 'New York Herald,' left the coast for Ujiji in February 1871, and, as has already been recorded, he found Livingstone and brought him much needed succour. Returning to England in the summer of 1872, after performing this great service, Mr. Stanley was cordially received by our President and Council. He was entertained at a great dinner on October 21st, 1872, and the unprecedented step was taken of conferring upon him the Society's Gold Medal some months before the appointed time. Meanwhile the Council had started a Livingstone Search and Relief Fund, large sums were subscribed, and a well-equipped expedition was sent to Zanzibar, and was on the point of starting for the interior, when Mr. Stanley returned with the news of Livingstone's safety.

But when Stanley announced that the aged explorer had once more started alone for the unknown interior, it was strongly felt that succouring expeditions should be despatched both to the east and to the west coasts. Lieut. Grandy, R.N., was sent to the Congo to meet Livingstone if he should emerge on the west coast, and Mr. James Young generously defrayed the heavy expenses of this part of the scheme. The conduct of the east-coast expedition was entrusted to Lieut. V. L. Cameron, R.N. On November 11th, 1872, these two young officers were entertained at dinner by the Geographical Club. Cameron's instructions were to deliver supplies to Dr. Livingstone wherever he might find him, and to place himself under the great traveller's orders. But after reaching Unyanyembe, the melancholy certainty of Livingstone's death necessarily altered Cameron's plans, and in October 1873 the faithful servants arrived there with the body and proceeded to the coast. Cameron resolved to achieve some geographical success. He pushed onwards, reached Ujiji in February 1874, explored the southern half of Lake Tanganyika in a boat, and solved the long doubtful problem of its outlet. He then advanced across the Manyuema country to the Lualaba or Congo, crossed that river, and reached the capital of Urua in October 1874. In the same month of the following year Cameron arrived at Benguela on the Atlantic, and was thus the first European traveller who had walked across tropical Africa from east to west. At a great meeting of the Society on April 11th, 1876, in St. James's Hall, Cameron gave an account of his memorable journey, and in May he was presented with our Founder's Medal. He was also promoted to the rank of Commander, and Her Majesty conferred upon him a Companionship of the Bath. The heavy expense of the expedition, upwards of 12,000*l.*, fell mainly upon the Society, being only partly refunded by liberal private subscriptions, and by a grant of 3000*l.* from the Government. Lieut. Grandy was recalled on the news of Livingstone's death, but not before he had done some useful exploring work in the Congo country.

While these resolute efforts were being made to increase our knowledge of tropical Africa, an accomplished German traveller had been engaged in exploring the south-western basin of the Nile. Dr. Schweinfurth, starting on his travels in 1868, succeeded in defining the limits of the basin of the Bahr Ghazal, crossed the water parting to the south, and reached the river Uelle, the course of which has not yet been explored. His work entitled 'The Heart of Africa,' is a most able description of the physical geography, ethnology, climate, botany, and resources of the Bahr Ghazal region. In recognition of its merits Dr. Schweinfurth received our Founder's Medal in 1874.

In 1874 Mr. Stanley undertook a second journey into the interior of Africa, to explore the equatorial lakes, and discover the course of the Congo. In March 1875 he reached the southern shore of the Victoria Nyanza, where he put a boat together, which he had conveyed from Zanzibar in pieces, and launched it on the lake. He circumnavigated the lake, visited the capital of Uganda, and returned to his camp after an absence of fifty-eight days. Having made some journeys in the direction of the Albert Nyanza, and in the kingdom of Rumanika, Stanley proceeded to Ujiji, and followed Cameron's route round the southern half of Lake Tanganyika. He then marched across Manyuema to Nyangwe and embarked on the Lualaba, which eventually proved to be identical with the Congo. Leaving Nyangwe on November 5th, 1876, Stanley and his party rapidly descended the river, encountering frequent opposition from hostile tribes, until the falls were reached, but it took the party five months to pass these cataracts. The distance from Nyangwe to the mouth of the Congo is calculated at 1800 miles, and Mr. Stanley was navigating the river from November 1876 to August 1877. Dangers in every form were met with intrepid resolution, while marvellous resource and ingenuity were exercised in combating the great physical obstacles. Sir Roderick Murchison, whose forecasts were seldom wrong, held the opinion that Livingstone's Lualaba was the Congo, and Stanley verified the fact.

The Council of the Society, while encouraging and assisting exploration in tropical Africa, was not unmindful of the useful if less known labours of those who were zealously working further south, and also on the west coast. Mr. R. B. N. Walker received a sum of 143*l*. in 1865, to aid him in his efforts to explore the Ogowé, 100*l*. was granted to Mr. St. Vincent Erskine in 1870 for exploring the Limpopo, Mr. Wakefield of Mombas was granted 35*l*. in 1871, and in 1872 the services of Karl Mauch were recognised by the grant of 25*l*. Landing at Natal almost destitute, Herr Mauch gradually worked his way northward to the region lying between the lower courses of the Limpopo and the Zambesi, the region of the semi-fabulous Monomotapa of the early Portuguese. Here the enthusiastic explorer brought to light the abandoned gold-fields, and the ruins of an ancient city. He carried on his investigations year after year amid many privations, and also fixed the positions of several points, and the courses and width of rivers by exact observations. In 1873 a gold watch was granted to that well-known traveller and painter of African scenery, Thomas Baines.

Born in 1822, the son of a Master Mariner at King's Lynn,
young Baines went out to the Cape in 1842, and remained there
until 1854.   He was next engaged as artist with Gregory's
N.W. Australian Expedition, and afterwards with Livingstone
on the Zambesi.   In 1861–62 he made a journey from Walfisch
Bay to Lake Ngami and the Victoria Falls, and from 1864 to
1868 he was again in England.   His large series of admirable
sketches in oils was divided between our Society and Kew
Museum.   His unselfishness and willingness to oblige were
only equalled by his extraordinary industry.   His time and
abilities were at the service of all who needed them, with or
without payment.   In 1868 Mr. Baines returned to Africa to
explore the gold-fields of Tatí, which were discovered by Karl
Mauch.   The results of his exploration of this region were
exceedingly valuable, but he gained nothing for himself, and
died very poor at Durban on May 8th, 1875.

That excellent man and most painstaking and accurate
explorer, Werner Munzinger, contributed several valuable papers
to our Journal, although he did not receive any special recognition from the Society for his services.   His career was prematurely cut short.   He rendered such essential service to the
Abyssinian Expedition that a Companionship of the Bath was
conferred upon him at its close, but his best geographical work
was the toilsome and arduous journey through the desert Afar
region, and the memoir and map which were its result.
Munzinger was making his way to the kingdom of Shoa when
he was murdered by a party of Gallas on November 14th,
1875.

The name of W. Winwood Reade must here find a place
among African explorers.   Born in 1838, the stories of Du
Chaillu led him to make a voyage to the Gaboon to hunt
gorillas, and on his return he published his ' Savage Africa.'
Afterwards he led an expedition from Sierra Leone to the upper
waters of the Niger in 1869 ; and his observations are recorded
in his ' African Sketch Book.'   This zealous explorer and
brilliant writer was cut off prematurely, dying at the early age
of 37, in 1875.

As regards the Niger region, a gold watch was presented to
Bishop Crowther in 1880, in recognition of the service to
geography which he has performed during his numerous voyages
up the river.

In consequence of the efforts made by His Majesty the King
of the Belgians to promote African discovery, the Council of
our Society resolved to raise an " African Exploration Fund,"
to be appropriated to the scientific examination of Africa.   A
Committee was appointed to carry the objects of the Fund into

effect, and the Council granted 500*l.* towards it, in March 1877. Seven routes were suggested for exploration :—

1st. From the gold-fields of South Africa, past the south end of Tanganyika, to Unyanyembe.
2nd. Along the east face of the coast range between the Zambesi and the Equator.
3rd. From the east coast to the north end of Nyassa.
4th. Between the north end of Nyassa and south end of Tanganyika.
5th. From the coast opposite Zanzibar to the south end of Lake Victoria; thence to the north end of Tanganyika.
6th. From Mombasa, by Kilimanjaro, to S.E. shore of Lake Victoria.
7th. From Formosa Bay, along the valley of the River Dana, by Mount Kenia, to N.E. shore of Lake Victoria.

In 1878 the Committee selected the 3rd and 4th, from Dar-es-Salaam, a few miles south of Zanzibar, to the northern end of Lake Nyassa, and thence to Tanganyika. The Council voted a further grant for the contemplated expedition, eventually raising their contribution to 2000*l.* Fellows and other well-wishers together subscribed 1989*l.* Young Mr. A. Keith Johnston, the only son of the eminent geographer of Edinburgh, was selected to command this expedition. Born in 1844, he had been carefully instructed in geography by his father, and afterwards completed his education in Germany. For about eighteen months, in 1872–73, he was Assistant-Curator in our Map Room, and until 1875 he was learning active field work in the wilds of Paraguay. After his return he was engaged on literary geographical work until he left England in November 1878. He was accompanied by Mr. Joseph Thomson, a young Scotch geologist, and at Zanzibar he secured the services of Livingstone's faithful servant Chuma. After a preliminary trip to the Usambara Mountains, the party landed at Dar-es-Salaam on May 19th, 1879. Ascending the course of the river Rufiji, Mr. Keith Johnston was attacked by fever, and he expired on the 23rd of June. " Thus," says his young companion, " was one of the most promising explorers who had ever set foot on African shores, numbered with the long list of geographical martyrs who have attempted to break through the barriers of disease and barbarism which make the interior of Africa almost impenetrable." Mr. Thomson, at the age of 22, now found himself alone in the wilds of Africa, charged with heavy responsibility, and at the head of work in which few have succeeded. The brave young fellow proved equal to the occasion. With his foot on the threshold of the unknown, he resolved to go forward and do his best. " Though the mantle of Mr. Johnston's knowledge could not descend upon me," he said, "yet he left his enthusiasm for the work of research, and I resolved to carry out his design as far as lay in my power."

On the 2nd of July Mr. Thomson resumed the journey, and after many long and perilous marches he reached the northern shore of Lake Nyassa. Thence he advanced northwards, and on November 2nd, 1879, he came in sight of Lake Tanganyika. His work, as traced out by the Society, was now finished ; but Mr. Thomson, on seeing the great expanse of waters, felt impelled to explore the Lukuga outlet discovered by Cameron. Encamping his men under command of Chuma, he started on his march northwards, along the western shore, with only thirty porters. Suffering from fever, the enthusiastic young explorer felt as if he had got a new lease of life when, on Christmas Day 1879, he beheld the noble river Lukuga bearing the drainage waters of the Tanganyika to the Congo and the Atlantic. For six days he advanced down the river's course, and reached a hill whence he could see the great plain of the Lualaba spread out below him. For a long time he was in constant danger from the fierce race of Waruas, but he eventually escaped and returned to his camp on April 4th. Mr. Thomson then made his way back to Zanzibar from the south end of Tanganyika, discovering a remarkable lake, which he named Lake Leopold, on his way. After resting for a few days at Unyanyembe, he finally reached the sea-shore at Bagamoyo. He thus concludes his modest and most interesting narrative : " I felt it to be my proudest boast that of the 150 men who left Dar-es-Salaam, only one did not survive to see the Indian Ocean again ; and it will ever be a pleasure to me to think that though often placed in critical positions, I never once required to fire a gun for either offensive or defensive purposes."

This expedition was organized by, and directed from first to last, under instructions from a Committee of the Society's' Council, the chairman of which was our former President, Sir Rutherford Alcock. It had a clearly defined aim, and it was conducted ably, economically, and with complete success, first by its lamented leader, and afterwards by a most competent successor, whose fortitude, energy, and sound judgment, combined with intelligent and instructed observation, are rare combinations in any man, and most remarkable in one so young as Mr. Joseph Thomson.

Finally, that gallant young Portuguese officer, Major Serpa Pinto, received our Gold Medal in 1881, for his discoveries and numerous astronomical observations, during the course of his march across Africa, from Benguela to Natal.

This long array of gallant and most brilliant achievements, with which our Society has been more or less closely connected, has wrought a marvellous change on the map of Africa. Yet this is only one great division of the world, and it will now be seen that our activity has not been confined to the African continent.

The Society, since it initiated the expedition of Lieuts. Grey and Lushington, has taken a leading part in advocating and planning the exploration of Australia. A general plan for exploring North Australia was advocated by our Society, in consequence of a project for colonizing Carpentaria put forward in a book by Mr. Trelawney Saunders, and in accordance with the suggestions of our Associates Admiral Stokes and Captain Sturt. Her Majesty's Government decided upon adopting our proposal, and they selected an experienced surveyor, Mr. Augustus C. Gregory, to carry out this important project. Mr. Gregory had previously unravelled the condition of the interior of Western Australia, and in 1848 he had proceeded from Perth and travelled over 1500 miles in search of good land. In 1856 his expedition went by sea from Sydney through Torres Strait, and landed on the Victoria River, about eighty miles from its mouth. He was accompanied by his brother Mr. F. Gregory, the botanist Dr. Muller, the geologist Mr. Wilson, and Mr. Baines the artist traveller. Ascending the Victoria to its source, the explorers crossed the water-parting at a height of 1660 feet, and descended a stream flowing south, ending in a desiccated salt lake, which he called Sturt Creek. Returning to the Victoria, he next advanced thence to the Gulf of Carpentaria, and explored the region between the eastern side of that gulf and the then northernmost station of our settlers, ending his labours at Brisbane. He had marched over 6500 miles in a country previously unknown, and received our Founder's Medal in 1857. The Patron's Medal was adjudicated to another Australian explorer, Mr. M'Douall Stuart in 1861, for having advanced across the continent from the south to within 245 miles of the Gulf of Carpentaria. Attempts to cross the continent were continuous, and Mr. Richard O'Hara Burke, with his companions Wills and Gray, at length traversed it from south and north. But they perished, and the Founder's Medal was awarded to the representative of O'Hara Burke in 1862. One man alone survived, Mr. John King, to whom a gold watch with a suitable inscription was presented. Meanwhile our Medallist, M'Douall Stuart, in 1861–62, successfully crossed the continent from Adelaide to Van Diemen Gulf, exploring the route along which the electric telegraph was subsequently laid. In 1863 our Gold Medal was presented to Mr. Frank Gregory for his successful explorations in Western Australia, and gold watches, with honorary inscriptions, were adjudged to Mr. William Landsborough, Mr. John M'Kinlay, and Mr. Frederick Walker, for valuable additions to our knowledge; the first for his journey from Carpentaria to Victoria, the second for exploring from Adelaide to Carpentaria, and the third for discoveries between the Nogoa and the Gulf of Carpentaria. Landsborough and M'Kinlay were leaders of expeditions for the relief of O'Hara Burke.

Our rewards for Australian work have since been bestowed upon gallant and resolute men who have traversed the trackless and arid wastes on the western side of the continent. In 1872 an overland telegraph line had been successfully laid across Australia from Port Augusta to Port Darwin. Central Mount Stuart is nearly on the centre of this line, and in April 1873 Colonel Egerton Warburton, of the good old Cheshire stock, started thence to reach the western settlements. After eight months' march, the latter portion of which was through an arid region where the party was supported by the meat of their slaughtered camels, and finally narrowly escaped death from starvation, the frontier settlements on the De Grey River were reached in the end of December, nearly 1000 miles of entirely new country having been traversed. For this service to geography Colonel Warburton received our Medal in 1874. Mr. J. Forrest had the same distinction conferred upon him in 1876, for his route survey across the interior from Murchison River to the line of the Overland Telegraph, when he marched, for the most part on foot, for 2000 miles, 600 of which was through a region covered with spinifex grass, and almost destitute of water. Lastly, our Patron's Medal was presented to Mr. Ernest Giles, in 1880, for having led several exploring expeditions between 1872 and 1876, the most important of which were from Beltana to Perth, and from Champion Bay to the Overland Line of Telegraph.

If our honours have not so frequently been bestowed on travellers for work in North and South America, it is not for want either of important and interesting undiscovered regions to be explored, or of accomplished travellers to describe them. Since 1850 only two of our medals have been conferred for work in North America, and but one for South American exploration. In 1858 the Patron's Medal was adjudicated to Professor Alexander Dallas Bache, who had been in charge of the Great Coast Survey of the United States since 1844. Sir Roderick Murchison did no more than justice to this national undertaking, when he said that "whether we regard the science, skill, and zeal of the operators, the perfection of their instruments, the able manner in which the Superintendent has enlisted all modern improvements into his service, the care taken to have the observations accurately registered, or the noble liberality of the Government, all unprejudiced persons must agree that the United States Coast Survey stands without a superior." Captain John Palliser received the Patron's Medal in 1859 for the successful results of the expedition under his command during 1857 and 1858, in exploring large tracts of British North America, and particularly for the determination of the existence of practicable passes across the Rocky Mountains within British territory. Palliser's Expedition originated in the pressing recommendation of our Society.

Since the days of Schomburgk, the Gold Medal has only been awarded to one traveller in South America. Mr. William Chandless received it in 1866, for his unaided exploration of the River Purus, one of the great southern tributaries of the Amazon, for a distance of 1866 miles, and for laying down the course of this previously undefined stream by a continuous series of astronomical observations for latitude and longitude, and true compass bearings. The great danger encountered in travelling for months through a country of interminable forest, in which lurk hordes of savage Indians, was shown in the treacherous slaughter of Mr. Chandless's servant, and his boat's crew, in descending the river. The result of his enterprise was the discovery of a vast tract of interesting country previously unknown, and a profound modification of all our maps of the interior of tropical South America. Commander Musters, R.N., was, in 1872, awarded a gold watch, with a suitable inscription, for his adventurous journey in Patagonia through 960 miles of latitude, in 780 of which he travelled over a country previously quite unknown to Europeans. But this by no means exhausts the list of accomplished and deserving South American travellers, the successors of Humboldt, of Woodbine Parish, and of Schomburgk. The names of Pentland, Poeppig, Martius, Maw, and Smyth; of Wallace, Spruce, and Bates; of Tschudi, Wertermann, and Raimondi; of Cox and Moreno, at once recur to the mind. South America is indeed the classic land of travellers; the land to the descriptions of which the writer of travels and the portrayer of scenery must go for his best models, the land which inspired our ablest geographical writers from the classic works of Humboldt to the charming narrative of Bates. No travellers have been more thoroughly fitted for their tasks by previous training, none have more resolutely faced dangers and privations, and some among them stand first as accurate scientific observers, while their works are the best models on which a book of travels can be written. Every geographical author should be a student of Humboldt, of Schomburgk, and of Bates.

The searches for Sir John Franklin's expedition, in which the whole nation took so deep an interest, were specially advocated by our Society. The expedition had been sent out through the influence of our Founder and former President, and was commanded by one of our Vice-Presidents. It is our pride, too, to be able to reflect that Sir Roderick Murchison stood by the noble-hearted widow of Franklin, supporting her efforts to the last when others, including the Government, fell away from her; and that the attempts made by Sir Roderick to obtain a renewal of the glorious work of Arctic discovery only ceased with his life.

When Sir James Ross returned, without tidings, in 1849, Captains Collinson and M'Clure were despatched in the *Enterprise* and *Investigator* to search by way of Behring Strait, while Captain Austin's expedition sailed in April 1850 to follow the footsteps of Franklin up Baffin Bay and Barrow Strait. No expedition was ever more ably and successfully commanded than that of Captain Austin, and its proceedings form a turning-point in the history of Arctic exploration on several grounds. It was the first in which steam power was efficiently used in ice navigation, and the work of Cator and Sherard Osborn on board the *Intrepid* and *Pioneer* in Baffin Bay pioneered the way to a revolution in the methods of encountering and overcoming ice obstacles. Then it was Captain Austin who brought the carefully calculated system for winter quarters to the highest perfection, and no one has since improved upon his methods and arrangements. Lastly, it was Captain Austin who inaugurated the system of extended sledge parties, depôts, and auxiliaries; which was developed, in its details, by the genius of M'Clintock. Thus, in 1851, a most complete system of search was carried out, consisting of six extended parties to be away sixty days each, marching in different directions, and each supported by an auxiliary sledge to lay out a depôt.

Captain Austin returned in the autumn of 1851, and when another expedition sailed in the next year, it merely followed exactly the arrangements of its predecessor. Indeed its leading spirits were Austin's old officers—M'Clintock and Sherard Osborn, Mecham and Hamilton, MacDougall and May. Sir Henry Kellett, in the *Resolute*, wintered at Melville Island in 1852-53, and Lieut. Mecham fortunately discovered a record left by Captain M'Clure which announced the position of the *Investigator* in a harbour of Banks Land. Knowing the position, Captain Kellett sent Lieut. Pim to communicate early in the spring of 1853, and the gallant crew of the *Investi-*

gator, just when the ship was about to be abandoned after three winters, were saved. By marching across to the *Resolute* and afterwards returning home by Baffin Bay, M'Clure, his officers, and crew traversed a North-West Passage. It was in 1853 and 1854 that the Arctic sledge travelling, developed and matured under Captain Austin, was still further extended. M'Clintock, in 1853, marched over 1328 miles, and was absent from the ship 105 days. Mecham was away 94 days and went over 1163 miles. Richards and Osborn discovered the northern shores of the Parry Islands. But the most brilliant feat in naval Arctic travelling was performed by our Associate Lieut. Mecham in 1854. He was travelling for 61 days, and marched over 1336 miles, at an average rate of 20 miles a day.

Sir Robert M'Clure, who received the honour of knighthood on his return, had our Patron's Medal adjudged to him in 1854, for his discovery of the North-West Passage, before it had been ascertained that Franklin's dying heroes were ahead of him in that great achievement. In presenting it, the Earl of Ellesmere said that when M'Clure sailed, the language in naval circles was—" that man will not return by the way he has gone, unless at least he should meet Franklin. He will return eastward or he will return no more." He died on October 17th, 1873, and was attended to his grave by the President and Secretary of our Society, and by many old Arctic officers. The author of the narrative of his voyage thus sums up his character: " M'Clure was stern, cool, and bold in all perils, severe as a disciplinarian, self-reliant, yet modest as became an officer. With a granite-like view of duty to his country and profession, he would in war have been a great leader; and it was his good fortune, during a period of profound peace, to find a field for all those valuable qualities and to add fresh glory to a navy, the life-blood of which is honour and renown. The name of M'Clure will be for all time associated with the most remarkable voyage of discovery of our generation." Captain Collinson, in the *Enterprise*, while prosecuting the search for Franklin during three winters and five summers, also made a most remarkable voyage. He penetrated further eastward from Behring Strait than any ship has ever done before or since, and his route, from Behring Strait, led him along that prescribed for Franklin, if successful in reaching the north coast of America. In 1858 he was awarded our Founder's Medal. Admiral Sir Richard Collinson has since worked hard for our Society as a most active Member of Council and Vice-President during eighteen years, from 1857 to 1875. In the latter year he was obliged to retire, owing to the pressure of his duties as Deputy-Master of the Trinity House.

The labours of the searching expeditions added largely to our knowledge of the Arctic Regions. Not only was a vast extent of land and sea added to our maps, but light was thrown on the physical geography and hydrography of a considerable area previously unknown, as well as on questions relating to its geology and the distribution of animal and vegetable life. Above all a bright page was added to the history of naval prowess ; and it was no small advantage that the historian of the Arctic searches was a prominent and zealous actor in the work of exploration. Sherard Osborn's ' Stray Leaves from an Arctic Journal,' his ' Discovery of a North-West Passage by Captain M'Clure,' and his ' Career and Last Voyage of Sir John Franklin' are classic works in the geographical literature of England. They will remain as the record of great events in naval chronicle, and will "awaken in the breasts of future Parrÿs, Franklins, or M'Clures that love for perilous adventure which must ever form the most valuable trait in the character of a great maritime people."

The heart of our President, Sir Roderick Murchison, was set upon never ceasing to search the Arctic Regions until true tidings were obtained of the fate of Sir John Franklin and his gallant companions. He, therefore (news having arrived from Dr. Rae that an Eskimo statement pointed to King William Island, a place not hitherto searched, as the scene of the disaster, and that relics had been obtained which corroborated the story), very cordially joined with Lady Franklin in her efforts to induce the Government to send out a small expedition to search the unvisited shores of King William Island. A memorial was presented to the Prime Minister by Sir Roderick, as President of the Society, dated June 5th, 1856, which was signed by Admirals Beaufort, Beechey, Austin, Collinson, Smyth, and FitzRoy, by General Sabine, by the Earl of Ellesmere, and by many other eminent Arctic officers and geographers. The Government refused its request. Then it was that Lady Franklin resolved, with the aid of her steadfast friends, to despatch an expedition on her own responsibility. The cost was 10,412*l.* ; the subscriptions amounted to 2981*l.* Sir Roderick Murchison gave 100*l.*, Sir Thomas Acland, 100*l.* ; the mother of Lieut. Fairholme of the *Erebus*, 150*l.* ; the relations of Lieut. Hornby of the *Terror*, 150*l.* ; an old and dear friend of the gallant Fitzjames, 100*l.* ; Sir Francis Beaufort, 50*l.* ; the Hydrographer, 20*l.* ; Captain Collinson, 20*l.* ; Sir James Ross, 20*l.*, and several other old Arctic officers, besides many Fellows of the Society were among the subscribers. Captain Allen Young gave 500*l.* besides his own valuable services. But the great bulk of the expense fell upon Lady Franklin. She was so fortunate as to obtain the willing services of Captain M‘Clintock, the most eminent among Arctic sledge travellers, to command her steamer, the *Fox*, and the expedition sailed on June 30th, 1857. In the first season the *Fox* was forced to winter in the pack of Baffin Bay and was exposed to extreme danger at the breaking up of the ice. But, undaunted by this disaster and resolved not to return home, M‘Clintock again turned the *Fox's* head northwards, and was rewarded by reaching a point whence King William Island could be searched by sledging parties in the spring of 1859. M‘Clintock marched entirely round the shores of King William Island and examined Montreal Island, at the mouth of the Great Fish River, while Allen Young completed the discovery of the southern side of Prince of Wales Land. The result was that, by finding the famous document at Point Victory (signed by Captains Crozier and Fitzjames), the fate of Sir John Franklin and his heroic followers was ascertained, while the skeleton *beyond* or south of Simpson's cairn, on Cape Herschel, was a silent but certain proof that to them belongs the glory of having solved the question of the North-West Passage. When M‘Clintock returned from this most successful expedition he received the honour of knighthood, while his time in the *Fox* was allowed to reckon as time served in one of Her Majesty's ships.

The Council desired to commemorate, in an especial manner, the great services to geography of our gallant Vice-President Sir John Franklin. They therefore awarded the Founder's Medal, in 1860, to his widow, in token of their admiration of her noble and self-sacrificing perseverance in sending out, at her own cost, several searching expeditions, until at length the fate of her husband was ascertained. It was adjudged to her not only as the merited recompense of her husband's discoveries, but also as a testimony of the admiration entertained by British geographers for her who devoted twelve years of her life to this glorious object, in accomplishing which she sacrificed so large a portion of her worldly means.

The Patron's Medal of 1860 was adjudged to Sir Leopold M‘Clintock, for the consummate skill and unflinching fortitude with which he and his gallant companions not only enlarged our acquaintance with Arctic geography, but also brought to light the precious Record which revealed the history of the voyage and of the final abandonment of the *Erebus* and *Terror*. His interesting narrative of the voyage of the *Fox*, entitled ' Fate of Sir John Franklin,' passed through four editions.

After the return of M‘Clintock there was very lamentable neglect of Arctic work in this country during several years ; but the Council never ceased to take an interest in the efforts of other nations, and to show their appreciation of useful work well done, in a tangible form.   In 1853 Dr. Kane, in the little brig *Advance* with a crew of seventeen men, led the first American expedition into Smith Sound, and the Founder's Medal was adjudged to him in 1856 for his discoveries and arduous labours during two winters in the ice.   Dr. Kane's companion, Dr. Hayes, led another expedition to Smith Sound in 1860, and made a very gallant attempt to advance northwards along the western shore with a dog sledge.   For this service to geography Dr. Hayes received the Patron's Medal in 1867.   The admiring attention of our Council was also turned to the achievements of the Swedish explorers in the Spitzbergen seas.   Professor Nordenskjöld received our Founder's Medal in 1869 for his valuable work in Spitzbergen, which was continued in subsequent years ; and when he succeeded in the glorious achievement of making the North-East Passage in 1879, the Medal was conferred upon the commander of his ship, the *Vega*, the gallant Captain Palander.   The Norwegian, Captain Carlsen, had, in 1873, received a gold watch for circumnavigating Spitzbergen in 1863, and Novaya Zemlya in 1871.

The discovery of Franz Josef Land by the Austro-Hungarian Expedition, under the command of Lieuts. Payer and Weyprecht, and the admirably conducted sledging expeditions of Payer excited the admiration of English geographers.   In 1875 the Founder's Medal was adjudged to Lieut. Weyprecht, and the Patron's Medal to M. Julius Payer.   The latter officer came over to England, and was entertained at dinner by the Geographical Club, on November 10th, 1874, and also by the Trinity House.

But in the meanwhile our Arctic Associates had, during ten years, been striving to obtain a renewal of Arctic exploration by the Government of this country.   It was in 1865 that Captain Sherard Osborn resolved to bring this important subject before the Society.   He fully recognised the fact that the great work could only be accomplished gradually, and that one expedition must follow another until all the knowledge attainable by human means, in this field of inquiry, had been secured.   He also saw that a mere quest for the Pole was not an aim which would secure influential or intelligent support, but that the objects of Arctic exploration, in these days, must be to obtain valuable scientific results.   Lastly he felt that the route for an expedition must be that which held out the best prospect of crossing the threshold of the unknown region and reaching new ground.   He therefore wisely and correctly selected Smith Sound, at the head of Baffin Bay, as the direction that ought to be taken in the first instance.

Sherard Osborn's memorable paper on the renewal of Arctic research, was read at the Meeting of the Royal Geographical Society on the 23rd of January, 1865, with Sir Roderick Murchison in the chair. Seldom has so influential an assembly been brought together to support our Chair, men of the highest eminence in science being as numerous as Arctic and other naval officers. The address was eloquent and conclusive, and stirred up the feelings of those who heard it to such purpose that the subject was never again allowed to drop. Our President espoused the cause most warmly, secured the adhesion of other scientific societies, and headed a deputation of our Council to the Duke of Somerset, then First Lord of the Admiralty. But in March 1865 Sherard Osborn had accepted an appointment which obliged him to go to Bombay, and the movement, for a time, lost its chief support. In private correspondence Sir Roderick deeply regretted Osborn's absence, speaking of him as " our right hand." Efforts were not, however, relaxed, and at last Osborn decided that the time had arrived for the formal renewal of his proposal. He read a second paper on the subject on April 22nd, 1872, and the Council appointed an Arctic Committee, with Admiral Sir George Back as its chairman, in that year. A second Committee, formed of Members appointed jointly by the Royal Society and by our Council, was formed in 1873; and the Reports of these two Committees laid down the canons for Arctic exploration, enumerated its important objects in great detail, and adopted the views which Sherard Osborn had advocated since 1865. Our President Sir Henry Rawlinson, accompanied by Sir Joseph Hooker and Admiral Sherard Osborn, armed with these Reports, had an interview with Mr. Disraeli on August 1st, 1874, and on the 17th of November the Prime Minister announced that the Society's petition had been successful. " Her Majesty's Government have had under consideration the representations of the Council of the Royal Geographical Society in favour of a renewed expedition under the conduct of Government, to explore the region of the North Pole, and having carefully weighed the reasons set forth in support of such an expedition, the scientific advantages to be derived from it, its chances of success as well as the importance of encouraging that spirit of maritime enterprise which has ever distinguished the English people, have determined to lose no time in organising a suitable expedition for the purpose in view." Accordingly the *Alert* and *Discovery*, Arctic exploring ships, were commissioned, under the command of Captain Nares, who had served under Kellett in 1852–54.

But a very serious loss to our Society and to the navy, saddened the departure of the Arctic Expedition. On May

6th, 1875, Admiral Sherard Osborn died very suddenly. His body was followed to the grave by the President and Secretary of our Society, and by a large concourse of Arctic and other naval friends. Osborn became a Fellow in 1856, and was on our Council from 1867 until his death. He was also Vice-President of the Bombay Geographical Society from 1865 to 1867. He read various interesting papers at our meetings, constantly joined in our discussions, while his munificent present to our library will be noticed in another chapter. The Society never had a warmer or a more zealous friend. His cheery voice and hearty joyous smile, which won upon men's feelings as much as his close reasoning and well-marshalled facts affected their judgments, will long be remembered.

The Arctic Expedition achieved all that our Council desired or expected in the face of greater dangers and obstacles than were ever anticipated. It succeeded in crossing the threshold of the unknown region, its ships attained a higher latitude than any other vessel has ever reached, they wintered further north than any human being has ever been known to have wintered before, and Captain Markham planted the Union Jack on the most northern point ever reached by man. Moreover the expedition explored that portion of the previously unknown Arctic region which could be reached from the direction of Smith Sound, with most valuable scientific results. On his return Sir George Nares and his officers were honoured with the warm approval of their Sovereign and of the Admiralty, and the leader was created a K.C.B. He and his officers had a magnificent reception at a special meeting of our Society, held at St. James's Hall, with the Prince of Wales in the chair, on December 12th, 1876. On the previous day they were entertained at dinner by the Geographical Club, when the largest number of Members assembled that had ever been brought together since its foundation. Sir George Nares was adjudged the Gold Medal of our Society for his great services to Arctic geography, and Captain Markham received a gold watch, with a suitable inscription, for having advanced his country's flag to the most northern point ever reached by man. The work of the expedition was done well, but geographers, who have studied the subject, are mindful that Arctic work cannot be completed by a single effort, and that the reasons for the continuance of northern exploration are as strong now as they ever were.

The most gratifying recognition of the merits of our explorers was the dinner given to them by the old Arctic officers, to the number of twenty-eight, on December 6th, 1876. The veteran Sir George Back, who presided at this dinner, gave expression to the feelings of old Arctics in a heart-stirring speech that will not soon be forgotten by those who heard it; and it was the last occasion on which the good old Admiral, the Father of Arctic explorers, spoke in public.

Born in 1796, George Back achieved undying fame in the Arctic Regions, first in the Spitzbergen Seas, next with Franklin on his two land journeys, then in his chivalrous attempt to succour the Rosses, when he discovered the Great Fish River, and lastly in the memorable voyage of the *Terror.* He was an accomplished artist, as well as an accurate observer, and an undaunted explorer. He received our Gold Medal in 1835, and became a Fellow in 1836. From that time he was constantly either a Member of Council or Vice-President, and was twice President of the Raleigh Club. He was a genial and most entertaining host, a steadfast and warm-hearted friend, and a hard-working Member of our Council. Sir George Back died, at a good old age, on June 23rd, 1878. He showed the regard he entertained for the Society and its objects, by his bequest of a legacy of 600*l.* and of the fine portrait of himself by Brockedon,* which now hangs in the Council Room of the Society.

After the return of our Arctic Expedition, the glorious work was, it is to be hoped only for a time, abandoned to private efforts and to other countries. In 1878–79, Nordenskjöld achieved the North-East Passage. The Dutch nation, inspired by the patriotic energy of Jansen and Koolemans Beynen, has sent the little schooner *Willem Barents* on three useful exploring voyages to the Arctic seas in 1878, 1879, and 1880. Captain Markham, in the little schooner *Isbjorn*, made a polar reconnaissance in 1879; and in 1880, Mr. Leigh Smith, in a steamer built specially for exploring, made important discoveries along the south coast of Franz Josef Land. For this great service to geography he received the Patron's Gold Medal in 1881.

The Council, remaining true to the principles originally laid down, has not confined its honours to geographers only who have worked in the field. Scholars and cartographers, those who have discussed and utilized the work of travellers, have also had their labours and their merits duly recognized.

The Society has adjudged the Royal Award to two of its Presidents. It is true that Admiral Smyth had fairly earned

---

* Mr. Wm. Brockedon, F.R.S., was on our Council in 1831, 1838, 1843, and 1844. He was an artist, and also a great Alpine traveller; author of 'The Passes of the Alps,' and Murray's 'Handbook of Switzerland.' He died in 1855.

the honour by his great geographical services in the field. But when, in 1854, he received the Founder's Medal, the Council and Fellows thought chiefly of the pilot who steered the Society's ship through a stormy sea and brought her safely into port, of him who had given the Society, from its origin, the great benefit of his assistance and advice, and his vigorous superintendence while he occupied the presidential chair. The presentation of the Founder's Medal to Sir Roderick Murchison, in 1871, was but a very slight acknowledgment of all that the Society owes to him who placed it amongst the foremost, the most active, the most popular, and the most widely known of our scientific bodies. The history of the award of a Gold Medal to Sir Roderick was thus related by Sir Henry Rawlinson. " When ill-health forced him to retire, the Council had under consideration the presentation to him of some fitting testimonial. But while they were deliberating on the best means of carrying out this resolution, it was ascertained that Sir Roderick, with a delicate and touching appreciation of the value of the Society's approbation, would prefer to any testimonial, however costly and elaborate, the simple medal which he had himself so often presented to others as the reward of merit."

Three eminent cartographers have been selected by the Council for the Royal Awards. Foremost was John Arrowsmith, an original Fellow of our Society, and a Member of the Council from 1851 to 1868. He was born at Winston, near Barnard Castle in Durham, on April 23rd, 1790, and in 1810 he came to London to join his uncle Aaron Arrowsmith, who was then the leading cartographer in this country. For many years young John aided his uncle in the construction of his large collection of maps, and soon after his uncle's death he commenced his admirable ' London Atlas,' the first edition of which appeared in 1834. From that time he worked earnestly and ardently to the last, although from 1861 he ceased publishing on his own account. While engaged on his Atlas he laboured with the greatest industry, and lived in the most frugal manner. When that work had achieved success he still continued his painstaking career. He purchased his uncle's house, No. 10, Soho Square, from his cousin Samuel in 1839, and continued to live there until 1861. A great number of his maps illustrate the papers in our Journals, and the perspicuity and fidelity with with which he laboured for many years in analysing and comparing the crude and hastily constructed sketch-maps which travellers brought home from distant lands, and the pains he took to delineate such fresh knowledge correctly, quite irrespective of any pecuniary profit, renders his name justly famous among practical geographers. It will long be remembered, how, for so many years, he pointed out the places on the wall-diagrams as the authors read their papers at our Meetings, "describit radio," as Lord Ellesmere said. John Arrowsmith was adjudged the Patron's Medal in 1863, for the very important services he had rendered to geographical science. He died at his house in Hereford Square, on May 2nd, 1873, in his 84th year.

In 1868 the Founder's Medal was awarded to Dr. Augustus Petermann for his services, as a writer and cartographer, in advancing geographical science, and for his well-known publication, the 'Geographische Mittheilungen,' commenced in 1856. Dr. Petermann was born at Bleicherode in Prussia in 1822, and first studied geography under Berghaus. In 1845 he came to Edinburgh to assist in the preparation of the English edition of the 'Physical Atlas' of Berghaus, published by Keith Johnston, and from 1847 to 1854 he was in London. Returning to Germany in 1855, he took the management of the geographical establishment of Justus Perthes at Gotha, including the editorship of the 'Mittheilungen.' From that time his life was one of ceaseless activity and usefulness in furthering the interests of geography. He died at Gotha on September 23rd, 1878. To Mr. A. Keith Johnston of Edinburgh the Patron's Medal was adjudged in 1871. The two editions of his great 'Physical Atlas' cost him ten years of the best period of his life; the result was that the study of physical geography at once took its place among the necessary branches of a liberal education. In 1860 he published his 'Dictionary of Geography.' Mr. Keith Johnston only survived a month, after the presentation of the Medal.

Mrs. Mary Somerville was, throughout a very long life, eminently distinguished by her proficiency in those branches of science which form the basis of physical geography, and, in 1869, the Council unanimously agreed that she had well earned a claim to the Patron's Medal, which was accordingly adjudged to her. Her first work, 'The Connection of the Physical Sciences,' appeared in 1834, and her 'Physical Geography' in 1848. It was Sir Bartle Frere who pointed out that, among the acts of Sir Roderick Murchison's Presidency, one of those of which he was most proud, was his having induced the Council to decree Gold Medals to two illustrious women : Mrs. Somerville as the pre-eminent geographer and physicist, and Lady Franklin for her heroic exertions in determining the real fate of her husband.

Colonel H. Yule, C.B., received the Founder's Medal in 1872 for the eminent services rendered by him to geography in the publication of his three great works, ' Narrative of a Mission to the Court of Ava in 1855,' ' Cathay and the Way Thither,' 1865, and his new edition of ' Marco Polo ' in 1871. ' Cathay and the Way Thither ' was one of the Hakluyt Society's series, and that the Geographical Society's Gold Medal should be adjudged to its editor, proves the close connection between the work and objects of the two Societies. Colonel Yule's exhaustive and masterly edition of ' Marco Polo ' is a work, the publication of which forms an epoch in geographical literature, and it is fitting that our Council should have conferred its highest honour on the first comparative geographer of this country. Since 1877, when he succeeded Sir David Dundas, Colonel Yule has been President of the Hakluyt Society. In 1880 the Council recorded their appreciation of the literary labours of Mr. E. H. Bunbury, in the production of his ' History of Ancient Geography,' a work of the highest value, combining accurate scholarship with large observation, and displaying a thorough acquaintance with modern geographical discovery, as well as with classical literature. A copy of the Council's Resolution was presented to Mr. Bunbury, by the President, with the best thanks of the Council for the service he had rendered to geographical science and culture.

This long roll of eminent explorers and geographers whom the Society has delighted to honour, this record of assistance given to expeditions in every part of the world, represents the main branch of the labours of an institution which has, during half a century, striven zealously and unceasingly to perform a duty which is of national importance.

CHAPTER X.

PUBLICATIONS OF THE SOCIETY.   LIBRARY AND MAP ROOM.
EDUCATIONAL MEASURES.

Next, in usefulness and importance, to the operations of the Geographical Society in the field, are the measures for recording the results of discoveries, for disseminating knowledge, for providing instruction and information, and for encouraging educational measures connected with the study of geography.

In the first year of the Society's existence the form of our 'Journal' was decided upon by the Council, and the first volume was published in octavo, as at present, containing 264 pages, illustrated by eight maps. The first six volumes were edited by the first Secretary, Captain Maconochie, R.N., and in addition to the papers, contained analyses of recent publications, and miscellaneous geographical information. The two succeeding Secretaries, Captain Washington, R.N., and Colonel Jackson, continued the same plan of giving analyses of books, and in 1837 it was resolved that all the maps should be engraved on copper. In order to supply the information as rapidly as possible, the 'Journal' was published in two parts, in May and November, and for a short time, in 1839 and 1840, it came out in three parts, in February, May and November. A very useful addition was also made, in those years, in the shape of lists of geographical works and maps recently published. But in 1842 the issue of two parts during the year was reverted to, and in 1847 the analyses and miscellaneous information were discontinued. Colonel Jackson completed an index of the first ten volumes in 1844.

Owing to the depressed state of the Society's affairs, the 'Journal' in 1848 only contained 144, and in 1849 only 200 pages; but as our prosperity increased, so the size and importance of the 'Journal' continued to grow, and in 1862 it consisted of 31 geographical papers, illustrated by 16 maps, and comprising 583 pages. The index of the second ten volumes of the 'Journal,' by Mr. G. S. Brent, was issued in 1853. From 1848 to 1855 the 'Journal,' issued once a year, was the only publication, and it began to be felt that the information received by the Society ought to be utilised more expeditiously, and more frequently. Moreover the papers which did not obtain a

H

place in the ‘Journal,’ as well as the discussions, were lost to the Fellows and to the public.

It was at the suggestion of Mr. Francis Galton, then the Honorary Secretary, that the series of ‘ PROCEEDINGS ’ was commenced in 1855. to be published periodically, and to contain all papers read at the Meetings, together with the discussions, and additional geographical notices. These ‘Proceedings’ were issued, in pamphlet form, at intervals of six weeks during the Session, and latterly six numbers formed a volume. The numbers did not appear at regular intervals, the first being published in about the middle of January and the last in September. There are twenty-two volumes of the ‘Proceedings’ (Old Series), from November 1855 to December 1878, and the average size of the three last yearly volumes was 580 pages.

This publication was capable of great improvement, and of being made the leading authority in the world on all subjects relating to geography. In the year 1872, as the Council did not contemplate any change at the moment, one of the Honorary Secretaries, when an opportunity offered, undertook to edit a Geographical Periodical independent of the Society, to embody all the information which such publication ought to contain. The sections into which it was divided were original articles or papers, reviews of books, reviews of new maps and charts, geographical news in concise paragraphs, correspondence, obituary and other personal notices, and reports of proceedings of Geographical Societies at home and abroad. It was a monthly publication, each number being illustrated by one or two maps. ‘The Geographical Magazine’ continued to have a steady constituency of 1000 to 1200 subscribers, and appeared regularly on the 1st of each month, under the editorship of Mr. Markham, from July 1872 to December 1878. But in the fulness of time the Council of the Royal Geographical Society felt the necessity for so enlarging and improving their ‘Proceedings’ as that they should cover the whole ground occupied by the Magazine. Thus the Magazine found its successor in a monthly periodical containing the same matter, and published by the Society. Its last number appeared in December 1878, and the first number of the New Series of the ‘Proceedings’ in January 1879. ‘The Geographical Magazine’ completed its work and fulfilled its mission. Its labours were not in vain, its objects did not die with it, but were actively and ably pursued by its successor.

The ‘ Proceedings of the Royal Geographical Society ’ (New Series) ‘ and Monthly Record of Geography ’ have since been published on the first day of every month with perfect regularity, and very ably edited by the Society’s zealous and accomplished Assistant-Secretary, Mr. H. W. Bates. Each number contains the papers read at the Society's Meetings, with the discussions, occasionally also a memoir or communication which has not been read, announcements, geographical news in concise paragraphs, proceedings of Foreign Societies, notices of new geographical books and of maps, and obituaries; and is illustrated by two or more good maps. Meanwhile the 'Journal' has continued to be issued, and to contain the more important papers illustrated by maps, so that it forms an unbroken series of annual volumes from 1831 to 1881. The 'Journals' contain the whole series of Council Reports and Presidential Addresses. From 1854 they have been accompanied by a Report on the progress of Admiralty Surveys annually supplied by the Hydrographer. An index to the third ten volumes (1850 to 1860) was prepared by our Gold Medallist, Colonel H. Yule, c.b., and issued in 1867, and a fourth index, now completed by Mr. Duffield Jones, brings that laborious work up to 1870.

The Society has, in addition to its periodical publications, occasionally issued separate volumes on special subjects. The first of these, printed at the Society's expense, appeared in 1837. It was a translation from the Danish of the 'Narrative of an Expedition to the East Coast of Greenland, by Captain Graah,' with an original chart. The translator, Mr. Gordon Macdougall, was accidentally drowned in 1835, but the work had the advantage of supervision by Sir James Ross, who added some explanatory notes. The second volume separately issued was a 'Grammar of the Cree Language, with which is combined an analysis of the Chippeway Dialect,' by Mr. Joseph Howse of Cirencester, published in 1844. But there was an interval of nearly thirty years before the Society undertook the issue of another separate volume. 'The Lands of Cazembe,' published in 1873, contains Lacerda's Journey to Cazembe, translated and annotated by our Gold Medallist, Captain R. F. Burton; the Journey of the Pombeiros across Africa; and a résumé of the journey of Monteiro and Gamitto, by Dr. Beke. The last separate volume that has thus been issued consists of a selection of papers on Arctic geographical and ethnological subjects, reprinted and presented to the Arctic Expedition of 1875 by the President, Council, and Fellows of the Royal Geographical Society. It proved useful on that occasion, and also in the Swedish Expedition of Professor Nordenskiöld, which discovered the north-east passage.

Great efforts have been made, from the foundation of the Society, to bring together a complete geographical library, and an equally extensive collection of maps. But for many years there were great difficulties owing to insufficient space, and for some time the want of funds offered another obstacle. The Council, and many of the Fellows, zealously exerted themselves, in days of adversity as in times of prosperity, and the means at the disposal of the Society were not unfrequently supplemented through the munificence of individual Fellows.

The following account of the progress of the Library has been prepared by Mr. Edward Caldwell Rye, the Society's very able and efficient Librarian.

" In the original prospectus of the Society, of the 24th of May, 1830, one of its primary objects is stated to be 'to accumulate gradually a library of the best books on geography, a selection of the best voyages and travels . . . as well as all such documents and materials as may convey the best information to persons intending to visit foreign countries'; it being also proposed ' to open a communication with all those philosophical and literary Societies with which geography is connected.' The subsequent regulations contain a clause that ' The Society shall also commence the formation of a Library, . . . to which all Members shall have access, and strangers by their orders, under such restrictions as may appear to the Council necessary.'

" The first practical step towards this object is recorded in the Council Minutes of 1832, from which it appears that the Library then consisted of about 400 volumes, chiefly contributed by friends and Members of the Society, a list of whose names is annexed to the Report. The names (81 in number) of these donors, the absolute founders of the present Library, are those of learned Associations, noblemen, men of science, and publishers, from whom it is invidious to make a selection, since nearly all are familiar as household words: Faraday, Humboldt, Horsburgh, Von Martius, Babbage, and the Court of Directors of the East India Company, amongst others, representing a past generation, and Mr. John Murray, so long associated with standard works of travel, still contributing. Small progress was made at first, the funds of the Society only permitting a trifling annual outlay on books; and in 1834 the Library was considered to be the least satisfactory part of the Society's work, an appeal for help being made to the liberality of Members and friends. In 1836 and 1837, progress was far from satisfactory, many geographical works of the first importance being entirely wanting, and no suitable apartments found in which books could be placed for consultation. Many accessions are recorded in 1838, chiefly owing to the liberality of Foreign Institutions (the Dépôt de la Marine, Paris, being the earliest to receive honourable acknowledgment),—the first fruits of

the wise extension beyond strictly geographical objects autho-
rised by the original prospectus. In 1839 and 1840 the increase
was still higher, and foreign academies and official departments
continued to assist. Suitable rooms at No. 3, Waterloo Place
being then obtained, the Council in 1841 made a strenuous
appeal to the Members for further aid, stating it to be their
object ' that no work relating to geography, no map or chart
extant, should be wanting to the Library.' This produced in
the following year a special gift of 50*l.* from Mr. James Alexander (who made two subsequent similar gifts), and some
donations of books, especially one by Mr. (afterwards Sir Walter)
Trevelyan, one of the original donors, and who not only subsequently gave more books to the Library, but on his death
bequeathed to the Society *all* his books that might be deemed of
geographical importance. The Library was of very considerable extent and value in 1843, from more accessions; and
further steady but slight increase was made until 1848, when,
in consequence of the pressing need of proper arrangement, a
careful inspection was made by a Committee, who took measures
for preserving the books and obtaining the necessary accommodation. A special subscription for defraying the cost of these
works was set on foot, and by the next year had reached nearly
250*l.*, whereof the greater part was expended.

" In 1850, the Library contained over 4000 volumes (Sir
Walter C. Trevelyan again, with Mr. C. Baring Young, having
specially made liberal gifts); in 1852 the first Catalogue,
prepared by the Secretary, Dr. Norton Shaw, was seen through
the press by Mr. Greenough, who also recouped to the Society
the honorarium awarded to Dr. Shaw. Relations of exchange
were in this last year established with many other Libraries
and Public Institutions at home and abroad, and large and
important accessions were recorded. In this year also was
commenced the system of special grants by the Council for the
Library use, as the balance of the subscribed fund above-
mentioned was then exhausted. From this time, the importance
of the Library was firmly established and recognised; and in
1856, on the lamented death of Mr. G. B. Greenough, one of
its earliest and most steadfast supporters, it received a large
and important addition in the bequest of that gentleman's books
and maps relating to geography, accompanied by a legacy of
500*l.* for the expense of accommodating the collection. Steady
accumulations continued during succeeding years (1858 being
marked by special improvement), and in 1865 the main
Catalogue now in use was completed and issued to the Fellows
gratis. In 1871, the supplementary Catalogue, including works
acquired between 1865 and 1870, and the Classified Catalogue

of the whole (both prepared by Mr. Evans of the British Museum) were completed and published, the supplement being distributed gratis. The Classified Catalogue is practically an amplification of a similar work prepared many years before for the Library by Mr. F. Galton. The large accumulations since 1870 have rendered it desirable that a second supplement, covering from that year to the end of 1880, should be prepared. This has been done by the present Librarian, and is now in the hands of the Printers.

" On the removal in 1872 to the premises now occupied by the Society, the accommodation for books was increased about one-fourth, and this has in subsequent years been still further and largely added to by the erection of new presses in all available places, and by the appropriation of a special room apart from the Library for duplicates and works not frequently consulted.

" The first Librarian of the Society was Mr. Charles Bradbury, appointed in December 1832, who also acted as draughtsman. He resigned in November 1836, and was succeeded by Mr. R. W. Clifton, who was followed in December 1837 by Mr. Webb, R.N. In December 1841 Mr. J. Shillinglaw became Librarian, resigning in November 1846. After him Mr. Cartwright discharged the duties, as well as those of clerk ; and in 1854 so distinguished a geographer as Mr. Trelawny Saunders acted as temporary Librarian, practically re-organizing the library. That work being accomplished, Mr. Wheeler, the Chief Clerk, continued in charge of the books, until succeeded in both offices by Mr. E. Street in 1862. Lieut. A. J. Clark, a Fellow of the Society, acted on an emergency in 1864, until Mr. H. Purrier was appointed. In November 1866 Mr. J. H. Lamprey was made Librarian ; and on his retirement in March 1874, the present Librarian was appointed. The duties had by that time so much increased, that an assistant (Mr. Vincent Hawkins) was engaged in the following October.

" The work of the Library is superintended by a separate Committee, originally indicated in 1853. It meets practically every month during the Session, and has been very constantly and zealously presided over by Mr. Fergusson who, from 1863 to 1881, has given his time and valuable aid to the Society's work. The expenditure is now, on the average of the past six years, about 150*l.* per annum for books, and 90*l.* for binding. During that period, a further sum of 200*l.* has also been expended. This was the munificent present of the lamented Admiral Sherard Osborn during his life, ' in recognition of the valuable assistance afforded to him by the use of the Library.'

" The Library now contains upwards of 20,000 books and pamphlets, for the most part either purely geographical or bearing upon the sciences with which geography is connected, as desired by the original promoters of the Society. This large number of volumes, still steadily increasing, represents exchanges of publications and important donations, besides regular and occasional purchases. In addition to the gifts above alluded to, which form as it were a part of the history of the Library, having been made at critical periods of the existence of the Society, there are some which it is impossible here to pass over, though to give a proper recognition of obligations of this nature would require far more space than is available. The Library is most especially indebted to the various Departments of Her Majesty's Government for invaluable and continued support, perhaps most of all to the Secretary of State for India and to the different branches of the Indian Administration, from whom have been received the costly series of Gazetteers, the voluminous Reports (frequently illustrated, and which under that modest name are often exhaustive scientific treatises), the lengthy accounts of Trigonometrical, Topographical, Marine, Geological, Statistical and Revenue Surveys, the selections from Government papers, and the confidential and early details of explorations which enrich the presses devoted to Asia. It is to the attention to the Society's welfare in this respect by Mr. Markham, while he was in charge of the Geographical Department at the India Office, from 1867 to 1877, that many of these acquisitions are due. To the Secretaries of State for Foreign Affairs and the Colonies (as also the separate Colonial administrations, notably those of Canada, Victoria and New Zealand), the Intelligence Department of the War Office and the Admiralty, we are also largely indebted. Nor are the Governments of foreign countries less generous in their aid. Of them, the United States authorities stand conspicuously in the front rank, their gifts being second only to those on Indian subjects above mentioned in mere extent, and perhaps even wider in scope. The many comprehensive publications of the various State Geographical and Geological Surveys under Hayden, Wheeler, Powell, King, and others, of the Engineer Department, and Naval Observatory, the Senate documents, and Coast Surveys, are but the chief among the mass of works, bearing more or less on geography, which we continue to receive from Transatlantic official sources. And, as the outcome of a truly national Institution, the numerous Smithsonian publications can here be fitly acknowledged.

" Of other foreign State benefactors, the French Marine Department and Minister of Public Instruction, the Prussian and Egyptian General Staffs, and various officials of the German, Russian, Netherlands, Scandinavian, Austrian, Mexican, Chilian.

and Peruvian Governments, deserve especial thanks for their donations.

"To the individual contributors above recorded must be added the names of John Crawfurd, who presented 'Purchas his Pilgrimes,' Lord Stanley, Sir Roderick Murchison and Kenneth R. Murchison, Sir W. Codrington, Desborough Cooley, J. P. Gassiot and C. H. Wallroth, as having either by costly gifts or continued support shown how much they cared for the Society's best interests; for Arctic works, the well-known names of Back, Barrow, and Hooper are to be in like way signalised; and valuable presents by Commodore Jansen, Dr. Forchhammer, Dr. Ziegler, Count Wilczek, General Kaufmann, Professor Raimondi, Capt. Vidal Gormaz, and the Archduke Ludwig Salvator of Austria, sufficiently attest a world-wide interest in our welfare. This short list would be still more incomplete, if mention were not made of the continuous interest in the Library shown by our Secretary Mr. Markham, whose gifts of the great works of Gay and Castelnau, the earliest (1589) publication by Hakluyt, Van der Aa's collection of voyages, and all the early histories and memoirs of Viceroys referring to Peru, signalise themselves among minor donations too numerous to be given here.

"The chief aim of the Library Committees has been to obtain books which are beyond the reach of most individual purchasers; and with this view they have secured such desiderata as the long and costly series of French Voyages, the 1599 edition of Hakluyt, Eden's Travels, the Journal of the Godeffroy Museum at Hamburg, &c. The collection is, however, least rich in old books of importance.

"Receiving the publications of over thirty other Geographical Societies, subscribing for or being presented with every geographical periodical of any value, purchasing every important work of travel or bearing on scientific geography as soon as possible, and with the series of all corresponding scientific bodies kept up to date, the Library may now perhaps fairly be considered as the best purely geographical one in existence. It is largely consulted by the Fellows, whose power of borrowing is constantly exercised (though for the most part on works of transitory interest), by the officers of public Departments, and by travellers, authors, teachers, students, missionaries, merchants, publishers, and artists, who find in its stores material not elsewhere obtainable. In connection with the sciences allied to geography, it may be noted that the fact of some members of the Staff being Fellows of other Societies, has on several occasions enabled our own Fellows to obtain ready access to authorities incidentally valuable, but not properly within the scope of our Library. The aid which in earlier times it was enabled to afford to the State (e.g. during the Abyssinian War and San Juan Boundary dispute) is now of a less direct nature, as the Intelligence Department of the War Office has acquired so great an official standing and value. But that Department makes the most constant and the largest demands upon our resources.

" From time to time the Library is consulted by foreign geographers, who on some occasions have for that purpose visited England; and as the extent of its possessions in the allied sciences is gradually getting better known, it is acquiring a reputation for referential purposes.

" The Bibliography of the present issue of the Society's ' Proceedings,' tending as it does not only to add to a knowledge of geography (for there is no similar abstract in English of geographical works), but to increase the area of the Society's influence, may also be properly mentioned here, as it is founded on books that come under the Librarian's notice in his official capacity."

The collection of maps and charts now contains 35,000 sheets, 500 atlases, numerous pictorial illustrations, 63 relief maps and models, and 240 large maps or diagrams suitable for the illustration of lectures. It has annually continued to increase by donations and purchase, receiving a very large and important accession in 1855, from the munificent bequest of Mr. Greenough. All the principal maps published by Mr. Edward Stanford were presented by that gentleman; and in 1880 a complete collection of the maps published by the late M. P. H. Vandermaelen of Brussels, through his executors. Donations are received from the Admiralty, the War Department, and the Ordnance Survey Department, from the Secretary of State for India, and from various Foreign Governments, of the sheets of national surveys. The complete catalogue of maps and charts, including all the maps in the 'Journal,' was finished in 1880 and is about to be published. The interest taken in the Society's labours led to the Map Room being raised to the position of a national institution. In 1854 Her Majesty's Ministers felt themselves justified in tendering a yearly grant of 500*l.* to the Society, in order that the collection of maps and charts might be rendered available for general reference. This proposition was gratefully accepted, and arrangements were promptly made in accordance with the Treasury Minute. Thus, through this grant, the Society's Map Room has become a valuable place of reference which is open to the public, and which has ever since been constantly utilised by the Intelligence Department of the War Office and by other Government Departments, as well as by numerous individual inquirers. It is a gratifying incident in connection with the grant that our Associate Mr. Joseph Hume, M.P., the rigid economist and jealous guardian of the public purse, raised his powerful voice in favour of a measure which he considered to be useful and desirable. From 1854 the Society's Map Room has been, as Sir Roderick Murchison had long maintained it should be, the " Map Office of the Nation."

The Society's collection of instruments was formed both to enable travellers to become familiar with their use ; * and in order that the Council may be in a position to lend sets or single instruments to explorers and travellers who may apply for such loans, and are found to be qualified to observe. The system of lending instruments has been very successful. Several travellers are now annually enabled, in this way, to add considerably to the value of their reports, and the supply of instruments has become a regular and very useful branch of the Society's work. A complete set of instruments, with other articles necessary for the equipment of an observer in the field, is placed under a glass case in the Map Room, as a guide to intending travellers, and to remind them of useful things which might otherwise be overlooked.

With the instruments, the Council has always seen the importance of furnishing instructions for their use, and suggestions to the explorer on all points relating to their work. The first book of the kind, was Colonel Jackson's 'What to observe, or the Traveller's Remembrancer,' a fourth edition of which was issued in 1861. Meanwhile the Council had appointed a Sub-Committee consisting of Captain FitzRoy, R.N., and Lieutenant H. Raper, R.N., to report upon the best form in which information could be furnished to inquirers. The result was the publication of a pamphlet entitled ' HINTS TO TRAVELLERS,' containing the report of the Sub-Committee, and papers by Admiral Smyth, Admiral Beechey, Colonel Sykes, and Mr. Francis Galton. The report gives a list of necessary instruments, instructions for drawing maps and plans, and for observing for latitude and longitude. Admirals Smyth and Beechey furnish many valuable hints ; Colonel Sykes's paper is on the use of thermometers to determine heights ; and Mr. Galton discusses a traveller's outfit, and gives instructions for describing a new country.

The second edition of ' HINTS TO TRAVELLERS ' was revised by a Committee, consisting of Sir George Back, Admiral Collinson, and Mr. Francis Galton, in 1864. Their information is prefaced by the remark that it is to be understood as addressed to a person who, for the first time in his life, proposes to explore a wild country, and who asks what astronomical and other scientific outfit he ought to take with him, and on what observations he

---

* See page 19.

ought chiefly to rely. It, therefore, commences with a descriptive list of needful instruments and other articles, which is followed by detailed instructions for observing for latitude and longitude, for rough triangulation, for ascertaining altitudes by boiling-point, for projecting routes, for constructing maps, with hints on photography by Professor Pole, and on collecting objects in natural history by Mr. Bates. This edition was extensively circulated, and was followed by a third edition in 1871.

The fourth edition of 'HINTS TO TRAVELLERS' appeared in a new form in 1878, under the sole editorship of Mr. Galton. Instead of being an ordinary 8vo. pamphlet, it is a little square volume of 104 pages, very compact, and easily fitting into a coat pocket. The principal additions are a " Memoir on Surveys" by Major Wilson, R.E., a paper on observations with theodolites or altazimuth instruments by Colonel J. T. Walker, R.E., and several useful tables. There was a rapid and extensive sale of the fourth edition, and a new and revised edition is now about to be prepared.

In 1876 the Council had under its consideration a series of proposals drawn up by several of its Members, and concurred in by eminent men of science among the Council, which had for their object the adoption of measures with a view to giving greater encouragement to the study of the more strictly scientific side of geography, and of the causes which, by their combined action, have made the earth what we find it. The result of a careful consideration of these proposals was that the Council recorded its willingness to set aside an annual sum of 500*l.* for scientific purposes. It was decided that three lectures should be delivered at Evening Meetings during each Session, by the most eminent physicists whose services could be secured. These valuable lectures were continued during the three following years :—

1876–77.	Major-Gen. STRACHEY, C.S.I. ..	*Introductory lecture on scientific geography.*
	Dr. CARPENTER, C.B.	*On the temperature of the deep sea bottom.*
	A. R. WALLACE, Esq.	*Comparative antiquity of continents.*
1877–78.	Professor DUNCAN	*On the main land masses.*
	Captain EVANS, R.N., C.B. ..	*On the magnetism of the earth.*
	W. J. THISTELTON DYER, Esq.	*Plant distribution as a field for geographical research.*
1878–79.	Professor GEIKIE	*Geographical evolution.*
	Professor ROLLESTON	*The modifications of the external aspects of organic nature produced by man's interference.*
	JOHN BALL, Esq. .. .. ••	*On the origin of the flora of the European Alps.*

But it was found that the lectures were not suited to the
large mixed audiences which assembled at the Geographical
Society's Meetings. The object of the Council would, it became
evident, be more satisfactorily attained by a system of instruction to those who were actually desirous of acquiring a knowledge of scientific geography with some practical object.

A very large number of Englishmen visit countries which
have never been geographically described or correctly mapped,
and traverse routes along which no observations have ever
been taken. Many more annually pass and repass over tracts
respecting which some previous contributions have been recorded, but which need additional and more correct observations
before they can be adequately described and mapped. Every
year these wanderers, in various professions and engaged upon
divers avocations, spread themselves over every quarter of the
globe; yet, for want of necessary training, they travel and return
without any or with few results that can be utilised for geographical purposes.

In many instances such travellers would gladly and even
zealously add the work of observing and of collecting geographical
information to the more direct objects of their journeys. It is
probable that nearly all would do so if they were made sensible
of the value of such work, and if the means of acquiring the
necessary training were within their reach. These considerations induced the Council of the Society to take steps for providing this preliminary training. It was believed that by
undertaking to make proper arrangements for the purpose, the
increase of valuable observations, for geographical purposes, in all
parts of the world would be promoted. Mr. John Coles, late R.N.,
the Curator of the Society's Maps, was accordingly appointed to
give instruction in practical astronomy, route surveying, and
mapping; and steps were taken to make it generally known
that such instruction was provided by the Council. At the
same time the construction of a small observatory on the roof
of the Society's house was sanctioned, which was finished and
in use by February 1880.

Mr. Coles began to give instruction in October 1879, and he
has since given 232 lessons to 24 students, down to the end of
1880. The subjects taught embrace nearly all the problems in
practical astronomy and surveying, the use of the transit-
theodolite, ordinary 5-inch theodolite, sextant and artificial
horizon, hypsometrical apparatus, manner of plotting a traverse-
survey by means of the prismatic compass, and map construction.
The students have included civil engineers, naval and military
officers, surgeons, magistrates, botanists, missionaries, and one
bishop.

This measure has answered perfectly, and is likely to be still more successful in the future. Its scope might hereafter be extended, and it is calculated directly to advance the interests and objects of the Society. For upon the careful and efficient training of explorers depends the value and accuracy of their work.

A system had been inaugurated, some years previously, for promoting the teaching of geography in our schools, and thus widely disseminating a taste for our pursuit, and sowing seeds, some of which might surely be expected to bear fruit in after years. In 1868 the Council resolved, at the suggestion of Mr. Francis Galton, to offer prizes for competition in the principal public schools, with the object of encouraging the study of geography. For some years previously an annual prize of 5*l.*, termed the "Royal Geographical Society's Prize," had been granted by the Council, with beneficial results, to the Society of Arts, and awarded at their annual examination. It was now further resolved to offer two gold and two bronze medals, one of each to successful candidates in an annual examination on subjects of political and physical geography respectively, the first examination to take place in 1869, and to be repeated in each succeeding year. The decision of the Council to take this step was influenced by the Report of the Royal Commission on Public School Education in 1864, in which an opinion is expressed that greater attention should be paid to geography and history, than they now receive at schools. After the Council's action had received the test of ten years' experience, Mr. Galton was able, in 1878, to announce the continued success of the Public Schools' competition. Most of the Schools which sent candidates for the first examinations continued to do so, showing that they had found by experience that the teaching of geography did not interfere with other branches of study. Out of the forty medals which had been given, twelve had been gained by Liverpool College, five by Eton, and four each by Rossall and Dulwich. There could be no doubt that the effect of the medals had been to increase the standard of geographical teaching in many schools, and ample testimony has been borne, both by schoolmasters and by medallists, to the great service rendered to the cause of education by these prizes.

A perusal of this chapter will have shown the nature of the measures adopted by the Society with the object of instructing and training explorers and geographers, and of utilising the results of their labours. We begin by striving to infuse a taste for geographical studies in our public schools. We next supply the means of efficient instruction to all who are about to visit distant lands, and are willing to benefit by the facilities offered by the Society. Through our annually increasing library and map collection, the geographer is enabled to prosecute his studies with peculiar advantages; and the results of the labours of explorers and of the researches of students receive wide publicity through our 'Journals' and 'Proceedings,' and are thus fully utilised.

CHAPTER XI.

PROGRESS OF THE SOCIETY.

Finance—Members—Meetings—House Accommodation.

THE power of forwarding the objects of the Society, of accumulating geographical information and making it available, of furthering and assisting exploration and discovery, depends upon the support received by the Society from the public. It is only on the condition that the Geographical Society's work is felt and recognised to be work of national importance, that it can be efficiently and continuously performed. The great object of the Founders of the Society, and of their Successors, has been, by activity and diligence, to establish the Society's reputation, and to prove the value of its labours. Through evil report and through good report, the work has been steadfastly pushed forward during half a century ; and successive Members of the Council have given their time and abilities, in ungrudging measure, to the Society's business. It is this unostentatious work, this attention to the measures for increasing the number of Members, to financial details, and to administrative business, upon which the prosperity and well-being of the Society is founded.

The Society commenced its operations with 460 Members in 1830, the admission fee being 3*l.*, the annual subscription 2*l.*, which might be compounded for by one payment of 20*l.** In the first two years, from July 1830 to March 1832, the receipts amounted to 5239*l.*, and it was the original plan of the Council to form a reserve fund by investing the sums received as compositions, and to meet current expenses with the amount represented by annual subscriptions. During the first ten years the receipts averaged 1500*l.* a year, and by 1840 a reserve fund of 4000*l.* had been invested. The number of Members increased to 700, but arrears of payment were very large. Through the kindness of Mr. Robert Brown, one of our seven Founders, the Society obtained shelter and a place of meeting, during those first ten years, at the rooms of the Horticultural Society in Regent Street, for which a house-rent of 110*l.* was paid. But, as the collection of books and maps increased, and the evening meetings became more popular and more numerously attended,

---

* The composition is now 28*l.* on entrance, or 25*l.* at any subsequent period if the entrance fee be already paid.

the want of better accommodation was more and more felt.   The
difficulty in obtaining suitable rooms was caused by want of
sufficient funds, and also by the Society's large expenditure in
furthering geographical exploration which, during the first ten
years, was munificent, considering the means at its disposal.

At last, in 1839, the Society took a lease of a suite of rooms
at No. 3, Waterloo Place, at a rent of 263*l*. a year, which it
continued to occupy until 1854.   There was an expenditure of
270*l*. in fitting up and furnishing these rooms.   The evening
meetings were still held in the public room of the Horticultural
Society, in Regent Street.

The most depressed period of the Society's affairs was from
1845 to 1850, when the arrears increased to alarming proportions, the deficits were chronic, and there was an annual necessity for selling out and encroaching upon the reserve fund, to
meet them.   In 1848 there was a diminution in the number of
Members.   The Financial Committee reported that the Society
was in a state of financial embarrassment, and a representation
was made to the Prime Minister, asking for Government support on the ground of the national character of the Society's
work.   The receipts had fallen to 583*l*., while the expenditure
was 755*l*.   No help was granted.   The Council had to face and
overcome its difficulties without assistance, and it did so with
most complete success.

During Admiral Smyth's tenure of office the most strenuous
and effectual efforts were made to give a healthy tone to the
Society's finances, and to increase its resources.   The number of
Members began to increase, and fresh interest was given to the
Society's meetings.   In 1850 the sums invested had been
reduced, by sales to meet annual deficits, to 1886*l*., while the
subscriptions and entrance fees only amounted to 1036*l*.   Continued efforts were made to induce the Government to grant
suitable apartments for the Society's use, but without result.
But Admiral Smyth did not lose heart.   "It is our part," he
said, "to deserve success by eschewing despondency.   I
therefore call upon you all, and severally, to stand by your
colours—

> " ' True as the dial to the sun
> Although it be not shin'd upon.' "

Meanwhile, through the kindness of the Principal and Council
of King's College, improved accommodation for the evening
meetings was provided at Somerset House.

The true foundation of the Society's success has been the close
attention to its finances which has been given since 1850.   In
addition to the care bestowed upon them by the Treasurers, the
Council has continuously had the great benefit of diligent

assistance, in its financial affairs, from eminent merchants or actuaries of ability and long experience. From 1846 to 1863 Mr. Osborne Smith was constantly a Member of the Finance Committee, Mr. Brooking from 1855 to 1868, Mr. Charles White from 1869 to 1871, and Mr. S. W. Silver from 1871 to 1881. Sir George Balfour was also a most valuable Member of the Finance Committee from 1863 to 1868.

From the time of Admiral Smyth the affairs of the Society continued to improve without any check. In 1853 the Council, in order most efficiently to carry out the objects of the Society, was divided into permanent working Committees under the following heads:—

1. Regulations and Bye-laws.
2. Finance and House.
3. Library and Maps.
4. Publications.
5. Expeditions.

In the following year the Society took the lease of 15, Whitehall Place, a commodious house with suitable Library and Map Room, at a rent of 500*l.* a year for 16 years. The work of removing the valuable collection of maps and charts, and properly arranging them in Whitehall Place, was ably performed by Mr. Trelawney Saunders. The establishment of the Society in a house of its own, added very materially to its usefulness, and to the convenience of the Fellows. At first the Library was fitted up for evening meetings, but it was very soon found that the accommodation was quite insufficient; and in 1858 the use of the large room in the west wing of old Burlington House was accorded by the Royal Society and the University of London. This long and handsome room, hung with portraits of the Presidents of the Royal Society, conspicuous among whom was Sir Joseph Banks, the Founder of the African Association and the great patron of geography, continued to be our place of meeting from 1858 to 1868. Here took place the crowded receptions of Livingstone and Speke, and here Sherard Osborn read his memorable paper on the renewal of Arctic research.

The number of Fellows continued to increase rapidly. In 1850 there were 700, in 1858 the number was over 1000, and by 1868 it had passed 2000. From that time the rate of increase was more marked, for the figure 3000 was reached by 1876, and in 1880 the number of Fellows was 3371. From 1830 to 1860 the elections took place by ballot among the general body of the Fellows at the evening meetings. But in 1861 the elections were entrusted to the Council. It had been found that very great inconvenience attended the method of ballot at the crowded evening meetings. It was impracticable to carry round the boxes to obtain the vote of each Fellow, and very few took the trouble of voting as they entered the hall. Consequently it was unanimously agreed, at a General Meeting, that the elections should be entrusted to the Council, the names of Candidates proposed and of Fellows elected being regularly announced at each evening meeting. Besides the 3371 ordinary Fellows, there are nine Honorary Members, consisting of Crowned Heads or Imperial or Royal Personages who take an interest in geographical pursuits; and 59 Honorary Corresponding Members who are distinguished foreign geographers and travellers.

By 1864 the finances of the Society may be considered to have been brought back to a satisfactory condition. The receipts were 5256*l*., and the expenditure only 3655*l*., leaving a large sum for investment. The funded capital of the Society was 10,500*l*.

There was a considerable annual increase to the funded capital, which was accumulated with a view mainly to the purchase of a freehold property, at the conclusion of the lease of 15 Whitehall Place. In 1870 the funded capital amounted to 19,250*l*. The freehold of the house at No. 1 Savile Row was purchased in this year for 14,527*l*. A further expenditure of 3798*l*. was incurred for alterations and building the Map Room, 1074*l*. for removal expenses, and 334*l*. for dilapidations on giving up the lease of 15 Whitehall Place. The extensive alterations were superintended by a Building Committee, consisting of Mr. James Fergusson, and the Treasurer, Mr. Reginald Cocks. The total sum sold out amounted to 18,250*l*. Thus the Society became possessed, for the first time, of suitable premises of its own, consisting of an Office, Council Room, large national Map Room, Library, rooms for the Assistant-Secretary and Office Keeper, Instrument Room, and rooms for draftsman, and for the binder and map-mounter. An Observatory has since been added, at the top of the house, for the convenience of students receiving instruction in practical astronomy. The value of the house and furniture, exclusive of library and map collections (insured for 10,000*l*.) is estimated at 20,000*l*.

After the wing of old Burlington House was pulled down in 1869, the evening meetings of the Society took place for a time at the Royal Institution in Albemarle Street. But since 1870 they have been held, by permission of the Chancellor and Senate of the University of London, in their grand hall in Burlington Gardens. On great occasions, such as the reception of Lieut. Cameron, and of the officers and men of the Arctic Expedition on their return in 1876, the accommodation in Burlington Gardens has been found to be insufficient, and it has been necessary to hire a still more spacious place of reception, namely St. James's Hall.

The great number of Fellows has ensured the financial prosperity of the Society. Since 1870 this prosperity has steadily increased. The receipts in 1880 amounted to 8600*l.*, and the actual expenditure was 8490*l.*; while the Society's funded capital had again risen to 18,500*l.* The expenditure on the house, including office expenses and salaries, was 1792*l.*; on the Library, 467*l.*; on the Map Room, 1125*l.*; on the evening meetings, 157*l.*; on lectures and instruction to travellers, 112*l.*; on awards, 207*l.*; and on the publications, 3197*l.* In most years the donations towards the expenses of travellers also forms a considerable item in the accounts.

Her Majesty the Queen is Patron of the Society, the Prince of Wales Vice-Patron, and the Duke of Edinburgh Honorary President. The Council consists of a President, six Vice-Presidents, a Treasurer, two Trustees, two Secretaries, a Foreign Secretary, and twenty-one Ordinary Members. Their meetings take place once every fortnight during the Session, from November to June, and they are also divided into the following Committees for the transaction of the Society's business :—

1. Finance and House.
2. Library and Map.
3. Expeditions.
4. Hints to Travellers.
5. School Prizes.
6. Scientific Purposes.

By this machinery, and by the work of the Society's able and zealous permanent staff, the objects and interests of geographical science are furthered and extended. Instruction is afforded to travellers and explorers, assistance and advice provided, the means of reference furnished by one of the largest collections of geographical books and maps in the world, which is constantly being improved and added to, and information is regularly disseminated at the evening meetings and through the Society's publications. While this ordinary work is thus provided for, the Council is always willing to consider any new proposal for increasing its usefulness, and for still further widening the sphere of operations which are of such vital importance to a great maritime and commercial people.

CHAPTER XII.

COMPARATIVE VIEW OF GEOGRAPHICAL KNOWLEDGE IN 1830 AND 1880, WITH A NOTICE OF THE WORK THAT STILL REMAINS TO BE DONE.

THE progress that has been made in the science of geography since the Society was founded is only partially shown by a comparison of an atlas of 1830 with the maps of the present day. For this progress is not alone comprised in the discovery and delineation of unknown countries. Its range is far wider. There have also been great improvements in the methods of investigation, in systematic arrangement of facts, in cartography, and in the construction and use of instruments.

At the same time the most striking advances have been made in the work of discovery, and in completing our general knowledge of the earth's surface, preliminary to more systematic and detailed surveys. Yet, bearing in mind that the first discoveries are merely reconnaissances, it may safely be said that, great as our progress has been during the last half century, it only represents a very small fraction of what remains to be done.

Glancing first at the Arctic Regions, which had attracted so much attention during the period from the peace in 1815 to the attempt of Parry to push northwards from Spitzbergen in 1827, in 1830 only unconnected strips of coast line had been traced along the coast of Arctic America, and it was unknown whether there was a passage along that coast to Fury and Hecla Straits. Baffin's Bay had been re-discovered, and Parry had pushed westward along Barrow Strait to Melville Island, but nothing was known of the region between Barrow Strait and the continent. Knowledge respecting the eastern sides of Greenland and Spitzbergen, the coasts of Novaya Zemlya, and the surrounding seas was vague and inaccurate, and an enormous area was entirely unknown.

Now the whole coast of Arctic America has been delineated, the remarkable archipelago to the north has been explored, and no less than seven north-west passages have been traced by our naval explorers.* The channels leading northwards from

---

* 1. Along the west coast of Banks Island to Melville Sound. 2. Through Princess Royal Strait to Melville Sound. 3. Down McClintock Channel.

Smith Sound, the shores of the Palæocrystic Sea, considerable portions of the east coast of Greenland, and the south shore of Franz Joseph Land, have been discovered. Captain Markham has advanced the Union Jack to 83° 20′ N., and Nordenskiöld has achieved the north-east passage.

Still much remains to be done in the Arctic Regions. The interior of Greenland presents a problem of the deepest interest, while the discovery of its northern shore has been an object of honourable ambition for three centuries. The line of the Palæocrystic Sea has been traced from the North American coast along Banks and Prince Patrick Islands, Grinnell Land, and North Greenland; while a stream of this tremendous ice flows down Melville Sound to press upon the coast of King William Island, and fragments find their way down the east coast of Greenland. But the extent of this ancient ice is still unknown, and a complete discovery of the area it occupies, and the causes of its accumulation, will be a most important addition to geographical knowledge. The exploration of the northern side of Franz Joseph Land, of the lands north of Siberia, and the solution of numerous scientific questions within the undiscovered area, furnish work to occupy many successive expeditions in the future. Every new discovery increases the interest of those which are to follow. At first mere isolated geographical facts were ascertained; but as discovery advances, and these facts become more numerous, they begin to explain each other. The whole physical economy of the Polar Region will thus gradually be brought to light, and generalisation will become possible. In the Arctic Regions there is still an important and most difficult piece of work to be done; and it is the duty of our Society to promote and further it by every means in its power.

In the Antarctic Regions there is another enormous field for discovery. When the Society was founded, our Antarctic knowledge was derived from the voyages of Cook and Bellingshausen, who ascertained that there was no land over a very extensive area in high latitudes, and from those of Bransfield, Powell, and Weddell. Our second royal award was granted to Captain Biscoe, who, in February 1831 and 1832, discovered Enderby and Graham Lands; and in 1839 Balleny made known the Balleny Islands and Sabrina Land. Dumont d'Urville discovered Terre Adelie and Coté Clarie, in 1841 Sir James Ross established the existence of a great southern continent, and in

---

4. Down Peel Sound and Franklin Strait, and round the west side of King William Island.   5. Round the east side of King William Island.   6. Down Prince Regent Inlet and through Bellot Strait.   7. Through Fury and Hecla Strait and Bellot Strait.

1842 he penetrated to 78° 11′ s., the furthest ever reached. Since that time nothing has been done in the Antarctic Regions. South of 78° there is an area of millions of square miles which is absolutely unknown.

Next to the regions of the Poles, the greatest undiscovered area, when the Society was founded, was in the continent of Africa. In the 17th century, the wide African spaces had been well covered with names derived from Ptolemy, Leo Africanus, Edrisi, Pigafetta, and De Barros and other Portuguese sources. But the more critical school of geographers, which flourished in the end of the 17th and in the 18th centuries, rejected all names and details for which no sufficient authority could be given. Delisle (1698), who was followed by D'Anville, left the greater part of inner Africa a blank, retaining only the single great lake of Lopez and De Barros (Tanganyika). The maps of 1830 show a lofty chain, Ptolemy's "Mountains of the Moon," running across the continent, near the equator, and the Nile flowing northwards from them.* The coast kingdoms and colonies are indicated, and the mouths and lower courses of some of the great rivers. A dotted line shows the conjectural position of a long lake named " Maravi," in 10° s. Fezzan also appears, and lake Chad, with the routes of Denham, Clapperton, and Lander. Otherwise interior Africa is a blank space; a mysterious region, well fitted to excite the interest of geographers, and the adventurous ambition of explorers.

Fifty years has seen a vast change in all this. The discoveries of Burton, Speke, and Baker, revolutionised the orography of equatorial Africa, and established the existence of great lakes—the reservoirs of the Nile and the Congo. Livingstone revealed to us the basin of the Zambesi, and by discovering Nyassa, cleared up the mystery of lake " Maravi." Stanley descended the Congo, and Cameron crossed Africa, from Zanzibar to Benguela. The course of the Niger was traced by many persevering efforts, as well as those of the Senegal, the Gambia, the Ogowé, the Limpopo, and the Orange river; while intermediate regions have been brought within our knowledge through the labours of dauntless explorers of several nations—Portuguese on both coasts and across the continent, French in the north and west, Germans mainly from the west and east coasts, and in the Nile and Niger valleys, Englishmen in all parts; and single travellers of all four nations have left their marks in every direction. Africa has been a glorious field of generous rivalry among civilised Europeans.

---

* But Ptolemy erroneously placed the Nile sources and the Mountains of the moon in about 12° s.

Yet much remains to be done. There is a wide field for discovery between Morocco and the Niger. The course of the Uelle, beyond the point reached by Schweinfurth, is entirely unknown, as well as the immense region between the Uelle and the Congo. The country between lake Tanganyika and Albert Nyanza is undiscovered. South of Abyssinia, there is a great mountainous region, drained by the Juba and the Godjeb or Sobat, of which we know next to nothing. D'Abbadie's journey to Enarea and Kaffa, and that of Father Massajah are the only ones on record in this direction. Here there is a region inhabited by a brave and industrious people, and reported to be fertile and productive. Even now the coffee from these highlands finds its way through Abyssinia to Massowah. Further south, the country east of the Victoria Nyanza, overlooked by the snowy peaks of Kenia and Kilimanjaro, is equally unknown; and still further south there are unexplored countries along the east coast to the Limpopo, in the interior, between the Congo and Zambesi, and along the course of the Cunene.

Moreover, it must be remembered that the work of the first discoverers, though the most difficult and perilous, and therefore the most glorious, is of the character of a reconnaissance. The whole must hereafter be systematically explored and surveyed before we can acquire accurate knowledge of the structure—the physical geography of inner Africa. This will be the work of many years, and will need the fostering support and help of our Society.

Asia is the seat of the most ancient civilisations. Great trade routes have traversed it from end to end during many centuries. Important cities and countries were well known in history, while their actual positions are uncertain. The exclusiveness of the Chinese, and the barbaric fanaticism of Muhammadans, render vast regions, once civilised and the centres of commerce, as inaccessible as the wildest parts of Africa. Consequently there was, and still is, a wide field for exploration in the interior of the Asiatic continent; and discovery of a most interesting kind. For no mere daring explorer is fitted for Asiatic discovery. Classical and oriental learning, critical acumen, and historical knowledge are as necessary here as the ordinary qualifications of a trained traveller. Comparative geography, one of the highest branches of our science, by identifying sites, and demonstrating, from history, the changes which have taken place in the course of ages, has been an essential auxiliary to the student of the physical aspects of Asiatic regions. Thus the knowledge that has been acquired since 1830, on the continent of Asia, is not only extensive, but also of the highest scientific and historical interest. It has not only made known to us the geography of new regions; but has also thrown light upon the history of our race. The writings of Arrian and Ptolemy, of the Chinese Pilgrims and the Arab geographers are as necessary to the student of Asiatic geography as the reports of recent explorers; for a mastery of comparative geography is essential for a due comprehension of the existing physical conditions of many parts of this continent.

In 1830 the Indian atlas had already been commenced, and Persian topography was based on the itineraries of Kinneir; while the Himalayan region had been explored by Moorcroft and Trebeck, Baillie Fraser, and Herbert and Webb. Bogle and Turner had penetrated into Tibet, China was known to us through the Jesuit survey published by Du Halde, and Arabia through the work of Burckhardt. But the great mountain system of Central Asia was not understood, and the fountains and courses of most of the great rivers were unknown.

During the fifty years of our Society's existence, the trigonometrical survey of British India has been almost completed, the height of the loftiest mountains in the world were fixed between 1845 and 1850, our officers have mapped the whole of Persia and Afghanistan, surveyed Mesopotamia, and explored the Pamír Steppe. Japan, Borneo, Siam, the Malay Peninsula, and the greater part of China have been brought more completely to our knowledge, Eastern Turkestan has been visited, and trained native explorers have penetrated to the remotest fountains of the Oxus, and the wild plateaux of Tibet. Over the northern half of the Asiatic Continent the Russians have displayed equal activity. They have traversed the wild steppes and deserts of what on old atlases was called Independent Tartary, have surveyed the courses of the Jaxartes, the Oxus, and the Amur, and have navigated the Caspian and the Sea of Aral. They have pushed their scientific investigations into the Pamir and Eastern Turkestan, until at last the British and Russian surveys have been connected.

Still, many years must elapse before our knowledge of the geography of Asia will approach completeness. The sources and upper courses of the great rivers Yang-tsze, Cambodia, and Irawadi, and part of the course of the Brahmaputra, are unknown. Our acquaintance with the head waters of the Oxus is still very far from being satisfactory, while the northern half of the Tibetan plateau, and much of the Kuen-Lun range are quite unknown. Coming nearer to our own dominions, Kafiristan is still a mystery, and even the Zhob and other valleys within the Sulimani Range have never been visited by

Europeans. There are also very extensive tracts in Arabia which no traveller has ever explored.

The survey and geographical description of North America is progressing under the admirably organised Departments of the United States Government, while good work is also being pushed forward in the Dominion of Canada. An enormous extension of our knowledge has taken place since 1830, when California was only settled by scattered *Misiones,* and the country to the north of it was unexplored, except by a few trappers. Our Society has watched the progress of these marvellous changes with the greatest interest, and has benefited by the fact that scientific research has gone hand in hand with the settlement of the country. It has conferred its highest honours on an eminent United States surveyor, and on two explorers of the Rocky Mountains ; but it has felt that the actual work in the field is already in good hands. This is not the case, to anything like the same extent, in Central and South America, where much exploring work remains to be done.

Commencing our review of South America from the south, there is much that remains undiscovered in Patagonia and the extreme south of Chile, although valuable progress is annually made by the Hydrographic Department of Chile, under the able and zealous lead of Captain Vidal Gormaz. As regards the interior of Patagonia, Captain Musters was the very first traveller who ever traversed that wild region from south to north, and this fact alone shows how much remains to be done there. Proceeding northwards, the labours of Mr. Minchin and others in the region through which the Bolivian-Brazilian frontier passes has quite recently increased our geographical knowledge ; and our science is no less indebted to Colonel Church for his work in the basins of the Beni and Mamoré. Still there is a vast extent of interesting country which is practically unexplored in the provinces of Lipez, Chichas, and Carangas, and especially round the western side of lake Poopo.

In many respects the Andean system is, to the physical geographer, the most interesting mountain mass in the world. Here the phenomena of earthquakes may be studied on the largest and most awful scale. Here are volcanic chains extending hundreds of miles, and fossiliferous Silurian rocks raised in the form of mountain peaks over 20,000 feet above the sea. Here, too, the meteorological and other physical phenomena of mountain chains are of peculiar interest. Yet the orography of western South America is very imperfectly understood, and this is particularly the case as regards the peaks and ridges of south-western Bolivia. In the vast region of the Madeira basin, which has been the scene of Colonel Church's invaluable labours, there is a yet more extensive unknown area, over which historical tradition has thrown a halo of romance. The course of the Madre de Dios, which drains the eastern slopes of the Andes of Cuzco, and of the Caravayan rivers, with their rich auriferous deposits, are unknown, and the work of discovery in this most interesting region remains to be completed.

There is a wholly undescribed Andean country, comprised in the Peruvian provinces of Lucanas, Parinacochas, Cangallo, Aymaraes, and Cotabambas, and in the coast valleys and deserts between Arequipa and Nasca. There is also much useful geographical work to be done in northern Peru and Ecuador, especially in the basins of the Pastasa, Morona, Santiago, Tigre, and Napo. The Putumayo was recently ascended in a steam launch by Mr. Simson; but the basins, both of the Putumayo and the Japura, need further examination. There is an enormous tract in Colombia, bounded by the slopes of the Cordillera on the west, on the east by the Orinoco and Rio Negro, on the north by the river Meta, and on the south by the Uaupés and Japura, which is practically unknown. This region is also surrounded with a halo of romance, for here the old conquerors of the 16th century believed that the far-famed El Dorado dwelt in golden abundance. Many parts of the Colombian Andes need exploration, as well as the whole region, from the Rio Branco to the Atlantic. Enough has been said to show that there still remains a vast amount of exploration, and even of discovery to be achieved in South America, and that, so far as that continent is concerned, geographers will have no need to sigh because there are no more worlds to conquer, for generations yet to come.

In Australia and New Zealand, the whole interior of those countries has been discovered and explored since the Society was founded. The maps of 1830 show very little more than inaccurate coast lines. Now, the arid wastes of Australia have been traversed in various directions, and the whole continent has been crossed from sea to sea, with an amount of brave endurance and indomitable courage which have excited the admiration of geographers, and gained for the explorers themselves the highest honours that the Society can bestow. Little now remains to be done on the mainland of Australia; but the interior of New Guinea has yet to be explored, as well as New Britain, the Solomon Group, and many islands to the north and north-east of New Guinea.

A large part of the world is still undiscovered, and it must be remembered that, even when the whole of this preliminary reconnoitring work is completed, the labours of the geographer are only commencing. It will then be necessary to push forward those more detailed surveys which are necessary before the physical configuration and aspects of a region can be correctly understood and described. Our work, as geographers, is to measure all parts of earth and sea, to ascertain the relative positions of all places upon the surface of the globe, and to delineate the varied features of that surface. This great work has been proceeding from the first dawn of civilisation, and it will probably be centuries longer before it is completed.

Nor are our labours confined to the land. Hydrography is an equally important branch of our work. Sir John Barrow, in his opening address in 1830, urged upon the Society that, on the exactitude of the minutest details of hydrography, mainly depended the safety of navigation, and he recommended its members to look forward to the completion of surveys, and to extended observations on prevailing winds and currents. " Every accession to hydrographical knowledge," he added, " must be of great importance to navigation and therefore a fit object for promulgation by the Society." Having the interests of hydrography at heart, and making it a part of its duties to advocate and watch over the execution of surveys, the Society was joined by all the eminent nautical surveyors. The hydrographer, Sir Francis Beaufort, was an active member of our Council for twenty-five years, making the work of his department known through the Society's publications, and sometimes inducing the Council to represent to the Government the urgency for undertaking some particular survey.* On four occasions the Society has conferred its highest honours upon naval surveyors, and the Society has been reminded of its duties relating to hydrography by successive Presidents, and by the reports which accompany their Addresses, as well as of the importance of increasing the accuracy of the surveys. For instance, Admiral Beechey, in 1856, told us that " rapid reconnaissance of a coast might have been tolerated half a century ago, but that such a survey of any shore cannot now be accepted."

---

* " A Deputation composed of the President, Captain Beaufort, and Mr. Murchison, waited upon Lord Glenelg, recommending a nautical survey to complete the parts of the north-west coasts of Australia left unfinished, and to examine more thoroughly Bass and Torres Straits. The Deputation was most favourably received; a survey of the coasts was ordered, and H.M.S. *Beagle*, commanded by Captain Wickham, will sail early in June."—R. G. S. ' Journal,' vol. vii. p. 10 ; 1837.

Great progress has been made in providing accurate charts for navigation during the last fifty years; but much remains to be done. Commander Hull, R.N., who was Superintendent of Charts at the Admiralty from 1873 to the end of 1879, read an admirable paper on this subject at the United Service Institution in 1874, entitled the "Unsurveyed World," in which he showed the coasts that have been surveyed, those that have been only partially surveyed, and those that have merely been explored. The first class of coasts still bears but a small proportion to the rest; and, in furthering the advance of the good work by all legitimate means, whether by inviting discussion, publishing information, rewarding and encouraging zealous and meritorious surveyors, or making well-considered representations, the Society will perform in the future, as it has done in the past, a useful national service.

Since the foundation of the Society a new branch of geographical investigation and study has come into existence, namely, the physical geography of the sea, which is an important extension of hydrography. Mathew Fontaine Maury, the Superintendent of the National Observatory at Washington, was the creator of this branch of our science. As Commodore Jansen truly said in his able memoir—" Maury threw a new light upon the ocean, and on its profoundest abysses, that will never be extinguished ; and it was through Maury's initiative that the naval profession now forms the most intelligent and active corps of co-operators in systematic research into the hidden chambers of the great deep. It was Maury who, by his wind and current charts, his trade-wind, storm, and rain charts, and last, but not least, by his work on the Physical Geography of the Sea, gave the first great impulse to all subsequent researches."

The progress of our knowledge of the bottom of the ocean has been nearly continuous since 1840, in which year Sir James Ross, on board the *Erebus,* obtained a sounding in 2677 fathoms. In 1847, on January 12th, Captain Owen Stanley, in the *Rattlesnake,* found bottom, near the equator, at a depth of 2600 fathoms. Then followed the work of officers of the United States; and in 1856 Derryman, with the Brooke machine, obtained twenty-four deep-sea soundings on a great circle from St. John's, Newfoundland, to Valentia. In 1857 Lieut. Dayman, in the *Cyclops,* obtained a complete series of deep-sea soundings across the Atlantic, showing the great fall of 7200 feet, and the " Telegraphic Plateau." In 1858 Lieut. Dayman sounded from Newfoundland to Fayal, and from Fayal to the English Channel, and in 1859 across the Bay of Biscay, and along the coast of Portugal, to Malta. Then followed the work of Sir

Leopold M'Clintock in 1860 in the *Bulldog,* of Captain Short-
land in the *Hydra* in 1867, from Malta to Bombay, and of the
Porcupine, Lightning, and *Gannet.* Finally, the important
voyage of the *Challenger* under Captain Nares, from 1873 to
1875, in the Atlantic, Indian, and Pacific Oceans, added enor-
mously to our knowledge of the physical geography of the
sea. The greatest depth was between St. Thomas and
Bermuda, where a sounding of 3875 fathoms was obtained.*
A line was taken across the Atlantic from Greenland to Ireland
by the *Valorous* in 1875; and many deep sea soundings have
been added by vessels employed by the Telegraph Maintenance
Company. Our lamented associate, Admiral Sherard Osborn,
who was the Managing Director of this Company, communicated a most interesting paper on the geography of the beds
of the Atlantic and Indian Oceans and Mediterranean Sea
in 1870. Osborn bore generous testimony to the great service
performed by Maury, and said that the geographer must not
be satisfied with observations on the surface of the ocean, but
must endeavour to probe mysteries down to the solid crust on
which the ocean rests. This then is a branch of geographical enquiry, in which much remains to be learnt, and which
has come into existence since the Society was founded.

This rapid glance at the unknown and unexplored parts of
the earth, shows that many years must elapse before all has
been discovered, and that there is abundant work before the
Society, even of this preliminary kind. In his Anniversary
Address of 1851, Admiral Smyth offered some remarks on the
duties of the Society which are as applicable now as they were
then. He said that "one by one the last remnants of the
unknown would yield to the efforts of explorers; but, had we
even actually arrived at so desirable a consummation, would
our labours then be terminated? Would Geographical Societies cease to be requisite? Certainly not. Our work might
then be said to be only beginning. Till we actually know the
whole extent and surface of the globe on which we move, its
peculiarities as a whole, and the mutual relations of its several
parts, it can never be thoroughly investigated or understood;
and much will long remain, as it now is, only a source of
wonder and confusion." When, in the far distant future, the
whole surface of the earth has been surveyed and mapped, the
study of physical geography may be recommenced on a sound
basis, and generalisations will become more accurate, and will

---

* Or 23,250 feet. This is 5752 feet less than the height of Mount Everest
above the level of the sea. So that the perpendicular height of Mount Everest
above the lowest depth of the ocean is 8 miles, or 52,252 feet.

be founded on more correct and reliable data. Until then, investigations in all the branches into which the science of geography is divided must be continued, with patience and industry, and with the best information that can be obtained.

Geography is a progressive science. Every year, with its discoveries and novelties, also brings forth a large crop of corrections and of information which modifies preconceived theories and opinions. It is this freshness, this constant supply of new material, which constitutes one of the many charms of geographical research.

The Geographical Society thus commences its second half-century of work with a bright prospect of continued usefulness. It has an honourable record of past labours to look back upon. It has now reached a high position as regards popular support and financial prosperity. It goes forward in the full assurance, which is justified by its former history, that it will have a long career of activity and success; and that its efforts to perform good work, and to encourage and assist the labours of others, will constitute a service of national value and importance.

APPENDIX.

CONTENTS.

APPENDIX

———•◦•———

PRESIDENTS

OF THE

ROYAL GEOGRAPHICAL SOCIETY.

(* *Gold Medallists.*)

1831–33. Viscount Goderich.
1833–35. General The Right Hon. Sir George Murray, G.C.B.
1835–37. Sir John Barrow, *Bart.*
1837–39. Mr. W. R. Hamilton.
1839–41. Mr. G. B. Greenough.
1841–43. Mr. W. R. Hamilton.
1843–45. Mr. R. I. Murchison.
1845–47. Admiral Lord Colchester.
1847–49. *Mr. W. J. Hamilton.
1849–51. *Admiral W. H. Smyth, C.B.
1851–53. Sir Roderick Murchison.
1853–55. The Earl of Ellesmere, K.G.
1855–56. Admiral Beechey.
1856–59. Sir Roderick Murchison.
1859–60. Earl de Grey and Ripon.
1860–62. Lord Ashburton.
1862–71. *Sir Roderick Murchison, *Bart.*, K.C.B.
1871–73. Major-General Sir Henry Rawliuson, K.C.B.
1873–74. The Right Hon. Sir H. Bartle Frere, *Bart.*, G.C.B., G.C.S.I.
1874–76. *Major-General Sir Henry Rawlinson, K.C.B.
1876–78. Sir Rutherford Alcock, K.C.B.
1878–79. The Earl of Dufferin, K.P., K.C.B.
1879–80. The Earl of Northbrook, G.C.S.I.
1880–81. Lord Aberdare.

———————————

HONORARY SECRETARIES.

1847–49. Mr. George Long, and Major Shadwell Clerke.
1850–51. Mr. John Hogg, F.R.S., and Dr. Trithen.
1851–53. Colonel Philip Yorke, F.R.S., and Dr. T. Hodgkin.
1853–54. Capt. F. P. Blackwood, R.N., and ,, ,,
1854–57. Sir Walter Trevelyan, *Bart.*, and ,, ,,
1857–62. *Mr. Francis Galton, F.R.S., and ,, ,,
1862–63. ,, ,, ,, and Mr. W. Spottiswoode, F.R.S.
1863–64. Mr. Wm. Spottiswoode, F.R.S., and Mr. Clements R. Markham.
1864–66. Mr. Clements R. Markham, C.B., F.R.S., and Mr. L. Oliphant.
1866–81. ,, ,, ,, ,, and Mr. R. H. Major.

K

HONORARY FOREIGN SECRETARIES.

1830–46. Rev. J. C. Renouard (1840, Editor of Journal to 1844).
1862–65. Dr. T. Hodgkin.
1865–66. *Mr. Francis Galton, F.R.S.
1866–71. Mr. Cyril Graham, C.M.G.
1871–75. Mr. John Ball, F.R.S.
1875–81. Lord Arthur Russell, M.P. (to 1881).

TRUSTEES.

1830. Sir George Staunton, *Bart.*, and Sir George Duckett.
1836.   „   „   „   and Mr. F. Baily.
1845.   „   „   „   and Mr. W. R. Hamilton.
1858.   „   „   „   and Mr. R. Monckton Milnes.
1859. Mr. R. Monckton Milnes (cr. Lord Houghton, 1863) and Sir Walter Trevelyan, *Bart.*
1878. Lord Houghton and Sir John Lubbock, *Bart.* (to 1881).

TREASURERS.

1831. Mr. John Biddulph ; also Trustee in 1839.
1845. Mr. Robert Biddulph.
1864. Mr. Reginald Cocks (to 1881).

PERMANENT STAFF.

PAID SECRETARIES, 1830–47,

AND

ASSISTANT-SECRETARIES, 1847–81.

1830—July.   Captain A. Maconochie, R.N., K.H.
1836—May 23.   Captain Washington, R.N.
1840—Nov. 9.   Colonel Jackson (1844, Editor of ' Journal ').
1847—April 3.   Dr. Humble.
1849—Jan. 22.   Dr. Norton Shaw.
1863—July 13.   Mr. Greenfield.
1864—April 25. Mr. H. W. Bates (to 1881).

LIBRARIANS.

1832—Dec. 15. Mr. Charles Bradbury.
1836—Nov. 14. Mr. R. W. Clifton.
1837—Dec. 11. Mr. Webb, R.N.
1841—Dec. 13. Mr. Shillinglaw.

CLERKS IN CHARGE OF THE LIBRARY.

1846—Nov. 23.   Mr. Cartwright, to 1851.
1854—Aug. 8.   Mr. Trelawney Saunders (Temporary Librarian).
1854—Nov. 23.   Mr. Wheeler.
1859—March 21. Mr. W. C. Street.
1863—Jan. 12.   Mr. E. B. Tattershall.
1864—Nov. 14.   Mr. A. J. Clark.

LIBRARIANS.

1864—Nov.   Mr. H. Purrier.
1866—Nov. 12.   Mr. J. H. Lamprey.
1874—Feb. 18.   Mr. E. C. Rye.
                (*Assistant*, Vincent Hawkins, Oct. 4, 1874.)

MAP CURATORS.

1854—Jan. 22.   Mr. Trelawney Saunders.
1857—June 15. Staff-Commander C. George, R.N.
1877—June 18. Mr. J. Coles, R.N.

Assistants :—1857—June 19. Mr. Oulet.
              1872—April.   Mr. A. Keith Johnston (to 1873).
              1878—June.   Mr. E. A. Reeves.

K 2

MAP DRAUGHTSMEN.

1873—Nov. 12. Mr. W. J. Turner.
1881—April. Mr. Henry Scharbau.

CHIEF CLERKS.

1846—Nov. 23. Mr. Cartwright.
1854—Nov. 23. Mr. Wheeler.
1862—Nov. Mr. E. Street.
1863—April 13. Mr. H. W. Farley.
1875—Feb. 15. Mr. A. E. Ball.
1876—May 15. Mr. E. Duffield Jones (to 1881).

CLERKS.

1854—Nov. 23. Mr. Price (to 1863).
1859—March 21. Mr. E. Street (to 1862).
1859—Oct. 24. Mr. Reginald Suggate (to 1881).
1863—Jan. 12. Mr. E. B. Tattershall (to 1864).
1866—Oct. 8. Mr. S. J. Evis (to 1881).

OFFICE KEEPERS.

1846—Dec. 28. Serjeant Lightfoot.
1853—July 24 Robert Suggate.
1876—Dec. 4. S. J. Evis (to 1881).

MAP MOUNTER.

1857—Sept. R. Burnett (to 1881).

MEMBERS

OF THE

COUNCIL

OF THE

ROYAL GEOGRAPHICAL SOCIETY,

1830-1880.

(*P.* President; *V.-P.* Vice-President; *C.* Council; *Treas.* Treasurer; *Sec.* Secretary;
For. Sec. Foreign Secretary; *Trust.* Trustee; PRESIDENTS in Small Capitals;
* *Gold Medallist.*)

ABERDARE, the Right Hon. Lord, *P.* 1880.
Acland, Sir Thomas Dyke, *Bart.*, C. 1840, 41, 42.
Addington, The Right Hon. H. U., C. 1862, 63, 64, 67, 68, 69.
Albemarle. (See *Keppel.*)
ALCOCK, Sir Rutherford, K.C.B., C. 1872; V.-P. 1873, 74, 75; *P.* 1876, 78;
 V.-P. 1878, 79, 80.
Althorp, The Right Hon. Lord, C. 1830.
* *Arrowsmith*, John, C. 1851, 52, 53, 54, 55, 56, 57, 58, 59, 60, 61, 62, 65,
 66, 67, 68.
ASHBURTON, Lord, *P.* 1860, 61; V.-P. 1862, 63.
Ayrton, Frederick, C. 1849, 50.

Bach, A., C. 1832.
* *Back*, Admiral Sir George, C. 1838, 39, 40; V.-P. 1844, 45; C. 1846, 47;
 V.-P. 1848; C. 1849; V.-P. 1850, 51, 52; C. 1853; V.-P. 1854–58;
 C. 1859–64; V.-P. 1865–69; C. 1870, 72, 73; V.-P. 1874, 75; C. 1876.
Backhouse, John, C., 1836, 37, 38, 40, 41.
Baily, F., C. 1830, 31; *Trustee*, 1836–44.
* *Baker*, Sir Samuel, C. 1866, 67, 68, 74.
Balfour, Lieut.-Gen. Sir George, K.C.B., C. 1863, 64, 65, 66, 67, 68.
Ball, John; *For. Sec.* 1871–74; C. 1875, 76, 77, 79, 80.
Bandinel, James, C. 1844, 45, 46.
Barkly, Sir Henry, G.C.M.G., K.C.B., V.-P. 1879, 80.
BARROW, Sir John, *Bart.*, V.-P. 1830, 31; *P.* 1835, 36; V.-P. 1837, 38,
 39, 40; C. 1841, 42, 43, 44; V. P. 1845–47.
Beaufort, Admiral Sir Francis, K.C.B., C. 1830, 31, 36, 37, 38, 39, 40, 41, 42,
 43, 44, 45, 46, 47, 48, 49, 50, 51, 52, 53, 54, 55.
Beckford, Francis, C. 1841, 47, 49.
BEECHEY, Rear-Admiral, C. 1854; *P.* 1855.
Berens, Joseph, C. 1840.
Biddulph, John, *Treas.* 1830–44; *Trustee*, 1839.
Biddulph, Robert, *Treas.* 1845–64.
Blaauw, W. H., C. 1847.
Blackwood, Captain Francis P., R.N., C. 1841, 47; *Sec.* 1852.
Borradaile, Abraham, C. 1836
Bowles, Admiral, C. 1836, 37, 38, 42, 43, 45, 46, 53, 54.

Brandreth, Major, R.E., C. 1847.
Britton, J., C. 1830, 31.
Brockedon, William, C. 1830, 31, 36, 37, 38, 42, 43, 44.
Brodie, Sir Benjamin, *Bart.*, C. 1859, 60.
Brodrick, The Hon. George, C. 1869, 70, 71, 72, 73, 74, 76, 77, 79.
Brooke, Sir Arthur de Capell, *Bart.*, C. 1830, 31.
Brooking, Thomas, C. 1855, 56, 57, 58, 59, 60, 61, 62, 64, 65, 66, 67, 68.
Broughton, The Right Hon. Lord, C. 1830, 31, 39, 57, 58.
Brown, Robert, C. 1830, 31, 38.
Buller, Captain Wentworth, R.N.., C. 1839.
Bunbury, Edward H., C. 1846, 47.
Burlington, Earl of, C. 1841 (now Duke of Devonshire).
Buxton, Sir T. Fowell, *Bart.*, C. 1871, 72, 73, 74, 75, 76, 77, 80.

Calthorpe, The Hon. F. H. W., C. 1859, 60.
Campbell, Sir George, K.C.S.I., C. 1870, 74, 75, 76.
Cardwell, The Right Hon. Edward, C. 1856, 57.
Carnarvon, The 3rd Earl of, C. 1842, 43 (d. 1849).
Chapman, Captain, R.A., C. 1841.
Charters, Major, R.A., C. 1840.
Chatterton, Sir William, *Bart.*, C. 1843, 46, 47.
*Chesney, General Francis Rawdon, C. 1839, 40, 41, 42.
Churchill, Lord Alfred, C. 1861, 62, 63, 64.
Clerke, Major Shadwell, C. 1845, 46; *Sec.* 1847.
Cockburn, Admiral The Right Hon. Sir George, G.C.B., C. 1837.
Cocks, Reginald, *Treas.* 1864–81.
COLCHESTER, Admiral The Right Hon. Lord, C. 1839, 40; V.-P. 1841, 42, 43; C. 1844; *P.* 1845, 47; V.-P. 1847, 48, 49; C. 1850, 51, 52; V.-P. 1853, 54; C. 1855, 56, 61, 62, 63, 64, 65, 66.
*Collinson, Admiral Sir Richard, K.C.B., C. 1857; V.-P. 1858, 59, 60, 61, 62, 63, 64; C. 1865, 66, 68, 69, 70, 71, 72, 73; V.-P. 1874, 75.
Colquhoun, Lieut.-Colonel, R.A., C. 1844, 45, 46, 47.
Cottesloe, The Right Hon. Lord, C. 1863, 64, 65, 66, 67, 68, 69, 72, 74; V.-P. 1875, 76, 77, 79.
Craufurd, W. P., C. 1832, 43, 44.
Crawford, R. W., C. 1865, 66.
Crawfurd, John, C. 1857, 58, 59, 60, 61, 62, 63; V.-P. 1864, 65, 66; C. 1867.
Curzon, The Hon. Robert, C. 1866.
Cust, Robert, C. 1877, 78, 79, 80.

Darwin, Charles, C. 1840.
DE GREY AND RIPON, The Earl of, *P.* 1859; V.-P. 1860; C. 1861 (now Marquis of *Ripon*).
De la Beche, Sir Henry, C. 1844, 45, 51.
De Mauley, Lord, C. 1851.
Denison, Sir William, K.C.B., C. 1866.
Denman, Captain The Hon. J., R.N., C. 1859.
Derby, The Earl of, C. 1871; V.-P. 1872, 73.   (See *Stanley*, Lord.)
Devonshire, The Duke of.   (See *Burlington*, Earl of.)
Dickson, Colonel Sir A., K.C.B., C. 1836, 37, 38, 39.
Dodd, George, C. 1843, 44, 45, 46, 47, 48, 49.
Donoughmore, The Earl of, C. 1864, 65.
Douglas, General Sir Howard, C. 1845.
Ducie, The Earl of, C. 1862, 73.
Duckett, Sir George, *Bart.*, *Trust.* 1832 to 1836.
DUFFERIN, The Earl of, K.P., K.C.B., C. 1858, 67; *P.* 1878.

Dundas, The Right Hon. Sir David, 1853, 54, 64, 65.
Eastnor, Viscount, C. 1846 (now Earl *Somers*).
ELLESMERE, The Earl of, K.G.. C. 1851, 52; *P.* 1853–55; V.-P. 1855, 56.
Elliot, Rear-Admiral The Hon. George, C. 1837.
Ellis, Sir Barrow, K.C.S.I., C. 1876, 77, 78, 79; V.-P. 1880.
Elphinstone, The Hon. Mountstuart, C. 1830, 31, 36, 37; V.-P. 1838-9, 40; C. 1841.
Enderby, Charles, C. 1836, 37, 38, 42, 43, 44, 45, 47.
Enniskillen, The Earl of, C. 1840.
Estcourt, Thomas Gorviston Bucknell, C. 1843.
Evans, Captain, R.N., C.B., 1874, 75, 76, 77, 78; V.-P. 1879, 80.
Everest, Colonel Sir George, C. 1853, 55, 56; V.-P. 1857, 58, 59, 60, 61, 62, 63.

Fanshawe, Colonel, V.-P. 1836, 37; C. 1838.
Fellowes, Sir Charles, C. 1841, 42, 43, 44, 45, 49, 50, 51, 52; V.-P. 1853, 54; C. 1855, 56.
Fergusson, James, C. 1863, 64, 65, 66, 67, 68, 69, 70, 71, 73, 74, 75, 76, 77, 78, 79, 80.
Findlay, A. G., C. 1857, 58, 59, 60, 61, 62, 63, 64, 67, 68, 69, 70, 71, 73, 74.
**FitzRoy,* Captain, R.N., C. 1837, 51, 52, 53, 56.
Forsyth, Sir Douglas, K.C.S.I., C.B., C. 1877, 78, 79, 80.
Fox, Lieut.-General, C. 1838, 39, 40, 41, 42, 43, 45, 46, 49, 50, 56, 57, 58, 60, 61, 64.
**Franklin,* Captain Sir John, R.N., V.-P. 1830, 44, 45.
Fraser, Colonel Sir Augustus, K.C.B., C. 1830, 31.
Fraser, J. Baillie, C. 1838, 39.
Fremantle. (See *Cottesloe.*)
Frere, Bartle, C. 1836, 37, 38, 39, 40, 41, 42, 43, 44, 45, 46, 47, 48, 49.
FRERE, The Right Hon. Sir H. Bartle, *Bart.*, G.C.B., G.C.S.I., C. 1868, 69; V.-P. 1870, 71, 72, 74; *P.* 1873; C. 1875; V.-P. 1876.
Freshfield, Douglas, C. 1879, 80.

Galton, Captain Douglas, C.B., C. 1876.
**Galton,* Francis, C. 1854, 55, 56; *Sec.* 1857–63; C. 1863, 64; *For. Sec.* 1865, 66; V.-P. 1866, 67, 68, 69, 70, 71, 72; C. 1873, 75, 76, 77; V.-P. 1879, 80.
Gibbs, H. H., C. 1872.
GODERICH, Viscount, P. 1830, 31, 32, 33. As Earl of Ripon, C. 1836, 37.
Godwin-Austen, Colonel, C. 1879, 80.
Goldsmid, Major-General Sir Frederic, K.C.S.I., C.B., C. 1873, 74, 75, 76.
Goodenough, Dr. (See *Wells,* Dean of.)
Graham, Cyril, C.M.G., C. 1862, 63, 64, 65; *For. Sec.* 1866–71.
**Grant,* Lieut.-Colonel, C.B., C.S.I., C. 1869, 70, 71, 72, 73, 74, 75, 76, 77, 78, 79.
Grant Duff, The Right Hon. Mountstuart Elphinstone, C. 1869, 70, 74, 75.
Green, Major-General Sir Henry, K.C.S.I., C.B., C. 1876, 77, 78, 79.
GREENOUGH, George Bellas, V.-P. 1830, 31; C. 1836; V.-P. 1837, 38; *P.* 1839–41; V.-P. 1841, 42, 43; C. 1844, 45, 46, 47, 49; C. 1850, 51, 52, 53, 54.
Grey, R. W., C. 1852.
Grey, Sir George, K.C.B., C. 1869.

Halford, Rev. Thomas, C. 1842.
Hall, Captain Basil, R.N., C. 1830, 31.
Hall, Admiral W. H., K.C.B., C. 1860, 61, 62, 63, 64, 70, 71, 72, 74, 75, 76.
Hallam, Henry, C. 1836.
HAMILTON, William R., C. 1830; V.-P. 1831; C. 1836; *P.* 1837–39; V.-P. 1839, 40; *P.* 1841–43; V.-P. 1843, 44; *Trust.* 1846–57.

Merewether, Colonel Sir William L., K.C.S.I., C.B., C. 1879, 80.
Merivale, Herman, C. 1850, 66, 67, 68.
Milne, Admiral Sir Alexander, *Bart.*, G.C.B.; V.-P. 1876, 77, 78, 79, 80.
Milnes, R. Monckton. (See *Houghton*.)
Monteith, General, C. 1831, 46.
Morier, James, C. 1836, 37, 38, 39.
*Murchison, Sir Roderick Impey, *Bart.*, K.C.B., C. 1833; V.-P. 1836;
    C. 1837, 38, 39, 40, 41; V.-P. 1842; *P.* 1843, 45; V.-P. 1845, 46; C.
    1847; V.-P. 1849, 50; *P.* 1851, 52; V.-P. 1853, 54, 55; *P.* 1856, 57,
    58; V.-P. 1859, 60, 61; *P.* 1862–70; V.-P. 1871.
Murchison, Kenneth, C. 1871, 72.
Murdoch, Thomas, C. 1830, 31; V.-P. 1836; C. 1837.
Murray, General, The Right Hon. Sir George, G.C.B., C. 1830, 31; *P.* 1833,
    35.
Murray, James, C. 1849, 50, 51, 52.
Murray, John, C. 1850, 72, 73, 74, 75, 77.
Murray, Rear-Admiral The Hon. H. A., R.N., C. 1858, 59, 60, 61, 62, 63.

Nares, Captain Sir George, R.N., K.C.B., C. 1880.
Nicholson, Sir Charles, *Bart.*, C. 1863, 64, 65, 66, 67, 68, 70, 71, 72, 73,
    74, 75.
Northbrook, The Earl of, G.C.S.I., *P.* 1879–80.
Northumberland, The Duke of. (See *Prudhoe*.)
Norwich, The Bishop of (Dr. Stanley), C. 1845.

O'Gorman, George, C. 1846, 47, 49, 50, 51, 52.
Oliphant, Laurence, C. 1859, 60; *Sec.* 1864, 65; C. 1866, 67.
Ommanney, Admiral Sir Erasmus, C.B., C. 1872, 73, 74, 75, 79, 80.
Osborn, Rear-Admiral Sherard, C.B., C. 1867, 68, 69, 70, 71, 72, 73, 74, 75.
Oswell, William Cotton, C. 1855.
Overstone, Lord, 1855. (See *Jones-Lloyd*.)
Owen, Captain W. F. W., R.N., C. 1832.
Oxford, Bishop of (Dr. Wilberforce), C. 1857, 58.

Parish, Sir Woodbine, V.-P. 1836, 37; C. 1839, 40, 42, 43, 49, 50; V.-P.
    1851, 52; C. 1853.
Parkyns, Mansfield, C. 1854.
Pelly, J. H., C. 1847.
Pelly, Colonel Sir Lewis, K.C.B., K.C.S.I., C. 1879, 80.
Phayre, Lieut.-Gen. Sir Arthur, C.B., K.C.S.I., C. 1879.
Pollington, Viscount, C. 1842 (now *Earl of Mexborough*).
Pollock, General Sir George, G.C.B., C. 1854–56, 57.
Portlock, Colonel, C. 1849, 53, 54, 55, 56, 59, 60; V.-P. 1861, 62.
Prince Lee, Dr. (See *Manchester*, Bishop of.)
Prudhoe, Captain Lord, R.N., C. 1830, 31, 36, 37, 39, 44, 45, 46, 50, 51,
    52. (Afterwards Duke of Northumberland.)

Rae, John, C. 1862, 70, 71, 72.
Raper, Lieut. Henry, R.N., C. 1846, 49, 50, 51, 52, 53, 57.
*Rawlinson, Major-General Sir Henry C. K.C.B., C. 1850, 51, 57, 58, 61, 62,
    63; V.-P. 1864, 65, 66, 67; C. 1868; V.-P. 1869, 70; *P.* 1871, 72, 73;
    P. 74, 76; V.-P. 76, 77, 78, 79, 80.
Rawson, Sir W. Rawson, K.C.M.G., C.B., C. 1841, 42, 76, 77, 78, 79.
Reay, Lord, C. 1880.
Rennie, George, C. 1836.
Rennie, Sir John, C. 1840, 41, 42; V.-P. 1843, 44; C. 1847.
Renouard, Rev. George Cecil, *For. Sec.* 1830–46; C. 1847, 49, 50, 51, 52.

Richards, Vice-Admiral Sir George, C.B., C. 1867, 68, 69, 70; V.-P. 71, 72, 73; C. 1875, 76, 77.
Richardson, Dr. Sir John, R.N., C.B., C. 1832.
Rigby, General, C. 1868, 69, 70, 71, 73, 74, 75, 76, 78, 79, 80.
RIPON, The Earl of. (See *Goderich.*)
RIPON, The Marquis of. (See *De Grey.*)
Rodd, Rear-Admiral Sir John Tremaine, C.B., C. 1837.
Rosse, The Earl of, C. 1845.
Russell, Lord Arthur, C. 1869, 70, 71, 72; *For. Sec.* 1876–81.
Ryder, Admiral Alfred Phillipps, C. 1863.

Sabine, General Sir Edward, K.C.B., C. 1852, 53, 57, 58, 59.
St. Asaph, Bishop of (Dr. Vowler Short), C. 1851, 52, 53.
Seymour, Henry Danby, C. 1856, 57, 58, 59, 60, 64, 65, 74, 75, 76, 77.
Sheffield, The Earl of, C. 1852, 53, 54, 55, 56, 57, 58, 59, 63, 64.
Sheil, Sir Justin, K.C.B., C. 1861.
Short, Dr. Vowler. (See *St. Asaph,* Bishop of.)
Silver, S. W., C. 1870–81.
Smith, E. Osborne, C. 1846–63.
*SMYTH, Admiral W. H., C.B., C. 1830, 31, 44; V.-P. 1845, 46, 47; *P.* 1849, 51; V.-P. 1851, 52; C. 1853; V.-P. 1855.
Smyth, Warington, C. 1871, 72, 73, 74.
Somers, Earl, C. 1855. (See *Eastnor.*)
Spottiswoode, William, C. 1860, 61; *Sec.* 1862, 63; C. 1864, 65, 66.
Stanley, C. 1854, 55. (See *Derby,* Earl of.)
Stanley, Dr. (See *Norwich,* Bishop of.)
Staunton, Sir George, *Bart., Trust.* 1832–60.
Staveley, Thomas, C. 1853, 54, 55, 56, 57, 58, 59.
Steele, Colonel Thomas, C.B., C. 1858.
Stephenson, B. C., C. 1871, 72.
Stephenson, Robert, C. 1858.
Stokes, Admiral J. L., C. 1856, 57.
Strachey, Lieut.-Gen. Richard, C.S.I., C. 1872, 73, 75, 76, 77, 78, 79, 80.
Strangford, Viscount, C. 1860, 61, 62; V.-P. 1863, 64, 65; C. 1866, 67.
Stratford de Redcliffe, Viscount, K.G., C. 1870.
Strzelecki, Count Sir Paul, K.C.M.G., C.B., C. 1855, 56, 57, 58, 59, 61, 62.
Sykes, Colonel, C. 1852, 55; V.-P. 1856, 57, 58, 59; C. 1860, 61.

Temple, Sir Richard, *Bart.,* G.C.S.I., C. 1880.
Thomson, Dr. Thomas, C. 1866, 67, 68, 69.
Thuillier, Lieut.-Gen. Sir Henry, C.S.I., C. 1879, 80.
Trevelyan, Sir Walter, *Bart.,* C. 1843, 52, 53; *Sec.* 1854, 55, 56; V.-P. 1857; *Trust.* 1860–78.
Trithen, Francis H., *Sec.* 1849, 50.

Vaughan, The Right Hon. Sir Charles, C. 1839.
Verney, Sir Harry, *Bart.,* C. 1842, 57, 68, 69, 73, 74, 75, 76; V.-P. 1877, 78; C. 1879, 80.
Vetch, Captain, R.E., C. 1836.

Walker, John, C. 1862, 63, 64.
Ward, H. G., C. 1830.
Ward, John, C. 1832.
Warre, J. A., C. 1859, 60.
Washington, Rear-Admiral, *Sec.* 1836–41; C. 1841, 42, 43, 44, 47, 49.
Waugh, Lieut.-Gen. Sir Andrew Scott, C. 1861, 62, 63, 64, 65, 66; V.-P. 1867, 68, 69, 70; C. 1871.

Wellington, The Duke of, K.G., C. 1869, 70.
Wells, The Dean of (Dr. Goodenough), C. 1831.
Wharncliffe, 3rd Lord, C. 1868. (See *Wortley.*)
Whewell, Dr., C. 1853, 54.
White, Charles, 1869, 70, 71.
Wilberforce, Dr. (See *Oxford,* Bishop of.)
Wilkinson, Sir Gardner, C. 1841, 52, 53, 54, 55.
Wilmot, Captain A. P. Eadley, R.N., C. 1867.
Wilson, Lieut.-Colonel, C.B., C. 1872, 73, 74, 75.
Wortley, The Hon. J. Stuart (afterwards 2nd Lord Wharncliffe), C. 1836, 37.

Yorke, Colonel Philip, C. 1847–49; *Sec.* 1851, 52; V.-P. 1853.
* *Yule,* Colonel Henry, C.B., C. 1863, 76, 77.

OBITUARY NOTICES

OF

DISTINGUISHED FELLOWS

OF THE ROYAL GEOGRAPHICAL SOCIETY

IN THE PRESIDENTIAL ADDRESSES AND PROCEEDINGS

(New Series).

*** The *first* number refers to the Volume of the 'Journal,' the *second* number
to the page.

LIST

OF

EXPLORERS AND GEOGRAPHERS

TO WHOM THE

ROYAL GEOGRAPHICAL SOCIETY

HAS GRANTED

HONORARY AWARDS.

ARCTIC.

1834. Captain Sir John Ross, R.N., C.B.	*(Royal Award)*
1836. Captain Sir George Back, R.N.	*(Royal Award)*
1839. Mr. George Simpson	*(Founder's Medal)*
1846. Professor Middendorf	*(Founder's Medal)*
1852. Dr. John Rae	*(Founder's Medal)*
1853. Captain Inglefield, R.N., C.B.	*(Patron's Medal)*
1854. Captain Sir Robert M'Clure, R.N., C.B.	*(Patron's Medal)*
1856. Dr. Elisha Kent Kane	*(Founder's Medal)*
1858. Captain Collinson, R.N., C.B.	*(Founder's Medal)*
1860. Lady Franklin	*(Founder's Medal)*
1860. Captain Sir Leopold M'Clintock, R.N.	*(Patron's Medal)*
1867. Dr. Hayes	*(Patron's Medal)*
1869. Professor Nordenskiöld	*(Founder's Medal)*
1873. Captain Carlsen	*(Gold Watch)*
1875. Lieut. Weyprecht	*(Founder's Medal)*
1875. Lieut. Julius Payer	*(Patron's Medal)*
1877. Captain Sir George Nares, K.C.B.	*(Founder's Medal)*
1877. Captain A. H. Markham, R.N.	*(Gold Watch)*
1880. Captain Palander	*(Founder's Medal)*
1881. Mr. B. Leigh Smith	*(Patron's Medal)*

ANTARCTIC.

1833. Mr. John Biscoe, R.N.	*(Royal Award)*
1842. Captain Sir James C. Ross, R.N.	*(Founder's Medal)*
1848. Captain Charles Wilkes, U.S.N.	*(Patron's Medal)*

AFRICA.

1832. Mr. Richard Lander	*(Royal Award)*
1839. Dr. Edward Rüppell	*(Patron's Medal)*
1845. Dr. Beke	*(Founder's Medal)*
1853. Mr. Francis Galton	*(Founder's Medal)*
1855. Rev. David Livingstone	*(Patron's Medal)*
1855. Mr. Charles J. Anderssen	*(Instruments)*

1856. Dr. Heinrich Barth, C.B. .. .. (*Patron's Medal*)
1856. Corporal J. F. Church .. .. (*Watch & Chain*)
1859. Captain Richard F. Burton.. .. .. (*Founder's Medal*)
1861. Captain John Hanning Speke .. .. (*Founder's Medal*)
1864. Captain J. A. Grant, C.B. .. .. (*Patron's Medal*)
1864. Baron C. von der Decken .. .. (*Founder's Medal*)
1865. Sir Samuel Baker.. .. .. (*Patron's Medal*)
1866. M. P. B. du Chaillu .. .. (100 *Guineas*)
1868. M. Gerhard Rohlfs .. .. (*Patron's Medal*)
1872. Herr Karl Mauch .. .. (*Sum of £20*)
1873. Mr. H. M. Stanley .. .. (*Patron's Medal*)
1873. Mr. Thomas Baines .. .. (*Gold Watch*)
1874. Dr. Georg Schweinfurth .. .. (*Founder's Medal*)
1876. Commander V. L. Cameron, R.N., C.B. .. .. (*Founder's Medal*)
1880. Bishop Crowther .. .. (*Gold Watch*)
1881. Major Serpa Pinto .. .. (*Founder's Medal*)

ASIA.

1835. Sir Alexander Burnes .. .. (*Royal Award*)
1838. Colonel Chesney, R.E. .. .. (*Royal Award*)
1840. Major-Gen. Sir Henry Rawlinson, K.C.B. .. .. (*Founder's Medal*)
1841. Lieut. John Wood, I.N. .. .. (*Patron's Medal*)
1843. Lieut. J. F. A. Symonds, R.E. .. .. (*Patron's Medal*)
1844. Mr. W. J. Hamilton .. .. (*Founder's Medal*)
1849. Austen H. Layard .. .. (*Founder's Medal*)
1849. Baron Hügel .. .. (*Patron's Medal*)
1851. Dr. George Wallin .. .. (25 *Guineas*)
1852. Captain Henry Strachey .. .. (*Patron's Medal*)
1857. Lieut.-General Sir Andrew Scott Waugh .. .. (*Patron's Medal*)
1862. Captain Thomas Blakiston .. .. (*Patron's Medal*)
1864. Mr. W. Gifford Palgrave .. .. (25 *Guineas*)
1865. Colonel T. G. Montgomerie, R. E. .. .. .. (*Founder's Medal*)
1865. Dr. Arminius Vambéry .. .. (40 *Guineas*)
1866. Dr. Thomas Thomson, M.D. .. .. (*Founder's Medal*)
1866. Moola Abdul Medjid .. .. (*Gold Watch*)
1867. Admiral Alexis Boutakoff .. .. (*Founder's Medal*)
1870. Lieut. Francis Garnier, F.I.N. .. .. (*Patron's Medal*)
1870. Mr. George W. Hayward .. .. (*Founder's Medal*)
1872. Mr. Robert Berkeley Shaw .. .. (*Patron's Medal*)
1873. Mr. Ney Elias .. .. (*Founder's Medal*)
1875. Mr. W. H. Johnson .. .. (*Gold Watch*)
1877. The Pundit Nain Singh .. .. (*Patron's Medal*)
1878. Baron F. von Richthofen .. .. (*Founder's Medal*)
1878. Captain Henry Trotter, R.E. .. .. (*Patron's Medal*)
1878. Colonel N. Prejevalsky.. .. .. (*Patron's Medal*)
1879. Captain W. J. Gill, R.E. .. .. (*Founder's Medal*)

INDIAN ARCHIPELAGO.

1848. Sir James Brooke, Rajah of Saráwak .. .. .. (*Founder's Medal*)

AUSTRALASIA.

1843. Mr. Edward John Eyre .. .. (*Founder's Medal*)
1846. Sir Paul Strzelecki, K.C.M.G., C.B. .. .. .. (*Founder's Medal*)
1847. Captain Charles Sturt .. .. (*Founder's Medal*)

1847. Dr. Ludwig Leichhardt	.. ..	.. (*Patron's Medal*)
1851. Mr. Thomas Brunner ..	.. ..	.. (*25 Guineas*)
1857. Mr. Augustus C. Gregory	.. ..	.. (*Founder's Medal*)
1861. Mr. John Macdouall Stuart ..	.. .. ..	.. (*Patron's Medal*)
1862. Mr. Robert O'Hara Burke ..	.. .. ..	.. (*Founder's Medal*)
1862. Mr. John King	.. .. ..	.. (*Gold Watch*)
1863. Mr. Frank T. Gregory	.. .. ..	.. (*Founder's Medal*)
1863. Mr. William Landsborough ..	.. .. ..	.. (*Gold Watch*)
1863. Mr. John M'Kinlay	.. .. ..	.. (*Gold Watch*)
1863. Mr. Frederick Walker	.. .. ..	.. (*Gold Watch*)
1874. Colonel P. Egerton Warburton	.. .. ..	.. (*Patron's Medal*)
1876. Mr. John Forrest	.. .. ..	.. (*Patron's Medal*)
1880. Mr. Ernest Giles	.. .. ..	.. (*Patron's Medal*)

NORTH AMERICA.

1850. General John C. Fremont ..	.. .. ..	.. (*Patron's Medal*)
1858. Professor Alexander D. Bache	.. .. ..	.. (*Patron's Medal*)
1859. Captain John Palliser	.. .. ..	.. (*Patron's Medal*)

SOUTH AMERICA.

1840. Sir Robert Schomburgk ..	.. .. ..	.. (*Patron's Medal*)
1866. Mr. William Chandless	.. .. ..	.. (*Patron's Medal*)
1872. Commander G. C. Musters, R.N.	.. ..	.. (*Gold Watch*)

MARINE SURVEYORS.

1837. Captain Robert FitzRoy, R.N., C.B.	.. ..	.. (*Royal Award*)
1854. Admiral W. H. Smyth, C.B.	.. ..	.. (*Founder's Medal*)

EMINENT GEOGRAPHERS.

1841. Lieut. Raper, R.N.	.. .. ..	.. (*Founder's Medal*)
1842. Rev. Dr. E. Robinson	.. .. ..	.. (*Patron's Medal*)
1844. Professor Adolph Erman ..	.. .. ..	.. (*Patron's Medal*)
1845. Herr Karl Ritter	.. .. ..	.. (*Patron's Medal*)
1863. Mr. John Arrowsmith	.. .. ..	.. (*Patron's Medal*)
1868. Dr. Augustus Petermann ..	.. .. ..	.. (*Founder's Medal*)
1869. Mrs. Mary Somerville	.. .. ..	.. (*Patron's Medal*)
1871. Mr. A. Keith Johnston, LL.D.	.. .. ..	.. (*Patron's Medal*)
1871. Sir Roderick I. Murchison, Bart., K.C.B.	.. ..	.. (*Founder's Medal*)
1872. Colonel Henry Yule, C.B. ..	.. .. ..	.. (*Founder's Medal*)
1880. Mr. E. H. Bunbury	.. .. ..	.. (*Letter of Thanks*)

ANALYSIS.

For Asia	28			English		72
„ Africa	22			Germans		16
„ Arctic	20	Civilians	51	Americans		7
„ Australasia	16	Sailors	23	Russians		3
Geographers	11	Soldiers	21	Swedes		3
Antarctic	3	Professors	5	French		1
N. America	3	Doctors	4	Portuguese		1
S. America	3	Clergymen	3	Norwegian		1
Marine Surveyors	2	Women	2	Magyar		1
Indian Archipelago	1			Natives of India		2
				Negro		1
					Total	109

THE SOCIETY'S GRANTS IN AID

TO

TRAVELLERS AND EXPEDITIONS.

		£	s.	d.
1832. Captain Back's Arctic Land Expedition		50	0	0
„ Instruments for travellers		11	14	0
1834. Delagoa Bay Expedition		170	16	4
„ Schomburgk's Guiana Expedition		50	0	0
1835. „ „ „		175	0	0
1836. „ „ „		490	0	0
„ Alexander's S. Africa Expedition		356	12	0
1837. Schomburgk's Guiana Expedition		156	4	0
1838. „ „ „		5	5	0
„ Alexander's S. Africa Expedition		223	0	0
„ Ainsworth's Kurdistan Expedition		298	0	0
1839. Schomburgk's Guiana Expedition		100	0	0
„ Ainsworth's Kurdistan Expedition		685	8	6
„ White Nile Expedition		50	0	0
„ New Zealand Expedition		9	9	0
1840. Ainsworth's Kurdistan Expedition		556	13	0
1841. „ „ „		313	12	9
„ Instruments for travellers		11	0	0
1842. Dr. Beke (Abyssinia)		100	0	0
„ Instruments for travellers		12	0	0
1843. Instruments for travellers		15	8	5
1844. Instruments for travellers		6	12	0
1861. Instruments for Consul Petherick.				
„ „ „ Dr. Rae.				
„ Consul Petherick for relief of Speke		100	0	0
(£1200 subscribed by Fellows.)				
1863. Instruments for Dr. D. Walker (N. America).				
„ „ „ Captain Bedford Pim, R.N.				
„ „ „ M. Jules Gerard.				
1864. Grant to M. Gerhard Rohlfs (N. Africa)		50	0	0
1865. Second Grant to „ „ „		50	0	0
„ Grant to Mr. R. B. N. Walker (Ogowé)		100	0	0
„ Instruments for „ „		43	0	0
„ Grant to Dr. Livingstone (Central Eq. Africa)		500	0	0
„ „ Captain Wilson, R.E. (Dead Sea)		107	7	9
„ „ Captains Wilson and Palmer (Sinai).				
1866. Leichhardt Search Expedition		200	0	0
1867. Instruments for Mr. Whymper (Greenland)		22	1	6
„ „ „ Mr. Whitely (S. America)		13	0	0
1868. Grant to Mr. Young, R.N. (Lake Nyassa)		160	0	0
„ Instruments for Rev. F. W. Holland (Sinai)		34	17	6
1869. „ „ Mr. Hayward (E. Turkistan)		14	8	6
„ Grant to „ „		300	0	0

			£	s.	d.
1870.	Grant to Mr. St. Vincent Erskine (Limpopo)		100	0	0
,,	Instruments for ,, ,, ,, ...		18	0	0
,,	Second Grant to Mr. Hayward (E. Turkistan)		300	0	0
,,	Instruments for Sir Samuel Baker		114	6	C
	,, ,, Mr. Palmer		4	1	C
1871.	,, ,, Mr. R. B. Shaw (E. Turkistan)		23	4	0
,,	,, ,, Rev. T. Wakefield (Mombas)..		35	5	0
	,, ,, C. Tyrwhitt Drake (Syria)		6	3	6
1872.	,, ,, Mr. St. Vincent Erskine (Limpopo) ..		18	2	0
,,	Livingstone Search and Relief Fund..		696	4	9
1873.	Instruments, outfit, &c., Lieutenant V. L. Cameron, R.N.	{	67	17	11
		{	416	0	0
,,	,, ,, Lieutenant Grandy, R.N.		123	11	4
,,	Outfit, Dr. Dillon, R.N.		100	0	0
,,	Meteorological Instruments, Consulate, Zanzibar		10	10	0
,,	Livingstone Search and Relief Expedition		416	8	0
,,	Instruments, Capt. A. H. Markham, R.N. (Whaling Cruise)		13	5	6
1874.	,, Dr. Beke (Midian)		30	1	6
,,	,, Mr. Ney Elias		8	10	0
,,	,, Mr. Hegan (Bolivia)		21	17	6
,,	Livingstone Search and Relief Fund..		1778	16	5
1875.	Cameron Expedition		500	0	0
,,	Instruments, Colonel Gordon	{	58	11	6
		{	99	5	6
,,	,, Captain Allen Young		13	0	0
,,	,, Arctic Expedition..		10	0	0
1876.	,, Mr. Watts (Iceland)		14	0	0
,,	,, Captain Allen Young	{	42	0	0
		{	29	0	0
,,	,, Mr. Cotterill (S. Africa)		24	0	0
,,	,, Mr. J. A. Skertchly (W. Africa).				
,,	,, Rev. Q. W. Thomson		5	0	0
,,	,, Lieutenant Congreve (Paraguay)		15	0	0
,,	Cameron Expedition Fund..		1000	0	0
1877.	Instruments, Rev. F. W. Holland (Sinai)		27	0	0
,,	African Exploration Fund		500	0	0
,,	Instruments for Mr. Keith Johnston		170	0	0
,,	,, ,, Mr. Young, R.N.		95	17	6
,,	Cameron Expedition Fund *		1012	2	6
1878.	African Exploration Fund		500	0	0
,,	Instruments for Mr. Keith Johnston (E. Africa)		170	0	0
1879.	,, ,, Mr. Forbes (Celebes)		9	0	0
,,	,, ,, Mr. Simons (Sta. Martha)		15	0	0
,,	,, ,, Rev. T. J. Comber (Congo)		57	0	0
,,	,, ,, Rev. J. Mullens		10	0	0
,,	,, ,, Captain A. H. Markham		5	18	0
1880.	African Exploration Fund. *Two Grants*		1000	0	0
,,	Instruments for Rev. W. P. Johnston (E. Africa)		35	5	0
,,	,, ,, Mr. Delmar Morgan (Kuldja)		15	15	0
,,	,, ,, Dr. Aitchison (Afghanistan)		24	11	0
,,	,, ,, Mr. A. M'Call (Congo)		33	3	0

* The total cost of the Cameron Expedition was 11,101*l.* 13*s.* 3*d.*, of which 3000*l.* was contributed by the Government.

	£	s.	d.
1880. Instruments for Captain Phipson-Wybrants	109	15	0
„ „ „ Dr. W. R. Peden (Shiré)	30	13	0
1881. Palestine Exploration Fund	100	0	0

TREASURY GRANTS RECEIVED.

	£	s.	d.
1836. For Guiana and South African Expeditions	1000	0	0
1856. For Captain Burton's Expedition	1000	0	0
1860. For Captain Speke's Expedition	2500	0	0
1873. For Dr. Livingstone's Funeral	500	19	1
1876. For Lieutenant Cameron's Expedition	3000	0	0

LIST OF PAPERS

IN THE

'JOURNALS' AND 'PROCEEDINGS'

OF THE

ROYAL GEOGRAPHICAL SOCIETY.

ARCTIC.

AMERICA, NORTH, Evidence for the discovery of, by the Scandinavians in the 10th century. viii. 114.
—— —— Arctic shores of. (*See* SIMPSON and RAE.)
ANDERSON, Mr. Journey to Montreal Island. xxvi. 18; xxvii. 321.
ANIMAL LIFE in the Arctic Regions, by P. L. Simmonds. (Proceedings, Vol. i. 53.) (*See* PETERMANN.)
" ARCTIC," whaler voyage of. C. R. Markham. (Proceedings, Vol. xviii. 12.)
ARCTIC EXPEDITIONS, Notes on the late, by S. Osborn. (Proceedings, Vol. i. 104.)
ARCTIC EXPEDITION, On the progress of and voyage of the "Valorous." By C. R. Markham. (Proceedings, Vol. xx. 55.)
—— —— of 1875–76. Results of. By C. R. Markham. (Proceedings, Vol. xxi. 536.)
ARCTIC EXPEDITIONS of 1878, by C. R. Markham. (Proceedings (N.S.) Vol. i. 16.)
ARCTIC EXPLORATION by Sherard Osborn. xxxvi. 279. (Proceedings, Vol. ix. 42; Vol. xii. 92; Vol. xvi. 227.) (*See* NORTH POLAR EXPLORATION.)
—— —— Sir Roderick Murchison's speech on. (Proceedings, Vol. ix. 87.)
AUSTRO-HUNGARIAN EXPEDITION of 1872–74. By Julius Payer. xlv. 1. (Proceedings, Vol. xix. 17.)
—— —— Scientific work of the second, 1872–74. By Lieut. Weyprecht. xlv. 19.

BACK, SIR GEO. Search for Capt. Ross. Account of his land expedition. ii. 336; iii. 64; v. 405; vi. i. Voyage of the "Terror," vii. 457, 460.
BAER, Professor. (*See* SIBERIA.)
BARENT'S SEA, Campaign of 1879, in. By Capt. A. H. Markham. (Proceedings (N.S.) Vol. ii. 1.)
BEHRING STRAIT TO CAMBRIDGE BAY, the proceedings of H.M.S. "Enterprise" from. By Capt. R. Collinson, R.N. xxv. 194.

CIRCUMPOLAR EXPLORATIONS. A. Petermann. (Proceedings, Vol. ix. 90.)
CIRCUMPOLAR REGIONS. Recent elevations of land. By H. H. Howorth. xliii. 240.

CIRCUMPOLAR SEA, on the. By Capt. G. S. Nares. (Proceedings, Vol. xxi. 96.) (*See* NARES.)

COLLINSON, Capt. Voyage of the "Enterprise." xxv. 194.

CURRENTS, On ocean. By Gen. Hauslab. xlv. 34. (*See* GREENLAND.)

DUTCH NAVIGATORS in Arctic Seas, by Commodore Jansen. (Proceedings, Vol. ix. 163.)

—— Arctic Expedition. (Proceedings, (N.S.) i. 26.)

FINDLAY, A. G. On route of Franklin. xxvi. 26. (Proceedings, Vol. i. 21.)

FRANKLIN, SIR JOHN. Sea of Spitzbergen, and Whale-fisheries in the Arctic Regions. By Aug. Petermann. xxiii. 129.

—— —— Narrative of the expedition in search of. By Sir F. L. McClintock, R.N. xxxi. i. (Proceedings, Vol. iv. 2.)

—— —— Arctic Explorations, with information respecting missing Party of. By Dr. John Rae. xxv. 246.

—— —— Report of the expedition in search of, during 53–55; chart showing Arctic discoveries. By E. Kent Kane. xxvi. 1.

—— —— On the probable course pursued by the expedition of. By A. G. Findlay. xxvi. 26. (Proceedings, Vol. i. 21.)

—— —— (search for.) Letter from Jas. Anderson to Sir Geo. Simpson. xxvi. 18.

—— —— Extracts from Jas. Anderson's Arctic Journal. xxvii. 321.

—— —— Memorial for continuance of search for. (Proceedings, Vol. i. 95.)

FRANZ JOSEF LAND. Discoveries by the Austro-Hungarian Expedition, xlv. 1; xlv. 19. (Proceedings, Vol. xix. 17.)

—— —— Discoveries along coast of, by B. Leigh Smith. (Proceedings (N.S.) Vol. iii. 129.)

FROBISHER. On the voyages of, by Commander Becher, R.N. xii. 1.

FROBISHER STRAIT. C. F. Hall. (Proceedings, Vol. vii. 99.)

FROZEN SOIL OF BRITISH N. AMERICA. Observations on the. Communicated by Dr. Richardson. ix. 117.

GERMAN ARCTIC EXPEDITION, Return of. Sir L. McClintock. (Proceedings, Vol. xv. 102.)

GREENLAND, the site of the lost colony of, determined. By R. H. Major. xliii. 156. (Proceedings, Vol. xvii. 312.)

—— On the large Continental Ice of, and origin of icebergs in the Arctic seas. By Dr. H. Rink. xxiii. 145.

—— The Arctic Current round coast of. By Capt. E. Irminger. xxvi. 36. (Proceedings, Vol. i. 61.)

—— On the supposed discovery by Dr. E. K. Kane of the North Coast of. By Henry Rink. xxviii. 272. (Proceedings, Vol. ii. 195.)

GREENLAND ESQUIMAUX, On the origin and migrations of the. By C. R. Markham. xxxv. 87. (Proceedings, Vol. ix. 88.)

GREENLAND, Discharge of water from glaciers in. Dr. Rink. (Proceedings, Vol. vii. 76.)

GREENLAND, FIORDS and GLACIERS, On. By J. W. Tayler. xl. 228. (Proceedings, Vol. v. 90; Vol. xiv. 156.)

GROUND ICE. (*See* SIBERIA.)

HALL, Captain. Arctic Expedition. (Proceedings, Vol. xv. 382.) (*See* FROBISHER ST. "POLARIS.")

NORTHUMBERLAND INLET, Journal of a whaling voyage. By Mr. Wareham, xii. 21.

NOVAIA ZEMLIA, On the recent Russian Expeditions to. By Professor K. E. von Baer, viii. 411. (See BARENTS SEA.)

OSBORN, Admiral S., On Arctic exploration, xxxvi. 279. (*See* ARCTIC EX-PLORATION, LIGHT, NORTH POLAR REGION.)

OPEN WATER in the Polar Basin, by R. V. Hamilton. (Proceedings, Vol. xiii. 234.)

PETERMANN, Dr., On distribution of animal life in the Arctic Regions, xxii. 118. (*See* FRANKLIN.)

—— On the proposed Polar Expedition. (Proceedings, Vol. ix. 90, 114.)

POLAR BASIN, Remarks on open sea in. By Robert White. (Proceedings, Vol. i. 27.)

"POLARIS," Discoveries of. By C. R. Markham. (Proceedings, Vol. xviii. 12.)

POLE. (See NORTH POLE.)

RAE, Dr., Information of missing expedition, xxv. 246. Victoria Land, xxii. 82. Wollaston Land, xxii. 73.

RINK, Dr. (See GREENLAND.)

Ross, Capt., Search for. (See BACK.)

Ross, expedition to ascertain fate of, ii. 336. (See BACK.)

SCHWATKA, Lieut. (*See* KING WILLIAM ISLAND.)

SIBERIA, On the frozen ground in. By Prof. K. E. von Baer, viii. 210.

SIBERIAN RIVERS, Ground ice in the. By Colonel Jackson, vi. 416.

SLEDGE TRAVELLING, On. By Capt. A. H. Markham. (Proceedings, Vol. xxi. 110).

—— —— By Sir L. M'Clintock. (Proceedings, Vol. xix. 464.)

SIMPSON AND DEASE, Account of recent Arctic Discoveries, viii. 213; ix. 325; x. 268.

SMITH SOUND, Discoveries of the "Polaris." By C. R. Markham. (Proceedings, Vol. xviii. 12.)

—— —— Expedition of Dr. Kane. xxvi. 1.

SOUTHAMPTON ISLAND, On the N.E. shore of. By Capt. Back, R.N., vii. 460. (See "TERROR.")

SPITZBERGEN, On discoveries East of. By C. R. Markham, xliii. 83. (Proceedings, Vol. xvii. 97.) (*See* NORDENSKIÖLD.)

STEPHENSON, Capt. H. F. On the winter quarters of the Discovery. (Proceedings, Vol. xxi. 106.)

SWEDISH, N. Polar Expedition, by Nordenskiöld and von Otter. (Proceedings, Vol. xiii. 151.)

"TERROR," H.M.S., Account of the late voyage of, vii. 457, 460.

THERMOMETRICAL OBSERVATIONS, made at Sir Edw. Parry's several wintering places. By Dr. Richardson, ix. 331.

UNKNOWN LANDS within the Arctic Circle. Probable existence of. By Capt. S. Osborn. (Proceedings, Vol. xvi. 227.)

VICTORIA LAND. (*See* RAE, Dr.)

WOLLASTON LAND. (*See* RAE, Dr.)
WRANGELL, Admiral von, On reaching the Pole, xviii. 19–24.

ZENI, Voyages of. By Capt. Zahrtmann, v. 102.
—— FRISLANDA is Iceland and not the Færoes. By Admiral Irminger. xlix. 398.
—— —— is not Iceland, but the Færoes; an answer to Admiral Irminger. By R. H. Major. xlix. 412.

ANTARCTIC.

ANTARCTIC DISCOVERY, On, and its connection with the Transit of Venus in 1882. By J. E. Davis. xxxix. 91. (Proceedings, Vol. xiii. 114.)
ANTARCTIC OCEAN, Recent discoveries in the. By John Biscoe, R.N. iii. 105.
—— —— Discoveries in the, by Balleny, in February 1839. ix. 517.

DECEPTION ISLAND, Account of, from private journal of Lieut. Kendal, R.N. i. 62.

ICEBERG. Note on a rock seen on an, in 61° S., by C. Darwin. ix. 528.

MORELL'S ANTARCTIC VOYAGE. Remarks on, by Capt. R. V. Hamilton, R.N. (Proceedings, Vol. xiv. 145.)

SABRINA LAND. C. Enderby. (Proceedings, Vol. ii. 171.)
SOUTHERN CIRCUMPOLAR REGION, Recent changes in the. By H. H. Howorth. xliv. 252.

EUROPE.

AITKINS ROCK. On the Vigia so called. By Captain Vidal, R.N. i. 51.
ALBANIA. Geographical Account of, from MS. of Count Karaczay. xii. 45
ALPS. Notes on the passage of Hannibal. By Professor Paul Chaix. xxv. 182.
—— European. On the origin of the flora of. By John Ball. (Proceedings, (N.S.) Vol. i. 564.
ARTA. Observations on the Gulf of, made in 1830. By Lieut. J. Wolfe, R.N. iii. 77.
ARVE. Hydrography of the valley of. By Professor Paul Chaix. xxvii. 224.
ATHOS, Mount, and its Monasteries, with notes of route from Constantinople to Salonica, in June 1836. By Lieut. Webber Smith, vii. 61.
—— —— Remarks on the Isthmus of. By Lieut. Spratt, R.N. xvii. 145.
AZORES. (*See* under OCEANIA.)
AZOV, On the Sea of, the Putrid Sea, and adjacent coasts of. By Capt. Sherard Osborn. xxvii. 133. (Proceedings, Vol. i. 305.)

ASIA.

AMUR, Notes on the River and its surroundings. By MM. Peschurof, Permikin, &c. xxviii. 376. (Proceedings, Vol. ii. 153 ; Vol. iii. 92.)

ANATOLIA, N.E., Tour in. By W. G. Palgrave. (Proceedings, xvi. 223.)

ANDAMAN ISLANDS, Narrative of an expedition to the, in 1857. By F. J. Mouat, M.D., F.R.G.S. xxxii. 109. (Proceedings, Vol. vi. 41.)

ANGORA, Journey from (by Kaisariyah), to Bir or Birehjik. By W. Ainsworth. x. 275.

ANTI-LIBANUS, Notes of a Reconnaissance of the. By R. F. Burton. xlii. 408.

ANTIOCH, on the Bay of, and the Ruins of Seleucia Pieria. By Lieut.-Col. Chesney, R.A. viii. 228.

ARABIA, Observations on the Coast of, between Ras Mohammed and Jiddah. By Lieut. R. Wellsted, I.N. vi. 51.

—— Remarks on manners of the inhabitants of Southern Arabia, and on ancient and modern geography of that part, and on desert route from Kosir to Keneh. By Jas. Bird, Esq. iv. 192.

—— Observations made in Central, Eastern, and Southern, during a journey in 1862 and 1863. By W. G. Palgrave. xxxiv. 111.

—— South Coast of. Journey from Tower of Ba'-l-haff to Ruins of Nakab el Hajar. By Lieut. Wellsted, E.I.C.S. vii. 20.

—— Visit to Jebel Shammar, New routes through Northern and Central. By W. S. Blunt. (Proceedings (N.S.) Vol. ii. 81.)

—— Memoir from the entrance of the Red Sea to Misenát, in 50° 43′ 25″ E. By Capt. Haines, I.N. ix. 125 ; xv. 104.

—— Proceedings of brig " Palinurus " whilst examining Coast between Ras Morbat and Ras Seger, &c. By Commander J. P. Saunders. xvi. 169.

—— Notes taken on a journey through a part of Northern Arabia. By Dr. Geo. A. Wallin. xx. 293.

—— Interior of, by W. Gifford Palgrave. (Proceedings, Vol. viii. 63.)

—— Visit to Wahabee capital. By Col. Pelly. xxxv. 169. (Proceedings, Vol. ix. 293.)

—— Account of a journey into interior of South. By W. Munzinger and Capt. Miles. xli. 210. (Proceedings, Vol. xv. 319.)

—— SOUTHERN, Geography of. By Baron von Maltzan. (Proceedings, Vol. xvi. 115.)

ARACAN, Extracts from a Journal up the Koladyne River. By Capt. S. R. Tickell, Bengal Native Infantry. xxiv. 86.

—— Hill trip on borders of, by Lieut. Lewin. (Proceedings, Vol. xi. 52.)

ARAL, Survey of the Sea of. By Commander Alexis Butakoff, Imperial Russian Navy. xxiii. 93.

ARARAT, Ascent of Mount, in 1856. By Major R. Stuart. (Proceedings, Vol. xxi. 77.)

ARMENIA and ASIA MINOR, Journey through a part of, in 1835. By Jas. Brant, Consul at Erz-Rum. vi. 187.

—— Notes of a tour, in 1851. By K. E. Abbott. xii. 207.

—— KURDISTAN, and UPPER MESOPOTAMIA, Journal of a tour in, with Notes of Researches in the Deyrsim Dagh, in 1866. By J. G. Taylor. xxxviii. 281.

—— and MOUNT ARARAT. By James Bryce. (Proceedings, Vol. xxii. 169.)

ARRACAN, General remarks on Coast. Transmitted by Capt. Laws, R.N. i. 175.

ASHTAROTH, On the Site of. By Capt. Newbold, H.E.I.M.S. xvi. 331.

---

* In the headings of the paper the name is erroneously given *J. T.* Jones.

BURMA. British and Western China, Trade routes between. By J. Coryton. xlv. 229. (Proceedings, Vol. xix. 264.)

BUSHIR to SHIRAZ, Notes on the routes from, &c. By Lieut.-Gen. Wm. Monteith. xxvii. 108.

BUSHIRE and TEHERAN, On the elevation of the country between. By Major St. John. xxxviii. 411.

BUSSORA to ALEPPO, Diary of a journey with Sir Eyre Coote. xxx. 198.

BUSTAR Dependency in British India, On the Mardian Hills and the Lower Indravati in. By Capt. Holdich. (Proceedings (N.S.) Vol. i. 372.)

CABUL. (*See* KABUL.)

CAMBAY, Tides in the Gulf of. By Capt. J. B. Jervis. viii. 202.

CAMBODIA, Notes on the Antiquities, Natural History, &c., of. By Jas. Campbell, Surgeon, R.N. xxx. 182.

—— A visit to the ruined cities and buildings of. By Dr. A. Bastian. xxxv. 74. (Proceedings, Vol. ix. 85.)

—— Travels in. By D. O. King. (Proceedings, Vol. iii. 365.)

—— The Lao country, &c., Notes on. By M. Henri Mouhot. xxxii. 142. (Proceedings, Vol. vi. 80.)

—— Southern Laos and. By H. G. Kennedy xxxvii. 298.

CANDAHAR. (*See* KANDAHAR.)

CANTON to HANKOW, Sketch of the journey. By Albert S. Bickmore, M.A. xxxviii. 50.

—— Boat journey to west of. By Lieut. Oliver. (Proceedings, Vol. vi. 85.)

CASHMERE. (*See* KASHMIR.)

CASPIAN and BLACK SEAS, Remarks on Country between the. By Prof. Hermann Abich. xxi. 1. (*See* BLACK SEA.)

CATHAY, Notes on. By Col. Yule. (Proceedings, Vol. x. 270.)

CAUCASUS, Journey in the, and ascent of Kasbek and Elbruz. By Douglas W. Freshfield. xxxix. 50.

CENTRAL ASIA, Note to Arrowsmith's Map of. xlv. 420.

—— —— The watershed of. By Col. Gordon. xlvi. 381.

—— —— In 1872. By Mr. R. B. Shaw. (Proceedings, Vol. xvi. 395.)

CEYLON, Papers concerning communication with India. Minute on the subject. By Governor of Madras. iv. 1.

CHAAB Arabs, Notes on. By Sir H. Rawlinson. xxvii. 185. (Proceedings, Vol. i. 351.)

CHINA, On Chinese and European Maps of. By Wm. Huttmann. xiv. 117.

—— On the frontiers of, toward Birmah. By Dr. Gutzlaff. xix. 85.

—— Report on Russian caravan trade with. By H. Parkes, Esq. xxiv. 306.

—— S.W. Exploration to, by way of the Irawadi and Bhamo. By Major Sladen. xli. 257. (Proceedings, Vol. xv. 343.)

—— A journey outside the Great Wall of. By S. W. Bushell. xliv. 73. (Proceedings, Vol. xviii. 149.)

—— Journey from Hankow to Ta-li-Fu. By A. R. Margary. xlvi. 172.

—— Visit to the Valley of the Shueli, in Western Yunnan. By Ney Elias. xlvi. 198.

—— Col. Sosnoffsky's expedition to, in 1874–75. xlvii. 150.

—— Western, Travels in and on Eastern borders of Tibet. By Capt. Gill. xlviii. 57. (Proceedings, Vol. xxii. 255.)

GHILAN, Province of, in Persia, Mr. Abbott on. (Proceedings, Vol. iii. 390.)

GILGIT and YASSIN, Letters from Mr. Haywood on exploration of. xli. 1.

—— and CHITRAL, Munful Mír Munshi on. (Proceedings, Vol. xiii. 130.)

GOBI, Buried Cities in the Desert of. By Sir D. Forsyth. xlvii. 1. (Proceedings, Vol. xxi. 27.)

GREAT TIBET, Travels in, and trade between, and Bengal. By C. R. Markham. xlv. 299. (Proceedings, Vol. xix. 327.)

—— Exploration of the Namcho. By Col. T. G. Montgomerie. xlv. 315.

—— Memorandum on the results of the exploration. By Col. T. G. Montgomerie. xlv. 325.

HADRAMAUT, Excursion in. By A. Baron von Wrede. xiv. 107.

HANKOW. (*See* CHINA.)

HARAN, in Padan Aram, Notes on an excursion to, and thence to Shechem. By C. T. Beke. xxxii. 76. (Proceedings, Vol. vi. 195.)

HAURAN, On. By C. Graham. (Proceedings, Vol. ii. 173.)

—— On. By F. A. Eaton. (Proceedings, Vol. viii. 29.)

HELMUND, The basin of. By C. R. Markham. (Proceedings (N.S.) i. 191.)

HERACLEA, from Constantinople by, to Angora, Notes of a journey, in 1838. By Wm. Ainsworth, Esq. ix. 216.

HERMON, The, and the physical features of Syria and Northern Palestine. By John Wortabet, M.D. xxxii. 100.

HIMALAYAN Valleys. Kulu, Labúl, and Spiti. By A. F. P. Harcourt. xli. 245. (Proceedings, Vol. xv. 336.)

HIMALAYA, Papers relating to the. (Proceedings, Vol. i. 345.)

HIMMA-LEH MOUNTAINS, Journey through the, to the sources of the Jumna, and thence to confines of Chinese Tartary, in 1827. By Capt. C. Johnson. iv. 41.

—— and Valley of Cashmir, Notice of a visit to, in 1835. By Baron Charles Hügel. vi. 343.

HIMYARITIC ALPHABET, The, and inscriptions. xi. 118.

HONG-KONG, Note on the Island of. By A. R. Johnston, Esq. xiv. 112.

ILI, Valley of the. By Ashton Dilke. (Proceedings, Vol. xviii. 246.) (*See* KULDJA.)

ILCHI. (*See* KHOTAN.)

ILIYATS, or wandering tribes of Persia, some account of. By Jas. Morier, Esq. vii. 230.

INDIA and CHINA, On Communication between, by the Burhampooter and Yang-tsze. By Gen. Sir Arthur Cotton, R.E. xxxvii. 231.

—— —— By Dr. McCosh. (Proceedings, Vol. v. 47.)

INDIA, Descriptive papers of the countries on the North West frontier of. By Lieut. Burnes. iv. 88.

—— On the maritime communications of, as carried on by natives. By Lieut. Burnes. vi. 23.

—— Observations on the ancient intercourse with, suggested by remarks of Lieut. Burnes. By Lieut. Dickinson. vi. 113.

—— On the progress and present state of survey in. By Capt. Thos. Best Jervis. vii. 127.

—— Routes in the Nizam's territory; from the journals of Capt. J. R. Wilson. xiii. 118.

INDIA, Overland telegraph route to. By Sir H. Rawlinson. (Proceedings, Vol. v. 219.)

—— Destruction of forests, and effect on water supply. By C. R. Markham. xxxvi. 180. (Proceedings, Vol. x. 266.)

—— Effects of forest destruction in Coorg. By Dr. Bidie. xxxix. 77. (Proceedings, Vol. xiii. 74.)

—— Geography and climate as regards site for a capital. Sir G. Campbell. (Proceedings, Vol. xi. 54.)

—— River communication between China and. Sir A. Cotton. xxxvii. 231. (Proceedings, Vol. xi. 255.)

—— On the Highland Region adjacent to the Trans-Indus frontier of. By Major James Walker. xxxii. 303.

INDIAN SURVEYS for the year 1878-9. (Proceedings (N.S.) vol. ii. 422.)

—— SEAPORTS. Duncan Macpherson. (Proceedings, Vol. vii. 95.)

INDRAVATI RIVER. (*See* BUSTAR.)

INDUS RIVER, Notes on the lower portion of the. By Col. W. Tremenheere. xxxvii. 68. (Proceedings, Vol, xi. 22.)

—— —— Substance of a geographical memoir on the. By Lieut. A Burnes. iii. 113.

—— —— Memoir to accompany the survey of the Delta of the, in 1837. By Lieut. T. G. Carless, I. N. viii. 328.

—— —— On the construction of the map of the. By Lieut. A. Burnes. iii. 287.

IRAWADY, The, and its sources. By Dr. J. Anderson. xl. 286. (Proceedings, Vol. xiv. 346. T. T. Cooper on. (Proceedings, Vol. xiii. 392.)

ISSYK-KUL EXPEDITION, Brief sketch of results of the. By Capt. A. Golubef. xxxi. 366.

—— ——, Notes on the Lake of, and the River Koshkar. By W. Veniukof. xxxii. 560.

—— Expedition to. By P. Semenoff. xxxix. 311.

JAPAN, Narrative of a journey in the interior of; ascent of Fusiyama, and visit to sulphur-baths at Atami in 1860. By Sir Rutherford Alcock, C.B., F.R.G.S. xxxi. 321.

—— Journey in Island of Yezo in 1873 ; and on Progress of geography in Japan. By R. G. Watson. xliv. 132. (Proceedings, Vol. xviii. 226.)

—— Narrative of a journey through the interior of, from NAGAZAKI to Yeddo in 1861. By Sir R. Alcock. xxxii. 280. (Proceedings, Vol. vi. 196.)

—— Report on the silk districts of. By Mr. F. O. Adams. xl. 339.

—— Island of Tsusima near. L. Oliphant. (Proceedings, Vol. vii. 61.)

—— Extract of a letter from Commander Mathison of H.M.S. *Mariner* in 1849. xx. 136.

—— A tour through parts of the Provinces of Echigo, Echiu, Kaga, and Noto. By J. Troup. 1871. xlii. 425.

—— Journey from Kiôto to Yeddo. By C. W. Lawrence. xliii. 54. (Proceedings, Vol. xvii. 80.)

—— Ascent of Fuji-Yama. By. J. H. Gubbins. (Proceedings, Vol. xvii. 78.)

—— Ascent of Fuji-Yama in the snow. By A. J. Jeffreys. (Proceedings, Vol. xix. 169.)

—— Ascent of Fusi-Yama. By Sir R. Alcock. (Proceedings, Vol. v. 132.)

—— Island of Yesso. Pemberton Hodgson. (Proceedings, Vol. v. 113.)

KHIVA. By Sir H. Rawlinson. (Proceedings, Vol. xvii. 162.)

KHORASAN, Northern, notes on a portion of. By Jas. Baillie Fraser. viii. 308.

—— Routes in, during 1831 and 1832. By Sarg. Gibbons. xi. 136.

—— Route from Turbat Haideri to the river Heri-Rud on the borders of Sistan. Extracted from Dr. Forbes' Journal. xiv. 145.

—— Diary of a tour in, and notes on the Eastern Alburz tract. By Capt. Napier. xlvi. 62.

—— Notes on the Yomut Tribe. By Kazi Syud Ahmad. xlvi. 142.

—— Tables of routes in the Eastern Alburz tract. xlvi. 145.

KHOTAN, Report on journey to Ilchí, capital of. By W. H. Johnson. xxxvii. 1. (Proceedings, Vol. xi. 6.)

—— Journey to, of the Brothers Schlagintweit. (Proceedings, Vol. i. 273.)

KHUZISTAN, Description of the province of. By A. H. Layard, Esq. xvi. 1.

KIACHTA, Route from Tientsin to. By W. A. Whyte. (Proceedings, xiv. 243).

KIRMAN, JEBAL, and KHORASAN, Routes in, during 1831 and 1832. By Sarg. Gibbons. xi. 136.

KOKAND, A journey to, in 1873. By E. Schuyler. (Proceedings, Vol. xviii. 408.)

KOREA. (*See* COREA.)

KRAW, Isthmus of. Route across. By Capts. Fraser and Furlong. (Proceedings, Vol. vii. 58.)

Kos and SYMI, Notice of the Gulfs of. By Lieuts. Graves and Brock, R.N. viii. 428.

—— —— in Anatolia, Notice of the gulfs of. By Lieut. Saumarez Brock, R.N. ix. 507.

KULDJA. By Major F. C. H. Clarke. (Proceedings (N.S.) Vol. ii. 489.)

—— By Ashton Dilke. (Proceedings, Vol. xviii. 246.)

—— By Delmar Morgan. (Proceedings (N.S.) Vol. iii. 150.)

KUMAON and GARHWAL, in the Himalaya Mountains, On the physical geography of, and of the adjoining parts of Tibet. By Capt. Strachey. xxi. 57.

KUMAOÑ, Altitude of places in. By Capt. W. S. Webb. iv. 376.

KURDISTAN, Notes of a journey through, in 1838. By Jas. Brant. x. 341.

—— Travels in, with notices of Eastern and Western Tigris and ancient ruins. By J. G. Taylor. xxxv. 21. (*See* ARMENIA.)

—— Visit to the Chaldeans of Central, and ascent of Peak of Rowandiz. By Wm. Ainsworth. xi. 21.

KURIA MURIA Isles. (*See* CURIA MURIA.)

KURRAM VALLEY, Survey operations in. By Capt. Gerald Martin. (Proceedings (N.S.) Vol. i. 617.)

"KUWEIK RIVER," The, an aqueduct. By D. J. Macgowan. xxxii. 74.

LADAKH, Notes on the Pangong Lake district of, made during survey in 1863. By Godwin Austen. xxxvii. 343.

LAKERADEEVH ARCHIPELAGO, Extract from Lieut. Wood's private journal of the. vi. 29.

LAOS, On the Country of the free. By Dr. Gutzlaff. xix. 33.

—— SOUTHERN, and Cambodia. By H. D. Kennedy. xxxvii. 298.

LEH to YARKAND and KASHGAR, Journey from, and exploration of the sources of the Yarkand. By G. W. Hayward. xl. 33.

LHASA, Nepal to. Route surveys. By Col. Montgomerie. (Proceedings, Vol. xii. 146.)

LINGAH, KISHM, and BUNDER ABBASS, Visit to. By Lieut.-Col. Lewis Pelly. xxxiv. 251.

LOB NOR, On position of.√ R. B. Shaw. (Proceedings, Vol. xvi. 242.)

LUSHAI Expedition. (Proceedings, Vol. xvii. 42.)

LYCUS, in Kurdistan, Sources and course of. By J. E. Taylor. (Proceedings, Vol. xi. 97.)

MAGHIAN, Notes on M. Fedchenko's Map of. By R. Michell. xliii. 263.

MAHANUDDY, On the basin of the river. A geographical abstract of a report by Mr. R. Temple. xxxv. 70. (Proceedings, Vol. ix. 81.)

MALAY STATES, Geography of Perak and Salangore. By W. B. D'Almeida. xlvi. 357.

MALDIVA ISLANDS, Some geographical remarks on, and the navigable channels between the Atolls. By J. Horsburgh. ii. 72.

—— —— On the. By Capt. Owen, R.N. ii. 81.

MARDIAN Hills. (*See* BUSTAR.)

MANCHURIA, Notes on. By Rev. A. Williamson, B.A. xxxix. 1. (Proceedings, Vol. xiii. 26.)

—— Palladius's Journey through. (Proceedings, Vol. xvi. 204.)

—— Notes on the Russian harbours on the coast of. By Rev. W. V. Lloyd, R.N. xxxvii. 212. (Proceedings, Vol. xi. 253.)

—— An expedition through, from Pekin to Blagovestchensk. By Palladius. xlii. 142.

MANGI, Notes on Southern. By Geo. Phillips. xliv. 97. (Proceedings, Vol. xviii. 168.)

MAZANDERAN, Memoranda to accompany part of a sketch of, &c., in April, 1836. By Major E. D'Arcy Todd. viii. 101.

MEDINA and MECCA, Journey from Cairo viâ Suez, &c., to, in 1845. By Dr. G. A. Wallin. xxiv. 115.

—— —— Journey to, with route from Yambu. By Lieut. Burton. xxiv. 208.

—— —— Journey from, to Mecca, down the Darb-el-sharki, or Eastern Road, in Sept. 1853. By Lieut. Burton. xxv. 121.

MEKRAN, Mission into, for political and survey purposes, in Dec. 1861. By Major Goldsmid. xxxiii. 181. (Proceedings, Vol. vii. 91.)

—— Coast, Journey from Gwadur to Karachi. By Capt. S. B. Miles. xliv. 163.

—— Route from Jask to Bampur. By E. A. Floyer. xlvii. 188.

—— Journey through. By Major E. C. Ross. (Proceedings, Vol. xvi. 139 and 219.)

MERV, The road to. By Sir H. Rawlinson. (Proceedings (N.S.) Vol. i. 161.)

MESOPOTAMIA, On part of, contained between Sheriat-el-Beytha, on the Tigris, and Tel Ibrahim. By Lieut. Bewsher. xxxvii. 160. (Proceedings, Vol. xi. 155.)

—— Notes of an excursion to Kalah Sherkat, the Ur of the Persians, and to the Ruins of Al Hadhr. By Wm. Ainsworth. xi. 1.

—— A journey from Baghdad to the ruins of Opis and the Median wall. By John Ross, M.D. xi. 121.

MIDIAN, Memoir explaining the new map of, made by the Egyptian Staff-officers. By R. F. Burton. xlix. 1.

MINICOY, Account of Island of. By Capt. J. Basevi. xlii. 368.

MINOA AND NISÆA, Remarks on the supposed situation of. By Mr. T. Spratt, R.N. viii. 205.

MOHAMRAH, and the vicinity, Notes on the ancient geography of. By Col. Sir H. Rawlinson. xxvii. 185. (Proceedings, Vol. i. 351.)

MOKHA to SANA, Narrative of journey from, in July and August 1836. By Mr. Chas. Cruttenden, I.N. viii. 267.

MONGOLIA, WESTERN, A journey through. By Ney Elias. xliii. 108. (Proceedings, Vol. xvii. 184.)

—— Route by, from Peking to St. Petersburg. By C. M. Grant. xxxiii. 167. (Proceedings, Vol. vii. 27.)

—— NORTH-WESTERN, Pévtsof's Expedition in. By E. D. Morgan. (Proceedings (N.S.) Vol. i. 701.)

MOSUL, Notes taken on a journey to, from Constantinople, in 1839 and 1840. By Ainsworth. x. 489.

MOUKDEN, MANCHURIA, Narrative of journey from Tientsin to, in July 1861. By A. Michie, Esq. xxxiii. 153. (Proceedings, Vol. vii. 25.)

MUSTAKH RANGE, On the glaciers of the. By Capt. Godwin-Austen, F.R.G.S. xxxiv. 19. (Proceedings, Vol. viii. 34.)

NAGASAKI TO YEDDO. Journey of Sir R. Alcock. (Proceedings, Vol. vi. 196, 200.)

NEPAL TO LHASA, thence to the source of the Brahmaputra. Report of a route-survey made by the Pundit. By Capt. G. T. Montgomerie, R.E. xxxviii. 129.

NEPAUL, On the Northern frontier of, from a member of the Nepaulese Embassy in London. xx. 252.

NOR-ZAISAN, The (Lake), and its vicinity. By Genl. Abramof. xxxv. 58.

OMAN, Narrative of a journey into the interior of, in 1835. By Lieut. Well-sted, E.I.C.S. vii. 102.

ORENBURGH, orographical survey of the country, from the Russian MSS. of M. J. Khanikoff. xiii. 278.

ORONTES, River (in Syria), Notes made on a journey to the sources of the. By W. Burckhardt Barker, Esq. vii. 95.

OXUS, Lower, The old channels of. By E. D. Morgan. xlviii. 301.

OXUS, Papers connected with the Upper. By Colonel H. Yule. xlii. 438.

—— Monograph on. By Sir Henry Rawlinson. xlii. 482.

—— Mouths of. By Adml. Boutakoff. (Proceedings, Vol. xi. 113.) (*See* AMU DARYA.)

PALESTINE, &c., Extracts from a journey of travels in, in 1838, undertaken for the illustration of Biblical Geography. By Rev. E. Robinson. ix. 295.

—— Notes on its physical geography, extracted from the letters of Col. von Wildenbruch. xx. 227.

—— Note on. By Mr. A. Petermann. xx. 232.

—— Outlines of a journey in, in 1852. By Dr. E. Robinson, E. Smith, &c. xxiv. 1.

PALESTINE. Report of a journey in. By Mr. Henry Poole. xxvi. 55.

—— Recent surveys. By Major Wilson. (Proceedings, xvii. 326.)

PAMIR, The, and the sources of the Amu-Daria. By M. Veniukof. xxxvi. 248.

—— Russian expedition to the Alai and. By R. Michell. xlvii. 17. (Proceedings, Vol. xxi. 122.)

—— M. Severtsof's journey in Ferghana and the. (Proceedings (N.S.) Vol. ii. 499.)

—— Pamir Region. By Sir Henry Rawlinson. (Proceedings, Vol. x. 134.)

PANGONG Lake. By Capt. Godwin-Austen. (Proceedings, Vol. xi. 32.)

PATKOI Range, Notes of a trip across. By H. L. Jenkins. xli. 342.

PECHELI Gulf, and the PEIHO. By Sherard Osborn. (Proceedings, Vol. iii. 55.)

PEKING, journey from, to St. Petersburg, across the Desert of Gobi. By C. M. Grant. xxxiii. 167. (Proceedings, Vol. vii. 27.)

—— Notes of a journey in the N.W. neighbourhood of. By Jones Lamprey, Esq., M.B., 67th Regt., F.R.G.S. xxxvii. 239. (Proceedings, Vol. xi. 259.)

—— Notes on, and its neighbourhood. By W. Lockhart, Esq. xxxvi. 128. (Proceedings, Vol. x. 154.)

PERSIA, KHORASSAN and AFGHANISTAN, Notes in. By Capt. Claude Clerk, F.R.G.S. xxxi. 37.

—— —— Notes. Shahrúd to Astrabad. (Proceedings, Vol. xvii. 193.)

—— Notes on Eastern and Western Beluchistan. By Col. F. J. Goldsmid, C.B., F.R.G.S. xxxvii. 269. (Proceedings, xvii. 86.)

—— Geographical notes taken during a journey in, in 1849 and 1850. By Keith E. Abbott, H.B.M. xxv. 1.

—— SOUTHERN, Observations on geography of. By Sir Henry Rawlinson. (Proceedings, Vol. i. 280.)

PERSIAN GULF. Notes made on a survey along the eastern shores, in 1828. By Lieut. Kempthorne, E.I.C. Marine. v. 263.

—— —— Concerning the pearl fisheries in the. By Col. D. Wilson. iii. 283.

—— —— As an area of trade. By Col. L. Pelly. (Proceedings, Vol. viii. 18.)

—— —— Descriptive sketch of the Islands and Coasts at the entrance. By Lieut. Whitelock, I.N. viii. 170.

PERSIAN TRAVEL, Notes on recent. By Major-Gen. F. Goldsmid. xliv. 183.

PERSO-KELAT frontier, Survey of. By Major B. Lovett. (Proceedings, Vol. xvi. 219.)

PETER-BOTTE MT. (Mauritius), account of the ascent of, Sept. 7th, 1832. By Lieut. Taylor, R.A. iii. 99.

PETRA, Extract from Baron Koller's Itinerary of his tour to, describing an overland route from Mount Sinai to Akabah. xii. 75.

PISHIN VALLEY. By Gen. Sir M. A. Biddulph. (Proceedings (N.S.) Vol. ii. 212.)

PUNJAB, KABUL, KASHMIR and LITTLE THIBET, Route through, in 1834–38. By G. T. Vigne. ix. 512.

RAGERY HILLS, MADRAS, Account of the. By Col. Monteith. v. 404.

RED SEA, On the physical geography of the. By Dr. Buist, of Bombay, F.R.G.S. xxiv. 227.

RUAD, On the Island of, North Syria. By Capt. W. Allen, R.N., F.R.G.S. xxiii. 154.

RUNN OF CUTCH, Notes on the, and neighbouring region. By Sir Bartle Frere, K.C.B. xl. 181. (Proceedings, Vol. xiv. 120.)

SAGHALIN, On the Island of. By Col. Veniukof. xlii. 373.

SAMARKAND. Notes on ruins of. By Fedchenko. (Proceedings, Vol. xv. 392.)

SEDASHEGHUR and seaports of India. By Duncan Macpherson. (Proceedings, Vol. vii. 95.)

SELEUCIA, IN PIERIA, the ancient harbour of. By Capt. W. Allen, R.N., F.R.S., F.R.G.S. xxiii. 157.

SEMIPALATINSK. By N. Abramof, member of the Imperial Russian Geographical Society. xxxii. 555.

SHAN STATES, Journey to. By C. O'Reily. xxxii. 164. (Proceedings, Vol. vi. 83.)

SHANTUNG, Notes on a journey through. By J. Markham, H.M. Consul at Chefoo. xl. 207. (Proceedings, Vol. xiv. 137.)

SHIRAZ to BAM, Surveys on the road from. By Major B. Lovett. xlii. 202. (Proceedings, Vol. xvi. 261.)

SHIRAZ to FEZZA and DARRAB, thence westward to Kazerun, Notes taken on a journey from, in 1850. By Consul Keith E. Abbott. xxvii. 149.

SIAM, Extracts from the 'Journal of a Residence in, and voyage along coast of China to Mantchou, 1832.' By Rev. Chas. Gutzlaff. iii. 291.

—— Trade of. Journey from Bangkok to Pecha-buri. By Sir R. Schomburgk. (Proceedings, Vol. iv. 211.)

—— Through, to Moulmein. By Sir R. Schomburgk. (Proceedings, Vol. v. 118.) *See* BANGKOK.

—— Geographical notes on, with new map of the lower part of the Menam River. By Harry Parkes, Esq., F.R.G.S. xxvi. 71.

—— Geographical Notes on. By H. Parkes. (Proceedings, Vol. i. 13.)

—— and CAMBODIA, travels in. By D. O. King, Esq. xxx. 177. (Proceedings, Vol. iii. 365.)

SIBERIA, Northern, narrative of M. Middendorf's journey in. Communicated by Admiral von Krusenstern. xiv. 247.

SINAI, Notes on the map of the Peninsula of. By Rev. F. W. Holland. xxxix. 342. (Proceedings, Vol. x. 158; xii. 190.)

—— On the Peninsula of. By Rev. F. W. Holland. xxxviii. 237. (Proceedings, xiii. 204.)

—— and PALESTINE, Recent surveys in. By Major C. W. Wilson. xliii. 206.

SIND. By Capt. A. Burnes, E.I.C.S. vii. 11.

SINGAPUR, Journal of an excursion from, to Malacca and Pinang. By J. R. Lagan. xvi. 304.

SINJAR HILLS, a visit to the, in 1838, with some account of the sect of Yezidis, &c. By F. Forbes, Esq., M.A. ix. 409.

SISTAN, Journey from Bandar Abbas to Mash-had, viâ. By F. J. Goldsmid. xliii. 65. (Proceedings, Vol. xvii. 86.)

—— Visit to the Kuh-i-Khwajah. By Major B. Lovett. xliv. 145.

—— Notes on. By Sir H. Rawlinson. xliii. 272. (Proceedings, Vol. xvii. 92.)

SOCOTRA, Memoir on the island of. By Lieut. J. R. Wellsted, E.I.C. Marine. v. 129.

SOUTHERN LAOS AND CAMBODIA, Notes of an expedition to, in 1866. By H. G. Kennedy. xxxvii. 298.

SUSA, On the site of. By George Long. iii. 257. *See* EULÆUS River.

SYMI, Sketch of the island and gulf of, on the S.W. coast of Anatolia, in 1837. By Jas. Brooke. viii. 129.

SYRIA, On parts of, and Dead Sea. vii. 456.

TABRIZ, Itinerary from, to Tehran, in 1837. By Major E. D'Arcy Todd. viii. 29.

—— Notes of a journey from, through Kurdistan, to Suleimaniyeh in 1836. By Lieut.-Col. J. Shiel. viii. 54.

—— Notes of a journey from, through Persian Kurdistan to the ruins of Takhti-Soleiman, thence to Gîlan in 1838; with memoir on site of Atropatenian Ecbatana. By H. C. Rawlinson. x. 1.

TADUM, Journey from Kumaon to, and back along the Kâli Gandak to British Territory. By Major T. G. Montgomerie. xlv. 350.

TAL—CHO'TIA'LI Field Force, Account of the country traversed by the second column of the. By Lieut. R. C. Temple. xlix. 190.

TALIFU. *See* CHINA.

TANGHI DARIA, a branch of the Jaxartes. On the desiccation of. By M. Khanikoff. xiv. 333.

TAVIUM, Observations on the position of. By W. J. Hamilton, Esq. vii. 74.

TEHAMA, Notes on a collection of plants from the. By John Lindley, F.R.S. v. 296.

TEHRAN to ALAMUT and KHURREM-ABAD, Itinerary from, in May 1837. By Lieut.-Col. Justin Shiel. viii. 430.

THÉCHÉS, Mount (of Xenophon), Identification of the. By M. P. Rorit. xl. 463.

THIBET. *See* TIBET.

TIAN-SHAN Celestial Range, A journey to the western portion of the, from western limits of the Trans-Ili Region to Tashkend. By N. Severtsof. xl. 343.

—— First ascent of the, and visit to upper course of the Jaxartes or Syr-Daria, in 1857. By P. P. Semenof. xxxi. 356.

TIBET and SEFAN. By Dr. Chas. Gutzlaff. xx. 191.

—— Physical Geography of Western. By Capt. Henry Strachey, Bengal Army. xxiii. 1.

—— Journey to Shigatze. By T. G. Montgomerie. xlv. 330.

—— A fourth Excursion to the passes into Tibet by the Donkiah Lah. By Dr. J. D. Hooker. xx. 49.

—— Visit to Daba in. By Capt. Bennet. (Proceedings, Vol. x. 165.)

—— GREAT, Travels in, and trade with Bengal. By C. R. Markham. xlv. 299. (Proceedings, Vol. xix. 327.)

—— —— Account of the Pundit's journey in. By Capt. H. Trotter. xlvii. 86.

—— Western. Exploration by Parties of the Indian Survey. (Proceedings (N.S.) Vol. i. 444.)

—— The Pundit's journey from Leh to Lhása and return to India *via* Assam. By Capt. H. Trotter. (Proceedings, Vol. xxi. 325.)

—— Attempt of Native Envoy to reach Missionaries in. By Capt. Gregory. (Proceedings, Vol. xiv. 214.) *See* GREAT TIBET.

—— T. T. Cooper on. (Proceedings, Vol. xiii. 392.)

TIGRIS, Note accompanying a survey of the, between Ctesiphon and Mosul. By Lieut. H. Blosse Lynch, I.N. ix. 441.

—— Note on a part of the, between Baghdad and Samarrah. By Lieut. H. B. Lynch, I.N. ix. 471.

—— Sources of. By J. G. Taylor. (Proceedings, Vol. ix. 36.)

TRANS-HIMALAYAN Explorations, Report of the, during 1867. By Capt. T. G. Montgomerie, R.E. xxxix. 146. (Proceedings, Vol. xiii. 183; xiv. 207.)

TRANS-INDUS FRONTIER OF BRITISH INDIA, Notes on the highland region adjacent to the. By Major James Walker. xxxii. 303.

TRANS-INDUS TERRITORIES, ETC. Notes on the Flora of the country passed through by Brigadier-Gen. Chamberlain's force in 1860. By Dr. J. L. Stuart. xxxii. 316.

TRANS-NARYN COUNTRY, Expedition to, in 1867. By Baron P. R. Osten-Sacken. xl. 250. (Proceedings, Vol. xiv. 221.)

TRAVANCORE, On the inland navigation of; an account of the Alipee Mud-bank and the Wurkallay Barrier. By C. R. Markham, F.S.A. xxxvi. 195. (Proceedings, Vol. xi. 78.)

TROY, Observations on the Topography of. By Dr. P. W. Forchhammer. xii. 28.

TSAI-SAN Lake. By General Abramof. (Proceedings, Vol. ix. 40.)

TSUSIMA, Japan, A visit to the Island of. By Laurence Oliphant, F.R.G.S. xxxiii. 178.

TURCOMAN frontier of Persia. Capt. the Hon. G. Napier's Journey. (Proceedings, Vol. xx. 166.)

TURKISTAN. Progress of Russian exploration. By E. D. Morgan. (Proceedings, Vol. xiv. 229.)

—— Astronomical Points fixed by Struve in, from 1865 to 1868. xxxix. 338.

—— EASTERN, A Prince of Kashgar on the geography of. By R. B. Shaw. xlvi. 277. (Proceedings, Vol. xx. 482; xvii. 195.)

—— Account of an Expedition to west shore of Issikul Lake. By P. Semenoff. xxxix. 311.

—— Trade between, and India. By Sir Henry Rawlinson. (Proceedings, xiii. 10.)

—— Transit of tea from N.W. India to. (Proceedings, Vol. xiii. 198.)

TURKOMANIA, Col. Stebnitzky's Report on his journey, in 1872, in Central and Southern. xliv. 217.

TYRE, Extract from a notice on the site of Ancient. By Count de Berton. ix. 286.

URAL MOUNTAINS, Observations on the, to accompany a new map of the southern portion of that chain. By Sir R. I. Murchison. xiii. 269.

—— —— Extract from the reports of M. Hoffman, Chief of an expedition to the North Ural. xix. 31.

UXIAN CITY, besieged by Alexander the Great; on its probable site. By the Baron C. A. de Bode. xiii. 108.

WADI-EL-ARABA, On the Watershed of. By Capt. W. Allen, R.N. xxiii. 166.

WAKHAN. By Sir H. Rawlinson. (Proceedings, Vol. xvii. 108.)

YANG-TSZE-KIANG, Notes on the, &c. By Dr. Alfred Barton, F.R.G.S. xxxii. 26.

AFRICA.

BAMANGWATO Country. By Capt. R. R. Patterson. (Proceedings (N.S.) Vol. i. 240.)

BATONGA Country, Elephant Mountains in. R. F. Burton. (Proceedings, Vol. vii. 104.)

BENGUELA to IBO and MOZAMBIQUE, journeys of Silva Porto with the Arabs from, through Africa, from 1852 to 1854. By Jas. Macqueen. xxx. 136. (Proceedings, Vol. i. 75.)

BAHR EL GHAZAL. Mme. Tinné. (Proceedings, Vol. viii. 12.)

BENIN and the Upper Course of the Quorra or Niger. By Capt. Becroft. xi. 184.

BENZERTA, Lakes of, in the Regency of Tunis. By Lieut. Spratt. R.N. xvi. 251.

BERENICE, Notice on the ruins of. By Lieut. Wellsted, I.N. vi. 96.

BIDA, in Nupé, to Kano, in Haussa, Notes of a journey from, in 1862. By Dr. Baikie, R.N. xxxvii. 92.

BINUÉ RIVER, Ascent of, in 1879, with remarks on the systems of the Shary and BINUÉ. By E. Hutchinson. (Proceedings (N.S.) Vol. ii. 289.)

BULAMA Island, west coast of Africa. Visit of Governor O'Conor to. (Proceedings, Vol. i. 42.)

BUSHMAN Land. By Dr. Moffatt. (Proceedings, Vol. ii. 77.)

CAIRO to I'FAT, Abstract of journal kept by Rev. Messrs. Isenberg and Krapf on the journey in 1839. Communicated by Church Missionary Society. x. 455.

CAMERON, Commander, R.N. Journey to Ujiji. (Proceedings, Vol. xix. 136.) Survey of Tanganyika. (Proceedings, Vol. xix. 246.)

—— Journey across Africa. Letter from. (Proceedings, Vol. xx. 118, 304.)

CAMEROONS, Excursion up the river of, to the Bay of Amboises. By Capt. Allen, R.N. xiii. 1.

—— Mount, Excursion Inland from. By Rev. T. J. Comber. (Proceedings (N.S.) Vol. i. 225.) Burton's ascent of. (Proceedings, Vol. vi. 238.)

CANARY ISLANDS, Survey of some of the, and of part of W. Coast of Africa in 1835. By Lieut. Arlett, R.N. vi. 285.

—— —— Ethnographical remarks on the original language of their inhabitants. By Don. J. J. da Costa de Macedo. xi. 171.

CAPE COLONY, On the roads and Kloofs in the. By Major Michell, R.E. vi. 168.

—— —— On steam communication with Australia and the Cape. By Capt. J. L. Stokes, R.N. xxvi. 183. (Proceedings, Vol. i. 79.)

—— —— Discovery of diamonds. Professor Tennant. (Proceedings. Vol. xii. 322.

CAPE COAST, Note of a journey from, to Whyddah on W. coast of Africa. By Mr. John Duncan. xvi. 143.

CAPE PALMAS, and the Mena or Kroomen. Communicated by Dr. Francis Bacon. xii. 196.

CARAVAN Journey from E. to W. coast of Africa. Notice of communication by Vice-Consul Brand, through the Foreign Office, with Remarks by W. D. Cooley. xxiv. 266.

CENTRAL AFRICA, Geographical notes of the Khedive's expedition to. By Lieut. Julian A. Baker, R.N. xliv. 37. (Proceedings, Vol. xviii, 50, 131.)

CENTRAL AFRICA, Discoveries by H. M. Stanley. Speech by the Prince of Wales. (Proceedings, Vol. xxii. 165.)

CENTRAL SOUTH AFRICA, Journey through, from the Diamond fields to the Upper Zambesi. By Dr. E. Holub. (Proceedings (N.S.) Vol. ii. 166.)

—— —— Notes on the Chobe River. By Dr. Bradshaw. (Proceedings (N.S.) Vol. iii. p. 208.)

CENTRAL AFRICA. Report of explorers under Dr. A. Smith. vi. 394.

—— —— Failure in exploring interior of, from original documents in the office of the R.G.S. ii. 305.

CENTRAL AFRICAN, New route and new mode of travelling into. By J. Mullens. (Proceedings, Vol. xxi. 233.)

CENTRAL AFRICAN EXPEDITION of Livingstone. (Proceedings, Vol. iv. 19.)

CENTRAL AFRICA, MISSION TO. Progress of the Misson, consisting of Messrs. Richardson, Barth, and Overweg. xxi. 130.

—— —— NORTH. By Dr. Barth. (Proceedings, Vol. ii. 217.)

—— —— Letters from Vogel's expedition. xxiv. 276. (Proceedings, Vol. ii. 30.)

—— —— Letter from Dr. Barth to Dr. Beke, from Timbuctoo. xxiv. 283.

—— —— Letters from Vogel. xxv. 237.

—— —— Notes on geography of. By James Macqueen. (Proceedings, Vol. i. 12 ; Vol. iii. 362.)

—— —— Expeditions by the Furanys. xxiii. 120.

—— —— Letters from Ladislaus Magyar. xxiv. 271.

—— —— Notes on geography of. By Macqueen. xxvi. 109. (Proceedings, Vol. iii. 208.)

—— —— Historical Description. By Barth. xxx. 112.

CHAD Lake, Journey to, and vicinity. By Dr. Nachtigal. xlvi. 396.

CHOBE RIVER. By Dr. Bradshaw. (Proceedings (N.S.) Vol. iii. 208.)

CINNAMOMIFERA (REGIO) of the Ancients. By D. Cooley. xix. 166.

COLESBERG to STEINKOPF, Journey in 1854–55. By R. Moffatt. xxviii. 153.

CONGO, Dr. Behm, on Livingstone's exploration of the Upper. (Proceedings, Vol. xvii. 21.)

—— Ascent by Comm. Hunt, R.N. (Proceedings, Vol. ii. 374.)

—— On. By Capt. Bedingfield. (Proceedings, Vol. iv. 66.)

—— Proceedings of Lieut. Grandy. (Proceedings, Vol. xix. 78.)

—— Account of recent journeys in the interior of. By Rev. T. J. Comber. (Proceedings (N.S.)Vol. iii. 20.)

—— Note on Lieut. Grandy's map of his journey from Ambriz to San Salvador and the. By W. J. Turner. xlvi. 428.

—— Journey through to Makuta. By Rev. T. J. Comber. (Proceedings, Vol. i. 225, N.S.)

—— Geographical sketch of basin of, and Nile. By H. M. Stanley. (Proceedings, Vol. xxii. 382.)

CUNENE RIVER, Green, Hahn, and Rath. (Proceedings, Vol. ii. 350.)

DAMARA LAND, Notes to accompany Andersen's map of. By Thos. Baines. xxxvi. 247.

DAMARAS of SOUTH AFRICA, Capt. Alexander's intended visit to the. vi. 443.

DAR ES SALAAM, Routes from, towards Lake Nyassa. By Keith Johnston. (Proceedings (N.S.) Vol. i. 417.)

EQUATORIAL AFRICA, EAST, Snowy Mountains of. By Baron von Decken. (Proceedings, Vol. viii. 5.)

EQUATORIAL WESTERN AFRICA. By Du Chaillu. (Proceedings, Vol. v. 108.)

FERNANDO NORONHA, A visit to. By A. Rattray. xlii. 431.

GAMBIA and CARSAMANZA RIVERS, Supposed junction, on W. Coast of Africa. By R. W. Hay. iii. 72.

—— —— Mohammed Sisei, a Mandingo of Nyani-Maru on the. By Capt. Washington. viii. 448.

—— RIVER, Abridged account of an expedition of about 200 miles up the. By Governor Ingram. xvii. 150.

GAZA LAND, Two journeys in. By St. Vincent Erskine. xlviii. 25. (Proceedings, Vol. xxii. 127.) (*See* MOZAMBIQUE.)

GHADAMAS, Journey from Tripoli to. By Vice-Consul C. H. Dickson. xxii. 131.

—— Account of. By Dickson. xxx. 255.

GHAT, Route from to Tawat, through the middle of the "Sahara." Communicated by Mr. Richardson. xvi. 258.

GOLD REGION. (*See* LIMPOPO.)

GORDON, Colonel. Expedition. On the progress of. By Sir H. Rawlinson. (Proceedings, Vol. xx. 50 ; Vol. xxi. 56 ; Vol. xxi. 63.) xlvi. 381.

HARAR, A trip to. By Lieut. Burton. xxv. 136.

—— Its probable position, with information relative to tribes in its vicinity. —— By Lieut. Barker, I.N. xii. 238.

IJEBU COUNTRY, Journey to Odé in. By Capt. Bedingfield. (Proceedings, Vol. vii. 105.)

IVORY TRADE. By Dr. Vogel. (Proceedings, Vol. i. 215.)

JAMOOR RIVER, On its mouths. By Rev. John Clark. xvi. 255.

JIMMA COUNTRY (S.W. of Berbera), Account of the. Communicated by Sir J. Gardner Wilkinson. xxv. 206.

JUBA RIVER, Death of Baron Von der Decken on the. (Proceedings, Vol. x. 109.)

KILIMANJARO and the WHITE NILE. By Macqueen. xxx. 128.

—— MOUNTAIN. Thornton. (Proceedings, Vol. vi. 47.; Vol. ix. 15.)

—— Ascent of, by Revs. New and Bushell. (Proceedings, Vol. xvi. 167.)

KINGANI River, East Africa. By F. Holmwood. xlvii. 253.

KORDOFAN. Notes of a journey to. By Holroyd. ix. 163.

—— and DARFUR, Astronomical observations in. By Major H. G. Prout. xlix. 392.

KOSTANTINAH, Heights obtained during the Campaign of September, 1837. viii. 226.

KROOMEN. (*See* CAPE PALMAS.)

KUBBABABISH ARABS, On the, between Dongola and Kordofan. By M. Parkyns xx. 254.

KWORA and CHADDA, Exploring trip up the rivers. By Dr. Baikie. xxv. 108.

Niger, Expedition to determine the course and termination of, from Yaaori to the Sea. By R. and J. Lauder. i. 179.

—— Delta, Notes accompanying a Chart of a portion of the. By R. D. Boler. xlvi. 411.

—— Voyage up, from Lagos to Bida. By Rev. J. Milum. (Proceedings, (N.S.) Vol. iii. 26.

—— Notes on. F. V. Robins. (Proceedings, Vol. x. 116.)

—— Notes on the River, by Bishop Crowther. (Proceedings, Vol. xxi. 481.)

—— Expedition. By Dr. Baikie. (Proceedings, Vol. ii. 83; vi. 22; vii. 66; xi. 49.)

Nile, White. On sources of. By A. W. Twyford. (Proceedings, Vol. i. 503.)

—— —— Land journey westward, by J. Petherick. xxxv. 289.

—— —— Notes to accompany a survey of the, from Lardo to Nyamyungo. By Col. Gordon. xlvi. 431.

—— —— Notes to accompany a Survey of, from Khartum to Rigaf. By Lieut. C. Watson. xlvi. 412.

—— —— Petherick on the. (Proceedings, Vol. iv. 39.)

—— —— Petherick on Sources. (Proceedings, Vol. iv. 223.)

—— —— Petherick (Proceedings, Vol. v. 27, 40, 41; vi. 18; vii. 20; viii. 122, 145.)

—— —— Lieut. Watson's astronomical observations at positions on the Nile. xlvi. 417.

—— —— Peney, expedition from Gondokoro. (Proceedings, Vol. vi. 18.)

—— —— Letter on exploration of Sir Samuel Baker. (Proceedings, Vol. xv. 92.)

—— —— Report on the calculations of heights from Watson's observations on the. By R. Strachan. xlvi. 421.

—— —— Meteorological Observations taken on the White Nile, between Khartum and Rigaf. By Lieut. Watson. xlvi. 424.

—— —— Above Gondokoro. By J. Kemp. (Proceedings, Vol. xix. 324.)

Nile, Livingstone's last journey to, and the probable ultimate sources of the. By Findlay. xxxvii. 193. (Proceedings, Vol. xi. 232.)

—— Upper Basin of, by inspection and information. By Capt. Speke. xxxiii. 322.

—— On the, and on the present and former levels of Egypt. By Sir J. G. Wilkinson. ix. 431.

—— and its Tributaries. By C. Beke. xvii. 1.

—— Comments on M. d'Abbadie's discovery of the sources of the White Nile. By F. Ayrton. xviii. 48.

—— Observations on, between Dufli and Magungo. By Col. Gordon. (Proceedings, Vol. xxi. 48.)

—— Notes on the Victoria Nile, between Magungo and Foweira. By Col. Gordon. (Proceedings, Vol. xxi. 49.)

—— Geographical notes on. By Prof. Paul Chaix. xix. 143.

—— H. M. Stanley's Geographical sketch of basin of, and that of Congo. (Proceedings, Vol. xxii. 382.)

North Africa, routes in. By John Bekr es Seddik. vi. 100.

Nuñez River, Report on its trade and resources. By Lieut. Comm. Lysaght. xix. 29.

Nyam Nyam Country. By Dr. Junker. (Proceedings (N.S.) Vol. iii. 301.)

NYASSA, Livingstone's expedition to Lake, in 1861-63. xxxiii. 250. Proceedings, iv. 87; vii. 18.

—— Explorations to W. of Lake in 1863. By Livingstone. xxxiv. 245.

—— Lake Mission. By E. D. Young. (Proceedings, Vol. xx. 451.)

—— second circumnavigation of. By Dr. Jas. Stewart. (Proceedings, (N.S.) Vol. i. 289.)

—— Report of expedition of Mr. Young. (Proceedings, Vol. xii. 79.)

—— Journey along part of W. side of. By Dr. Laws. (Proceedings (N.S.) Vol. i. 305.)

—— Routes towards, by Keith Johnston. (Proceedings (N. S.) Vol. i. 417.)

—— On the, and journey to Zanzibar. By H. B. Cotterill. (Proceedings, Vol. xxii. 233.)

—— Observations on W. side of, and on the country between, and Tanganyika. By G. James Stewart. (Proceedings (N.S.) Vol. ii. 428.)

—— On a recent sojourn at Lake. By E. D. Young. (Proceedings, Vol. xxi. 225.)

—— Lake, and the water route to the lake region of Africa. By J. Stewart, c.e. (Proceedings (N.S.) iii. 257.)

N'YASSI, or the Great lake of S. Africa, its geography investigated. By Cooley. xv. 185.

—— Further explanations in geography of. By Cooley. xvi. 138.

OLD CALABAR, Ascent of, in 1836. By Oldfield. vii. 195.

—— Is it a branch of the river Quorra? By Capt. Allen, R.N. vii. 198.

OLD CALABAR RIVER, Explorations of, in 1841 and 1842. By Capt. Becroft and King. xiv. 260.

—— By Capt. J. B. Walker. (Proceedings, Vol. xvi. 135.)

OGOWÉ River, Journey of R. B. Walker up. (Proceedings, Vol. xvii. 354.)

ORANGE, or 'GARIEP RIVER, South Africa, Water Supply in the Basin of the. By Jas. Fox Wilson. xxxv. 106. (Proceedings, Vol. ix. 106.)

ORANGE RIVER, Journey from Little Namaqua-Land eastward, in Aug., 1856. By Robert Moffatt. xxviii. 174.

—— —— Free State, and country of Transvaal Boers; a trading trip into. By John Sanderson. xxx. 233.

PALMAS. (*See* CAPE PALMAS.)

PETHERICK. (*See* NILE.)

PIGAFETTA'S Map of. By R. H. Major. (Proceedings, Vol. xi. 246.)

PRINCE'S ISLAND and ANNO BOM, In the Bight of Biafra; memoir descriptive of. By Capt. Boteler, R.N. ii. 274.

QUANZA, On the River. By Carl Alexanderson. xlvi. 428.

QUILIMANE River, Note on. By Capt. Hyde Parker. (Proceedings, Vol. i. 312.)

QUORRA, is it the same river as the Niger of the Ancients? By W. Martin Leake. ii. 1.

—— Letter from J. Becroft. vi. 424. (*See* NIGER.) (*See* KWORA.)

RED SEA, Notes on Bruce's Chart of Coasts of. By Lieut. J. R. Wellsted. v. 286.

—— —— Notes on names of places on shores of. By A. Thompson D'Abbadie. ix. 317.

—— —— Physical geography of. (*See* under ASIA.) xxiv. 227.

Suez Canal and its pilotage. By Capt. G. S. Nares. (Proceedings, Vol. xiv. 75.)

—— —— Opening of. By Lord Houghton. (Proceedings, Vol. xiv. 88.)

—— —— Report of Capt. Richards and Col. Clarke. (Proceedings, Vol. xiv. 259.)

Tanganyika, On Lake, Ptolemy's Western-Lake Reservoir of " Nile." By Richard F. Burton. xxix. 231. xxxv. 1. (Proceedings, Vol. iii. 111; Vol. ix. 6.)

—— On the Southern half of. By Lieut. Cameron. xlv. 184.

—— Lieut. Cameron's Diary. xlv. 197.

Timbuktu, Trade route from Gambia to. By H. Cooper. (Proceedings, xx. 78.)

Transvaal, Geographical and economic features of. By F. B. Fynney. xlviii. 16. (Proceedings, Vol. xxii. 114.)

—— Notes on physical and geological features of, to accompany his new map of. By F. Jeppe. xlvii. 217.

—— From the gold region in, to Delagoa Bay. By Capt. C. Warren. xlviii. 283. (*See* Orange Free State.)

Tripoli, An account of. By Col. G. H. Warrington. xiv. 104.

Uganda. *See* Victoria.

Ukerewe Lake, On. By Capt. R. F. Burton. (Proceedings, Vol. xvi. 129.)

Umzila's, South East Africa, journey to in 1871–72. By Mr. St. Vincent Erskine. xlv. 45. (Proceedings, Vol. xix. 110.)

Unyamwezi, Description of. By P. Broyon Mirambo. (Proceedings, Vol. xxii. 28.)

Upper Egypt, Notes on part of Eastern Desert of. By J. Wilkinson. ii. 28.

Usambara Country in East Africa. By Rev. J. P. Farler. (Proceedings (N.S.) Vol. i. 81.)

—— —— Notes of a trip from Zanzibar to. By Keith Johnston. (Proceedings (N.S.) Vol. i. 545.)

—— —— Notes on geology of. By J. Thomson. (Proceedings (N.S.) Vol. i. 558.)

—— —— Journey to Magila on borders of. By A. Bellville. (Proceedings, Vol. xx. 74.)

Vei Language, Discovery of a native written character at Bohmar, on W. coast of Africa, with vocabulary of the Vatice or Vei Tongue. By Lieut. F. E. Forbes. xx. 89.

—— —— Notes on the language and alphabet. By E. Norris. xx. 101.

Victoria Nyanza, Note on height of. By Staff Com. George. (Proceedings, Vol. xx. 159.)

—— —— Journey to, and back *via* the Nile. By R. W. Felkin. (Proceedings (N.S.) Vol. ii. 357.)

—— —— On H. M. Stanley's exploration of. By Col. J. Grant. xlvi. 10. (Proceedings, Vol. xx. 34.)

Victoria and Uganda Lake. By Rev. C. T. Wilson. (Proceedings (N.S.) Vol. ii. 353.)

Victoria Nyanza Expedition, Progress of the, of the Church Missionary Society. By E. Hutchinson. (Proceedings, Vol. xxi. 498.)

Vogel, Dr., fate of. (Proceedings, Vol. ii. 79.) *See* Central Africa (North).

VOLTA RIVER, Doblen. (Proceedings, Vol. vi. 49.)
—— —— Notes on. By Capt. Croft. (Proceedings, Vol. xviii. 183.)
—— —— Country between, and Niger. By Sir John Glover. (Proceedings, Vol. xviii. 286.

WADY HALFEH, On the country between, and Gebel-Berkel, in Ethiopia, with remarks on the level of the Nile. By Sir G. Wilkinson. xx. 154.
WAMI RIVER, Boat journey by Clement Hill. (Proceedings, Vol. xvii. 337.)
WASSAW, Visit to the gold fields of. By J. A. Skertchly. xlviii. 274.
WEDNOON, Letter of Mr. Davidson from. vi. 429.
WEST AFRICA, On a map showing the possibility of the rivers Yeu and Chadda being the outlet of Lake Chad. By Capt. Allen. viii. 289.
—— —— On the coast of, surveyed by H.M.S. "Ætna" in 1830–32. By Capt. Belcher, R.N. ii. 278.
—— —— British Settlements. By O'Connor. (Proceedings, Vol. vi. 15.)
—— —— Mr. Winwood Reade in. (Proceedings, Vol. vii. 106.)
—— —— Second journey into. By M. P. B. du Chaillu. xxxvi. 64. (Proceedings, Vol. x. 71; Vol. v. 108.)
—— —— Oil rivers. By W. N. Thomas. (Proceedings, Vol. xvii. 148.)
WESTERN EQUATORIAL AFRICA, An exploration of the Elephant Mountains in. By R. F. Burton. xxxiii. 241.
WHITE NILE. (*See* NILE.)
WHYDDAH, A journey from, to Adofoodiah. By J. Duncan. xvi. 154.

YORUBA AND NUPE COUNTRIES, Journey in, in 1858. By Daniel J. May. xxx. 212.

ZAMBESI, On the Gradient of the, on the level of Lake Nyassa, on the Murchison Rapids, and on Lake Shirwa. By John Kirk. xxxv. 167.
—— DELTA, On fossil bones from the alluvial strata of the. By John Kirk. xxxiv. 199. (Proceedings, Vol. viii. 151.)
—— AND SHIRE RIVERS, Extracts from despatches of Dr. D. Livingstone, 1858–61. xxxi. 256.
—— —— —— Notes on the. By the late Richard Thornton. xxxiv. 196.
—— An expedition up the, to Senna, by three officers of H.M.S. "Leven," when surveying E. coast of Africa in 1823. ii. 136.
—— A visit to the River. By T. S. Leigh. xix. i.
—— Note on, by Capt. Hyde Parker. (Proceedings, Vol. i. 312.)
—— McLeod on. (Proceedings, Vol. ii. 363.)
—— Journey of Galvão da Silva to Manica Gold fields, in 1788, with description of country south of the Lower. By Macqueen. xxx. 155.
—— Expedition. (Proceedings, Vol. iii. 99.)
—— Dr. Livingstone on. (Proceedings, Vol. v. 128.)
—— Mackenzie. Missionary Expedition. (Proceedings, Vol. v. 131.)
ZANZIBAR, On the possessions of the Imaum of Muskat, on climate and productions of, and on the prospects of African discovery from Mombas. By Col. Sykes. xxiii. 101.
—— Remarks by Sir Bartle Frere. (Proceedings, Vol. xvii. 343.)
ZULU AND AMATONGA COUNTRIES, Notes to accompany maps of, and of the country between Aliwal and Natal. By John Sanderson. xxxii. 335.

ZULU LAND. Books, Memoirs, and Map of. (Proceedings (N.S.) Vol. i. 201 and 205.)

—— —— Notes on physical geography of, by Rev. G. Blencowe. (Proceedings (N.S.) Vol. i. 324.)

AMERICA.

ACONCAGUA, Mt. in Chili, Notice of. By Capt. R. FitzRoy, R.N. vii. 143.

AMAZONS RIVER, On the southern affluents of the, on the rivers which flow from the Cordilleras of Peru into the Marañon or Amazons. Report of river Beni and surroundings, by Thadeus Haenke. v. 90.

—— AND NEGRO RIVERS, Account of the, from recent observations. By Lieut. Smyth, R.N. vi. 11.

—— Notes on the rivers Maué-assú, Abacaxis, and Canumá. By W. Chandless. xl. 419.

—— River, Table of distances on. By L. Nash. (Proceedings, Vol. xxi. 595.)

—— Geographical positions on the. (Proceedings, Vol. xvi. 271.)

AMERICA, Telegraphic communication with. Shaffner. (Proceedings, Vol. iv. 101.)

—— — (North), Evidence for the discovery of, by the Scandinavians in 10th century. viii. 114.

AMERICA, CENTRAL, On. By Col. Don Juan Galindo. vi. 119.

—— —— Sketch of the eastern coast of. By Capt. Bird Allen, R.N. xi. 76.

—— —— Considerations on the great Isthmus of. By Capt. R. FitzRoy, R.N. xx. 161.

—— —— Note upon the language of. By R. G. Latham. xx. 189.

—— SOUTH, Tierra del Fuego, and the Strait of Magelhaens, On the geography of. By Capt. Philip Parker King. i. 155.

—— NORTH, Remarks on the freezing of streams in. By A. C. Anderson. xv. 367.

—— —— Remarks on the physical geography of. By C. S. Rafinesque. xi. 165.

—— —— Palliser's expedition. (Proceedings, Vol. ii. 38–146; Vol. iv. 228.) (*See* ROCKY MOUNTAINS.)

—— —— Observations on the indigenous tribes of the N.W. coast. By John Scouler. xi. 215.

—— —— Barometric and thermometric measurements of heights in. By Capt. J. H. Lefroy. xvi. 263.

—— SOUTH, and OCEANIA, Notes on. By Gen. W. Miller. xii. 137.

AMERICAN ANTIQUITIES, On the Museum for, in Copenhagen. By Prof. C. Rafn. xiv. 316.

ANDES, SOUTHERN, of CHILI, Expedition across the, to open a new line from the Pacific to the Atlantic Ocean. By Don Gulliermo Cox, of Chili. xxxiv. 205.

—— —— —— Proposed railway route across the, from Caldera, in Chili, to Rosario, on the Parana. Report of E. A. Flint's survey. By W. Wheelwright. xxxi. 155 . (Proceedings, Vol. iv. 45.)

—— —— —— On a projected railway route over the, from the Argentine Republic. By R. Crawford. xliii. 46. (Proceedings, Vol. xvii. 57.)

ANDES, BOLIVIAN, On the general outline and physical conformation of the ; on the line of perpetual snow between 15° and 20° S. Lat. By J. B. Pentland. v. 70.

—— A journey across the, between Cochabamba and Chimoré. By J. A. Lloyd. Remarks on communication between Bolivia and the Atlantic, viâ the Amazon. xxiv. 259.

ANEGADA, Remarks on. By R. H. Schomburgk. ii. 152.

APURIMAC and Mantaro, Confluence of. By Don Antonio Raimondi. xxxviii. 413. (Proceedings, Vol. xiii. 112.)

AQUIRY, Notes on the River. By W. Chandless. xxxvi. 119. (Proceedings, Vol. xi. 100.)

ARIZONA, Notes on. By C. D. Postans. (Proceedings, Vol. xix. 302.)

ATACAMA, Journey into the Desert of. By Dr. R. Philippi. xxv. 158.

—— The Desert of. By J. Harding. xlvii. 250.

ATRATO, From the Bay of, to the Bay of Cupica on the Pacific, in 1827. By Comm. Chas. Friend. R.N. xxiii. 191.

—— Through the Valley of, to the Pacific, in search of a route for a ship canal. Under F. M. Kelley. xxvi. 174. (Proceedings, Vol. i. 63.)

BAYANOS RIVER on the Isthmus of Panama. By Laurence Oliphant. xxxv. 142. (Proceedings, Vol. ix. 276.)

BELIZE TO GUATEMALA, A journey from, and return by the river Polochic in 1834. By E. Legh Page. viii. 317.

BELIZE RIVER, Physical Geography of. By A. S. Cockburn. (Proceedings, Vol. xii. 72.)

BERBICE, in BRITISH GUAYANA, Diary of an ascent of the, in 1836–37. By Robert H. Schomburgk. vii. 302.

BOLIVIA, Notes on, to accompany original maps. By G. C. Musters. xlvii. 201. (Proceedings, Vol. xxii. 40.)

—— Boundary of Chili and. (Proceedings (N.S.) Vol. i. 785.)

BOGOTA, Journey from Chimborazo to. By R. Cross. (Proceedings, Vol. ix. 277.)

BOUNDARY (NORTH AMERICA), from the Lake of the Woods to the Rocky Mountains. By Capt. S. Anderson. xlvi. 228. (Proceedings, Vol. xx. 274.)

BRAZIL, Journey from River St. Francisco to the River Tocantins and to city of Maranhâo. By J. W. Wells. xlvi. 308.

—— Letter on the Abrohlos Bank off coast of. By Capt. FitzRoy. ii. 315.

—— The valley of the Tibagy. By T. P. Bigg-Wither. xlvi. 263. (Proceedings, Vol. xx. 455.)

BRITISH COLUMBIA, Exploration in Jarvis Inlet and Desolation Sound. By W. Downie. xxxi. 249.

—— —— Journey into the interior of. By Mathew B. Begbie. xxxi. 237. (Proceedings, Vol. iv. 33.)

—— —— On the geography and mountain passes of, in connection with an overland route. By A.Waddington. xxxviii. 118. (Proceedings, xii. 121.)

—— —— Remarks on the geography and natural capabilities of, and its gold fields. By Lieut. H. S. Palmer, R.E. xxxiv. 171. (Proceedings, Vol. iv. 33 ; Vol. viii. 87.)

—— —— A journey through the districts bordering on the Thompson, Fraser, and Harrison Rivers. By Lieut. R. C. Mayne, R.N. xxxi. 297. (Proceedings, Vol. iv. 33.)

BRITISH COLUMBIA. Report on the Harrison and Lilloet route. By Lieut. H. S. Palmer, R.E. xxxi. 224.

—— —— W. Kelly on. (Proceedings, Vol. vi. 107.)

—— —— Sketch of the country between Jervis Inlet and Fort Pemberton; with a map. By Lieut. R. C. Mayne. xxxi. 297.

—— —— "Benches" or valley terraces in. By Chief Justice Begbie. (Proceedings, Vol. xv. 133.)

BRITISH NORTH AMERICAN EXPLORING EXPEDITION, Progress of the, under Capt. J. Palliser. xxx. 267. (*See* ROCKY MOUNTAINS.)

CALIFORNIA, Notes on Upper. By Dr. Thos. Coulter. v. 59.

—— The Modoc Regions. By Wm. Simpson. (Proceedings, Vol. xix. 292.)

CARAVAYA, The Province of. By C. R. Markham. xxxi. 190.

—— Rivers of San Gavan and Ayapata in. Raimondi. (Proceedings, Vol. xi. 102.)

CARIBS, Notice of. By Don Juan Galindo. iii. 290.

CARMEN, On the town of, and the Rio Negro. By Murrell R. Robinson. xiv. 130.

CENTRAL AMERICA, New transit across. By Bedford Pim. (Proceedings, Vol. vi. 75, 112.)

—— —— Exploration in. By J. Collinson. (Proceedings, Vol. xii. 25.)

—— —— On the ruined cities of. By Capt. Lindesay Brine, R.N. xlii. 354. (Proceedings, Vol. xvii. 67.)

—— —— On Lake Yojoa. By Mr. Squier. (Proceedings, Vol. iii. 106.)

CHILI. (*See* ANDES.)

CHILE, Observations on the Coal Formation in. By W. Bollaert. xxv. 172.

—— Boundary of Bolivia and. (Proceedings (N.S.) Vol. i. 785.)

CHILOE, Account of Island and Province of. By Capt. Blankley, R.N. iv. 344.

COCOS, Isle. Note on. By Admiral Sir George Seymour. xix. 20.

COLORADO, On the basin of the, and the great basin of N. America. By W. A. Bell. xxxix. 95. (Procceedings, Vol. xiii. 140.)

COLUMBIA. Notes on the topography of the Sierra Nevada of Santa Marta. By F. A. A. Simons. (Proceedings (N.S.) Vol. i. 689.)

—— RIVER, Notes on the geography of. By the late Dr. Gairdner, M.D. xi. 250.

COMMUNICATION between the populations of Europe and Asia, Plan for a Direct. By Asa Whitney. xxi. 86.

—— with the East, viâ British N. America. By Capt. Synge, R.E. xxii. 174.

—— in Southern Peru. By C. R. Markham. xliv. 127. (Proceedings, Vol. xviii. 212.)

CORENTYN, Diary of an ascent of the. By R. H. Schomburgk. vii. 285.

CORDOVA to MENDOZA, Notes on the route from, in 1837. By Capt. Gosselman. ix. 407.

COSIGUINA, Volcano of (1835). v. 387.

CUPICA, Isthmus of. By Admiral Illingworth. (Proceedings, Vol. i. 86.)

CUYUNY RIVER, Expedition up, in 1837. By Wm. Hilhouse. vii. 446.

CUZCO, Journeys to the northward and eastward of, and among the Chunchos Indians, in July 1835. By Gen. Miller. vi. 174.

—— On the site of. By J. Pentland. viii. 427.

DARIEN Indians. (*See* TULE.)
—— Exploration of. By H. C. Caldwell. (Proceedings, Vol i. 484.)
—— Scientific explorations in the, in 1861 and 1865. By M. Lucien de Puydt. xxxviii. 69. (Proceedings, Vol. xii. 63.)
—— Report of party sent to cross the Isthmus of, under Comm. J. C. Prevost. xxiv. 249.
—— Summary of the survey of the. By L. Gisborne. xxvii. 191. (Proceedings, Vol. i. 88.)
—— of Central America, further considerations on the great. By Capt. R. FitzRoy. xxiii. 171.
DOMINICA, Island of, Recent volcanic eruption at the Grand Souffriere. (Proceedings (N.S.) Vol. ii. 363.)
DOMINICAN REPUBLIC, On the peninsula and Bay of Samana in the. By Sir R. Schomburgk. xxiii. 264.

ECUADOR, Explorations in, in 1856 and 1857. By Geo. Jas. Pritchett. xxx. 64. (Proceedings, Vol. iii. 93.)
ESMERALDA, Journey from, to San Carlos and Moura, thence to Demerara, in 1839. By R. H. Schomburgk. x. 248.
ESSEQUIBO and MASSAROONY RIVERS, Expeditions up the, in 1830–1831. By Capt. J. E. Alexander. ii. 65.

FALKLAND ISLAND, East, Account of. By Sir Woodbine Parish. iii. 94.
FROZEN SOIL of BRITISH N. AMERICA, Observations on the. By Sir J. Richardson. ix. 117.

GALAPAGOS ISLANDS, A visit to, in 1880. By Capt. A. H. Markham. (Proceedings (N.S.) Vol. ii. 742.)
—— Notes on Capt. Markham's paper. (Proceedings (N.S.) Vol. ii. 755.)
—— By Sir G. Seymour. xix. 20.
GORGON BAY, in Central America. By Capt. Bedford Pim, R.N. (Proceedings, Vol. vi. 112.)
GRANADA, Lake of, on the Isthmus between it and the Pacific Ocean. By J. Baily. xiv. 127.
GUATEMALA, on the latitude and longitude of important places in the Republic of. By A. Van de Gehuchte. xxviii. 359. (*See* USAMASINTA RIVER.)
GUIANA, BRITISH, Memoir on the Warow-Land of. By Wm. Hilhouse. iv. 321.
—— —— Expedition into interior of, in 1835–1836. By R. H. Schomburgk. vi. 224.
—— —— The third expedition into interior of, to the sources of the Essequibo, &c. By R. H. Schomburgk. x. 159.
—— —— A journey in the interior of. By E. F. im Thurn. (Proceedings (N.S.) Vol. ii. 465.)
—— —— Expedition to the Barima and Guiana Rivers. By R. H. Schomburgk. xii. 169.
—— —— Excursion up the Barima and Cuyuni Rivers in 1841. By R. H. Schomburgk. xii. 178.
—— —— Visit to the sources of the Takutu in 1842. By Sir Robert Schomburgk. xiii. 18.

NICARAGUA, Notes on Lake of, and the Province of Chontales. By Chevalier Emanuel Friedrichsthal. xi. 97.

—— Gerald Raoul Perry on. (Proceedings, Vol. vi. 74.)

—— Survey for a canal from Lake of, to the Port of Salinas or Bolaños. By Magister Andreas Oersted. xxi. 96.

—— Communication between Atlantic and Pacific Oceans by way of Lake. By Capt. Phillips, R.N. iii. 275.

—— Transit route across. By Capt. Bedford Pim, R.N. (Proceedings, Vol. vi. 75, 112.)

NORTH AMERICAN BOUNDARY, from Lake of the Woods to the Rocky Mountains. By Capt. Anderson. xlvi. 228. (Proceedings, Vol. xx. 274.)

NORTON SOUND, A journey from, to Fort Youkon. By F. W. Whymper. xxxviii. 219. (Proceedings, Vol. xii. 186.)

OLD PROVIDENCE, On the Island of. By C. F. Collet, R.N. vii. 203. (Proceedings, Vol. xxi. 148.)

OREGON, The exploration of, in 1878, by the Wheeler Survey. By J. W. Goad. (Proceedings (N.S.) Vol. i. 694.)

—— Ascent of Mount Hood. By Rev. H. K. Hines. (Proceedings, Vol. xi. 80.)

—— Journey across Cascade Mountains into E. Oregon. By R. Brown. (Proceedings, Vol. xi. 84.)

ORINOCO. Proposed expedition by Admiral Sir Charles Elliot. (Proceedings, Vol. i. 251.)

PANAMA, Notes on Isthmus of. Communicated by J. A. Lloyd. i. 69.

—— On the territory of Burica, in the Province of Chiriqui, Isthmus of. By. J. H. Smith. xxiv. 256.

PARANA, Report on the Brazilian Province of the. By H. P. Vereker. xxxii. 137. (Proceedings, Vol. vi. 74.)

PARAGUAY, Geography and resources of. By Leone Levi. (Proceedings, Vol. xviii. 117.)

—— Notes on physical geography of. By Keith Johnston. (Proceedings, Vol. xx. 494.)

PATAGONIA, Explanatory notes on maps of. By H. L. Jones. xxxi. 204.

—— A year in. By Commander Musters, R.N. xli. 59. (Proceedings, Vol. xv. 41.)

PEEL RIVER, Account of. By A. K. Isbister. xv. 332.

PERU, Geography of Southern. By Wm. Bollaert. xxi. 99. (Proceedings, Vol. xii. 126.)

—— Railroad and steam communication in Southern. By C. R. Markham. xliv. 127. (Proceedings, Vol. xviii. 212.)

—— Outlines of the Geography of. By Don Valentine Ledesma. xxvi. 210.

—— On the Province of Tarapaca, in South. By Don M. B. de la Fuente. xxvi. 229.

—— On Loreto in N. Peru. By Antonio Raimondi. (Proceedings, Vol. viii. 58.)

—— On the Rivers San Gavan and Ayapata, in the Province of Carabaya. By Professor Antonio Raimondi. (*See* CARAVAYA.) xxxvii. 116.

—— Geographical Position of tribes which formed the Empire of the Yncas of. By C. R. Markham. xli. 281. (Proceedings, Vol. xv. 367.)

PERU, Yncas of, Note on Map of Empire of. By T. Saunders. xlii. 513.

PURUS, Ascent of the river. By W. Chandless. xxxvi. 86. (Proceedings, Vol. x. 103.)

—— On the supposed sources of the. By C. R. Markham. xxv. 151. (Proceedings, Vol. v. 224.)

QUEEN CHARLOTTE ISLANDS. By Torrens. (Proceedings, Vol. iv. 226.) By R. Brown. (Proceedings, Vol. xiii. 381.)

QUITO, Journey from, to Cayambe. By Dr. Wm. Jameson, 1859. xxxi. 184.

—— To the River NAPO, Excursion from, Jan.—May, 1857. By Dr. Wm. Jameson. xxviii. 337.

RAILROADS. (*See* COMMUNICATIONS.)

RED RIVER and Saskatchewan. By Dr. John Rae. (Proceedings, Vol. vii. 102.)

RIO NEGRO, On the. By A. R. Wallace. xxiii. 212.

RIOJA, On the Province of, in South America; to accompany a map. By J. O. French. ix. 381.

ROCKY MOUNTAINS. By Palliser and Hector. xxx. 267. (Proceedings, Vol. iii. 122 ; Vol. iv. 73.)

—— —— By Lord Milton and Dr. Cheadle. (Proceedings, Vol. ix. 17.)

RUPERT LAND. By Capt. Synge. (Proceedings, Vol. vii. 71.)

SALADO VALLEY, Journey through and across the Argentine Provinces. By T. J. Hutchinson. xxxiv. 226.

SAN SALVADOR, Description of the State of. Communicated by John Power. xxviii. 349.

SAN JOAQUIM, FORT, Journey from, to Roraima, thence to Esmeralda, in 1838–1839. By R. H. Schomburgk. x. 191.

SANTA CRUZ RIVER, An attempt to ascend. By Capt. R. FitzRoy, R.N. vii. 114.

SKYRING WATER. (*See* MAGELLAN STRAIT.)

SOUTH AMERICA, On the Geographical position of W. coast of. By Carlos Moesta. xxviii. 333.

—— On the still unexplored parts of. By C. R. Markham. (Proceedings, Vol. xxii. 40.)

TAPAJOS, Notes on the rivers Arinos, Juruena, and. By W. Chandless. xxxii. 268.

TEHUANTEPEC, On the Isthmus of. By Herr M. G. Hermesdorf. xxxii. 536.

TEMPERATURE of the air, the best points in British N. America for observing the. By Dr. Richardson. ix. 121.

TEXAS AND NEW MEXICO, Journey through, in 1841 and 1842. By Thomas Falconer. xiii. 199.

—— —— Notes on coast of Texas, taken in 1842. By Wm. Bollaert. xiii. 226.

—— —— On Geography of Texas. By Wm. Bollaert. xx. 113.

TULE INDIANS on Darien coast, Vocabulary. By Dr. Cullen. xxi. 241.

UCAYALI, Peruvian exploration of the. By J. R. Tucker. (Proceedings, Vol. xiii. 133.)

URUGUAY, On the gold-fields of. By H. Bankart. xxxix. 339.

—— Central, A journey to. By Dr. D. Christison. (Proceedings (N.S.) Vol. ii. 663.)

USAMASINTA RIVER, Description of. By Don Juan Galindo. iii 59.

VALPARAISO AND CALLAO, on the longitude of. ix. 502.

VANCOUVER ISLAND, Route in exploring a road from Albernie Canal to Nanaimo in 1861, with a Track chart. By Commander Richard C. Mayne, R.N. xxxii. 529.

—— —— Report of an expedition along East coast of. By Governor Jas. Douglas. xxiv. 245.

—— —— Notes on physical geography of. By C. Forbes. xxxiv. 154.

—— —— Description of. By its first Colonist, W. Colquhoun Grant. xxvii. 268. (Proceedings, Vol. i. 487.)

—— —— By Mayne. (Proceedings, Vol. vi. 107.)

—— —— By Dr. Forbes, R.N. (Proceedings, Vol. viii. 83.)

—— —— Remarks on, concerning Town sites and Native Population. By W. C. Grant. xxxi. 208.

—— —— To Hudson's Bay. Proposed communication. By J. Banister. (Proceedings, Vol. i. 263.)

VERA PAZ, Account of the Province of. By Padre F. A. de Escobar. xi. 89.

VIRGINIA, Account of the Mound at Grove Creek Flats, in. By Schoolcraft. xii. 259.

WEST INDIA ISLANDS, Remarks on the Heavy Swell, on the set and velocity of the tides. By R. H. Schomburgk. v. 23.

YULE Indians. (*See* TULE.)

AUSTRALASIA.

ALPS, Australian. By Muller. (Proceedings, Vol. i. 3.)

AUSTRALIA, Recent Information from. (1832.) ii. 318.

—— Latest accounts from. (1835.) vi. 433.

—— Account of the recent exploration to the interior of. By Major J. L. Mitchell, vii. 271.

—— Considerations on the political Geography and geographical Nomenclature of. By Capt. Vetch, R.E. viii. 157.

—— Exploring excursions in. By H. S. Russell. xv. 305.

—— On the Languages of. xv. 365.

—— Considerations against the existence of a Great Sea in its Interior. By E. J. Eyre. xvi. 200.

—— On Steam communication with. By Capt. J. L. Stokes, R.N. xxvi. 183. (Proceedings, Vol. i. 79.)

—— An Exploration into its interior in 1844–45. By Capt. C. Sturt. xvii. 85.

GIPPS' LAND, Mr. Orr's Report to Governor Latrobe of an expedition to. xi. 192.

GREAT BARRIER REEF, Survey within. (Proceedings, Vol. viii. 114.)

GREY AND STANLEY RANGE, Cadell on. (Proceedings, Vol. vi. 55.)

HUME RIVER, On the course of, from the Hilly Districts to junction of the Morumbidgee. By Capt. C. Sturt. xiv. 141.

KING GEORGE'S SOUND, Descriptions of the Natives of. By Scott Nind. i. 21.

LEICHHARDT, Expedition in search of the remains of Dr., and party. By John Forrest. xl. 231. (Proceedings, Vol. xv. 190.)

        By Gregory. (Proceedings, Vol. iii. 18.)

        By Clarke. (Proceedings, Vol. iii. 87.)

        Search Expedition. (Proceedings, Vol. x. 58.)

LIVERPOOL PLAINS AND MORETON BAY, On the country between. Letters from Comm. H. G. Hamilton, R.N. xiii. 245.

LORD HOWE ISLAND, Visit to. By Dr. Corrie. (Proceedings, Vol. xxii. 136.)

MELVILLE ISLAND AND PORT ESSINGTON, Geographical Memoir of, on Cobourg Peninsula; on settlements on N. coast of New Holland. By Major Campbell, 57th Foot. iv. 129.

MORETON BAY TO PORT ESSINGTON, Account of Ludwig Leichhardt's expedition from. xvi. 212.

MURCHISON RANGE, John M'Douall Stuart's explorations to the North of, in 1860–61. xxxii. 340.

MURRAY RIVER, On the navigation of the. By Capt. Thos. Cadell. xxv. 177. (Proceedings, Vol. vi. 55.)

NEW GUINEA. (*See* under OCEANIA.)

NEW SOUTH WALES, The Progress of interior discovery in. By Allan Cunningham. ii. 99.

NEW ZEALAND, Notices of, from original Documents in the Colonial Office. ii. 133.

—— —— Recent surveys in the middle Island of. By Capt. J. L. Stokes, R.N. xxi. 25.

—— —— On the physique of the inhabitants. By Dr. A. S. Thomson. xxiii. 87.

—— —— On Otago in. By J. T. Thomson. (Proceedings, Vol. ii. 354.)

—— —— Thos. Brunner's exploration of interior of Middle Island. xx. 344.

—— —— Progress of discovery in Middle Island of. xiii. 344.

—— —— West coast of Middle Island. By Dr. Hector. (Proceedings, Vol. viii. 47.)

—— —— A reconnaissance survey of the southern districts of Otago. By J. T. Thomson. xxviii. 298.

—— —— Altitude sections of routes between East and West coasts of Canterbury. By Julius Haast. xxxvii. 328.

—— —— Expedition to W. coast of Otago. By Jas. Hector. xxxiv. 96. (Proceedings, Vol. ix. 32.)

—— —— Two expeditions to W. coast of Middle Island, in 1859. By John Rochfort. xxxii. 292.

OCEANIA.

NEW GUINEA, Voyage of the "Ellangowan" to China Strait in. By Rev. S. Macfarlane. (Proceedings, Vol. xxi. 350.)

—— —— Fly River. By D'Albertis. (Proceedings, Vol. xx. 343; (N.S.) i. 4.)

—— —— Fly River. By Rev. S. Macfarlane. (Proceedings, Vol. xx. 253.)

—— —— Travels of Mikluko Maklay in. (Proceedings, Vol. xix. 517.)

NEW HEBRIDES and SANTA CRUZ GROUPS. By Comm. A. H. Markham. xlii. 213. (Proceedings, Vol. xvi. 388.)

NEW IRELAND, Journey along Coast. By Rev. G. Brown. (Proceedings (N.S.) Vol. iii. 213.)

PACIFIC OCEAN, Notes on the Cocos, and two of the Galapagos Group. By Rear-Admiral Sir G. Seymour. xix. 20.

—— —— Extracts from a private journal kept on board H.M.S. "Seringapatam,' (1830). By Capt. W. Waldegrave, R.N. iii. 168.

—— New Ireland in the. vi. 441.

—— Newly discovered Islands in. vii. 454.

PITCAIRN ISLANDERS, Recent accounts of the. By Capt. W. Waldegrave, R.N. iii. 156.

—— —— Removal of. (Proceedings, Vol. i. 60.)

RAPA. Description of the island of. By Capt. Vine Hall. (Proceedings, Vol. xiii. 83.)

SADDLE ISLAND, Volcano of, extract from log of H.C. steam vessel "Victoria," xvi. 338.

SANDWICH ISLANDS, On the geography and recent volcanic eruption of the. By Rev. Thos. Staley. xxxviii. 361. (Proceedings, Vol. xii. 305.)

—— —— Letter dated Oahu, from Mr. Douglas to Capt. Sabine. iv. 333. (*See* HAWAII.)

SANTA CRUZ Group, Commander A. H. Markham on. xlii. 213. (Proceedings, Vol. xvi. 388.)

SKETCH of the surveying voyage of H.M. ships "Adventure" and "Beagle," 1825–36. By Capts. P. P. King, P. Stokes, and R. FitzRoy, R.N. vi. 311.

SOUTH SEA ISLANDS, Proceedings at the. By Capt. J. E. Erskine, R.N. xxi. 222.

INDIAN OCEAN.

ARRU ISLANDS. By A. R. Wallace. (Proceedings, Vol. ii. 163.)

ASIATIC ARCHIPELAGO, Proposed exploring expedition to the. By Jas. Brooke. viii. 443.

BAY OF BENGAL, surface currents of, during the South-West Monsoon. By J. A. Heathcote. xxxii. 234. (Proceedings, Vol. vi. 101, 114.)

BORNEO, Observations on N.W. coast. By Spencer St. John. xxxii. 217. (Proceedings, Vol. vi. 83.)

—— Sketch of the geography of. By John Crawfurd. xxiii. 69.

—— New Maharajabate of Sabak in. By P. L. Sclater. (Proceedings (N.S.) Vol. i. 121.)

—— On rivers Mukah and Oyah in. By Lieut. De Crespigny. (Proceedings, Vol. i. 205; ii. 342; xvii. 133.)

BORNEO, On Northern. By Lieut. De Crespigny. (Proceedings, Vol. xvi. 171.)
—— Journey up the Sadong River. By A. R. Wallace. (Proceedings, Vol. i. 193.)
—— CAYAGAN SULU, near Borneo, Account of. By Capt. Chimmo. (Proceedings, Vol. xv. 384.)
—— SARAWAK and NORTHERN BORNEO. By W. M. Crocker. (Proceedings (N.S.) Vol. iii. 193.)

CEYLON, Positions in. x. 579.

COCOS or KEELING ISLANDS, Account of. Transmitted by Sir E. W. C. R. Owen. i. 66.
—— —— Notes on. By H. O. Forbes. (Proceedings (N.S.) Vol. i. 777.)
COMORO ISLANDS. By Capt. A. De Horsey, R.N. xxxiv. 258.
—— —— By T. S. Leigh. xix. 7.

EASTERN ARCHIPELAGO, Notes of a cruise in, in 1841. By Capt. O. Stanley, R.N. xii. 262.

INDIAN ARCHIPELAGO, Voyages of steamer " Egeron " in, including discovery of Strait Egeron. xlviii. 294.
—— —— On the physical structure and arrangement of the Islands of the. By G. W. Earl. xv. 358.
INDIAN OCEAN, Geography of the bed of. By S. Osborn. xli. 46. (Proceedings, Vol. xv. 28.)
—— —— On the course of the hurricane on the Malabar Coast in April, 1847, and on the position of the " Cleopatra " at the time. By Capt. T. G. Carless. xix. 76.

KALATOA and PULOWEH Isles. By J. Cameron. (Proceedings, Vol. ix. 30.)
KISSER, one of the Serawatti Group, Account of a visit to. By G. W. Earl. Vol. xi. 108.

MADAGASCAR. Account of the Ovahs; sketch of their country, dress, &c. By Capt. Lewis, R.E. v. 230.
—— A memoir on. By Lloyd. xx. 53.
—— Abstract of MSS. books, &c., respecting, during the possession of Mauritius by the French. By W. J. Hamilton. xx. 75.
—— A boat voyage along the coast lakes of East. By Capt. Brooke. xxxvi. 52. (Proceedings, Vol. x. 54.)
—— A visit to the N.E. province of. By Rev. H. Maundrell. xxxvii. 108.
—— Ankova and the Royal Cities. By Rev. W. Ellis. (Proceedings, Vol. x. 55.)
—— Notes on W. coast of. By Capt. Wilson, R.N. xxxvi. 244.
—— By Lieut. Oliver. (Proceedings, Vol. vii. 68.)
—— Explorations in North of. By Dr. Gunst. (Proceedings, Vol. ix. 289.)
—— On the central provinces of. By J. Mullens. xlv. 128. (Proceedings, Vol. xxi. 155.)
—— Visit to Vohimarina. By Bishop of Mauritius. (Proceedings, Vol. xi. 50.)
—— Recent journeys in. By Rev. J. Mullens. xlvii. 47. (Proceedings, Vol. xix. 182.)
—— Journey from Antananarivo to Mojunga. By J. H. Maynard. (Proceedings, Vol. xx. 110.)

MADAGASCAR. History of geographical knowledge of. By Rev. James Sibree, (Proceedings (N.S.) Vol. i. 646.)

MALAY ARCHIPELAGO. On the Physical Geography of the. By A. R. Wallace. xxxiii. 217. (Proceedings, Vol. vii. 206.)

MALDIVES, Commodore Moresby's Report on the Northern Atolls of the. v. 398.

RODRIGUEZ, Island of. Remarks on the country, products, &c. By E. Higgin. xix. 17.

SERAWATTI Group. (*See* KISSER.)

SEYCHELLES. On the Island of Mahi. By Lieut.-Col. Lewis Pelly. xxxv. 231.

SUMATRA, Dutch expedition to Central. By Professor Veth. (Proceedings (N.S.) Vol. i. 759.)

MISCELLANEOUS.

ANEROID BAROMETER, Remarks on. By Col. P. Yorke. xxi. 35.

—— for the purposes of surveying in India. By Dr. Geo. Buist. xxi. 42.

ANTIQUITY OF CONTINENTS, Lecture on comparative, as indicated by distribution of animals. By A. Wallace. (Proceedings, Vol. xxi. 505.)

ARID COUNTRIES, On certain, and causes of their dryness. By Thos. Hopkins. xxvi. 158. (Proceedings, Vol. i. 58.)

—— —— Exploration of. By F. Galton. (Proceedings, Vol. ii. 60.)

ATLANTIC OCEAN, Geography of the bed of. By S. Osborn. xli. 46. (Proceedings, Vol. xv. 28.)

—— —— Sea bed of. Proposed survey. By Dr. Wallich. (Proceedings, vii. 53.)

AURORA BOREALIS. By J. W. Tayler. (Proceedings, Vol. iii. 117.)

BIFURCATE STREAM, Notice of, at Glen Lednoch Head, Perthshire. By T. P. White. (Proceedings, Vol. xiii. 352.)

BREAD PLANTS, The geography of. By Ph. Dr. Michelsen. xxxii. 565.

"BULLDOG," H.M.S., Surveys of. By Sir Leopold M'Clintock. (Proceedings, Vol. v. 62.)

CAÑONS and FJORDS, Remarks on formation of. By R. Brown. xli. 348.

COLUMBUS, Landfall of. By R. H. Major. xli. 193. (Proceedings, Vol. xv. 210.)

—— By Capt. Becher, R.N. xxvi. 189. (Proceedings, Vol. i. 94.)

CURRENTS (Oceanic). On their connection with proposed Central American Canal. By A. G. Findlay. xxiii. 217.

—— (Oceanic) on N.E. coast of S. America. By J. A. Mann. (Proceedings, Vol. vii. 50.)

—— Gibraltar. By Dr. Carpenter. (Proceedings, Vol. xv. 54.) (*See* IRMINGER, under ARCTIC and OCEAN CIRCULATION, GULF STREAM.)

CYCLONES, On the formation of, and tracks they pursue. By Capt. A. Parish. xxvi. 154. (Proceedings, Vol. i. 36.)

CYCLONIC HURRICANES, Chronological Table of 400, in West Indies and North Atlantic. By Andrés Poey. xxv. 291.

LIST OF MAPS AND OTHER ILLUSTRATIONS

CONTAINED IN THE

'JOURNAL' AND 'PROCEEDINGS'

OF THE

ROYAL GEOGRAPHICAL SOCIETY.

I.—THE WORLD.

GEOGRAPHICAL ARRANGEMENT AND NOMENCLATURE, Illustrations to Col. Jackson's Paper on. (Journal, Vol. iv.)

LAND-MASSES.—5 Diagrams to illustrate the paper by Prof. P. Martin Duncan, " On the Formation of the Main Land-Masses." (Proceedings, Vol. xxii.)

OCEANIC CIRCULATION.—Further inquiries on. Diagrams to illustrate Dr. Carpenter's Paper on. (Proceedings, Vol. xviii.)

OCEANIC CURRENTS.—Map to illustrate Findlay's Paper on. (Journal, Vol. xxiii.)

PROJECTION.—Col. James's Projection. (Journal, Vol. xxx.)

—— New Projection of the Sphere. Herschel. (Journal, Vol. xxx.)

SALTNESS OF THE OCEAN.—Chart showing the Distribution of. (Journal, Vol. xlvii.)

VERTICAL DISTANCES.—Table to illustrate Miss Coulthurst's Comparative View of the various Standards used to express Vertical Distances. (Journal, Vol. xix.)

WORLD.—1. Lines of Equal Magnetic Variation or Declination (Isogonic Lines) 1878.
    2. Terrestrial Magnetic Meridians, and Curves or Equal Dip, or Inclination (Isoclinal Lines) 1878. (With the Magnetic Pole in each Hemisphere.)
    3. The Earth's Magnetism.
To accompany the Paper by Capt. F. J. Evans, Hydrographer of the Admiralty. (Proceedings, Vol. xxii.)

II.—POLAR REGIONS.

ARCTIC COASTS.—Examined by Dr. J. Rae. (Journal, Vol. xxii.)

ARCTIC DISCOVERIES.—Map of. (Journal, Vol. viii.)

ARCTIC EXPLORATIONS.—Map to illustrate Dr. Rink's Paper on Dr. Kane's Arctic Explorations.—(Journal, Vol. xxviii.)

ARCTIC LAND EXPEDITION.—Map showing the Route of the recent Arctic Land Expedition. (Journal, Vol. v.)

ARCTIC LAND EXPEDITION.—Map of the Route of the. (Journal, Vol. vi.)

ARCTIC REGIONS.—Map of the range of Temperature in the. 2 Maps. (Journal, Vol. ix.)

—— —— Map to illustrate Inglefield's Route in the. (Journal, Vol. xxiii.)

—— —— Chart illustrating the remarks of Mr. Findlay, on the probable course pursued by Sir John Franklin's expedition, and of Capt. Irminger, on the Arctic Current around Greenland. (Journal. Vol. xxvi.)

—— —— Map to illustrate Kennedy's Route in the. (Journal, Vol. xxiii.)

—— —— Map to illustrate Dr. Rae's Arctic Explorations. (Journal, Vol. xxv.)

—— —— Map to illustrate Capt. Sherard Osborn's Paper on Light in the. (Journal, Vol. xxviii.)

—— —— Map showing the Coasts explored in 1859, in search of the lost ships of Sir John Franklin in 1845. (Journal, Vol. xxxi.)

—— —— Map of the North Polar Regions : to illustrate the paper on the origin and migrations of the Greenland Esquimaux by C. R. Markham, Esq. (Journal, Vol. xxxv.)

—— —— Chart of Coast from Cape York to Smith's Channel. Drawn by Kallihirua (*alias* Erasmus York). Supplement to the Journal, "Arctic Papers for the Expedition of 1875."

—— —— Circumpolar Map. (Proceedings, Vol. xxi.)

—— —— Chart of the Ice-Field between Spitzbergen and Nova Zembla in 1676. (Proceedings, Vol. ix.)

—— —— The Swedish and Dutch Arctic Expeditions of 1878. (Proceedings, Vol. i., New Series.)

—— —— Map of the Barents and Kara Seas, illustrating the Arctic Campaign of 1879. (Proceedings, Vol. ii., New Series.)

BALLENY ISLANDS.—View of the. Antarctic Ocean. (Journal, Vol. ix.)

DECEPTION ISLAND, NEW SOUTH SHETLAND.—By Lieut. E. N. Kendall, 1829. (Journal, Vol. i.)

FRANZ JOSEF LAND, Map of : from a Survey by Julius Payer. (Journal, Vol. xli.)

—— —— SOUTH COAST OF. (Proceedings, Vol. iii., New Series, p. 129.)

GREENLAND.—Map illustrating Rink's Paper on the Continental Ice of. (Journal, Vol. xxiii.)

—— From "Purchas his Pilgrimes." Vol. iii. To illustrate Mr. Markham's Paper. (Journal, Vol. xliii.)

—— SOUTH COAST OF.—Sketch Chart of the : from the Danish Admiralty Survey, corrected to 1873. Supplement to the Journal, "Arctic Papers for the expedition of 1875."

—— SOUTH WEST.—Sketch Chart of : from the Danish Admiralty Survey, corrected to 1873. With Prof. Rafn's adaptation of the ancient Sites from Ivar Bardsen's Chorography. (Journal, Vol. xliii.)

KING WILLIAM LAND.—Showing the Line of retreat of the Franklin Expedition. (Proceedings, Vol. ii., New Series.)

NORTH-WEST PASSAGE.—Map to illustrate McClure's Discovery of the. (Journal, Vol. xxiv.)

NOVAIA ZEMLIA.—Map of. (Journal, Vol. viii.)

NOVAYA ZEMLYA.—The Matyushin Shar (Matotschkin Schar) and part of the East Coast of Novaya Zemlya. (Proceedings, Vol. ii., New Series.)

SMITH SOUND.—Map to illustrate Dr. Kane's Expedition up. (Journal, Vol. xxvi.)

SOUTHERN HEMISPHERE.—Part of the Southern Hemisphere, showing recent discoveries. (Journal, Vol. iii.)

SOUTH POLAR REGIONS.—To illustrate the Paper by Staff-Commander J. E. Davis. (Journal, Vol. xxxix.)

SPITZBERGEN.—Map of: to illustrate the Paper by Prof. Nordenskiöld and Capt. von Otter. (Journal, Vol. xxxix.)

—— Map to illustrate Petermann's Paper on the Sea of. (Journal, Vol. xxiii.)

—— Fac-simile of the latest Edition of Van Keulen's Chart of. 1707. To illustrate Mr. Markham's Paper. (Journal, Vol. xliii.)

ZENO MAP.—(Fac-simile.)　1. To accompany Mr. Major's Paper on the "Site of the lost Colony of Greenland and the Pre-Columbian Discoveries of America." (Journal, Vol. xliii.)

　　　　2. Sketch Map of the Countries referred to in the Zeno narrative. To accompany Mr. Major's Paper. (Journal, Vol. xliii.)

III.— EUROPE.

ADRIATIC SEA.—1. Appearance of the bottom of the.
　　　　2. Course of the descending River.
　　　　3. Currents in the. (Journal, Vol. xlv.)

AITKIN'S ROCK.—Track of H. M. Sloop "Onyx," in search of Aitkin's Rock, under the command of Capt. A. T. E. Vidal, R.N., 1830. (Journal, Vol. i.)

ALBANIA.—Count Karaczay's Map of. (Journal, Vol. xii.)

ATHOS, MOUNT.—(Journal, Vol. vii.)

—— —— Map of the Isthmus of. (Journal, Vol. xvii.)

ARTA, THE GULF OF.—Surveyed in 1830. Drawn by Lieut. James Wolfe, R.N. (Journal, Vol. iii.)

—— —— Argos Amphilochicum. Wall of Limnœa, S.W. Side. Ruins of Limnœa. Ruins at Camarina. (Journal, Vol. iii.)

AZOV, SEA OF.—Capt. Sherard Osborn's Paper on the. (Journal, Vol. xxvii.)

BALKAN.—Map to illustrate Jochmus's Journey in the. (Journal, Vol. xxiv.)

BEAUFORT, VALLEY OF.—Map to illustrate Prof. Chaix's Paper on the. (Journal, Vol. xxv.)

COLUMBRETES ROCKS, near the Coast of Valencia, Spain, by Capt. W. H. Smyth, R.N., K.S.F., F.R.S. (Journal, Vol. i.)

DANUBE, RIVER.—Map to accompany Notes on the Lower Course of the. By Major J. Stokes, R.E., 1859. (Journal, Vol. xxx.)

EPIRUS.—Map of. To accompany the Paper by Major R. Stuart. (Journal, Vol. xxxix.)

FÆRÖE ISLANDS.—Map of the. To illustrate the Route of Nicolo Zeno. (Journal, Vol. xliii.)

GRAHAM ISLAND.—Sketch of the appearance of Graham Island on the 18th of July, 1831, when examined by H.M.S. "Rapid." (Journal, Vol. i.)

GREECE.—Map of the Northern Frontier of. (Journal, Vol. vii.)

—— Maps, etc., to illustrate General Jochmus's Commentaries (seven in number). 1. Taking of Thermus. 2. Defile of Ménélaïon. 3. Brennus against Thermopylæ, etc. 4. Battle of Marathon. 5. Plan of Sellasia. 6. Antiquities in Laconia, etc. 7. Sketch of Laconia and Cynuria, etc. (Journal, Vol. xxvii.)

ICELAND.—Map of. To illustrate the Paper by W. L. Watts, Esq. (Journal, Vol. xlvi.)
—— Map to illustrate the Paper by Admiral Irminger. (Journal, Vol. xliv.)
KUSTENJE AND THE DANUBE.—Map to illustrate Capt. Spratt's Route between. (Journal, Vol. xxvi.)
MILO GROUP, ETC.—Map of the Volcanic Group of Milo, etc., and of the Ancient Town of Melos, by Lieut. Leycester. (Journal, Vol. xxii.)
MINOA AND NISŒA.—Map of. (Journal, Vol. viii.)
NEVA.—Tables illustrating a Memoir on the Congelation of the Neva. (Journal, Vol. v.)
NORWAY AND LAPLAND.—Map of the Coasts of. To illustrate Lieut. G. T. Temple's Paper. (Proceedings, Vol. ii., New Series.)
SANTORIN.—Admiralty Map of. (Journal, Vol. xx.)
—— Views of. To illustrate Lieut. Leycester's Paper. (Journal, Vol. xx.)
URAL MOUNTAINS.—Map of the Southern Ural. Communicated by R. I. Murchison, Esq. (Journal, Vol. xiii.)

IV.—ASIA.

ADEN.—Map of the vicinity of. To accompany the Paper by G. J. Stevens. (Journal, Vol. xliii.)
AFGHANISTAN, ETC.—Map showing Route from Peshawur, through Chitral to Faizabad in Badakshan. From the Exploration made by a Sapper Havildar during 1870. To accompany the Paper by Major T. G. Montgomerie, R.E., F.R.G.S. (Journal, Vol. xlii.)
—— 10 Sketches to illustrate Sir Richard Temple's Paper, "The Highway from the Indus to Candahar." (Proceedings, Vol. ii., New Series.)
—— Map of the Country between Sind and Candahar, showing the course of the proposed Railway. To illustrate Sir Richard Temple's Paper. (Proceedings, Vol. ii., New Series.)
—— 12 Views, etc., illustrating Sir Michael A. Biddulph's Paper, "Pishin and the Routes between India and Candahar." (Proceedings, Vol. ii., New Series.)
AL HADHR, RUINS AT.—(Journal, Vol. xi.)
AMU-DARIA.—Map of the Delta and Mouths of the. From a Sketch Map by Admiral A. Boutakoff (Russian Navy). (Journal, Vol. xxvii.)
AMÚ-DARYA, R.—Mouths and Lower Courses of Amú (17th Century and subsequently). Lower courses of Amú-darya, 1848–59 (after Boutakoff). (Journal, Vol. xlv.)
—— 19 Diagrams, Sections, etc., of the. To illustrate Wood's Notes on the Lower Amú-darya. (Journal, Vol. xlv.)
AMUR RIVER.—Map to illustrate Notes on the. (Journal, Vol. xxviii.)
ANTI-LIBANUS.—Sketch Map of the. From Observations taken in 1878, by C. F. Tyrwhitt Drake, F.R.G.S. To accompany Capt. Burton's Paper. (Journal, Vol. xlii.)
ARABIA.—Map of. Showing the Routes of W. G. Palgrave, Esq., in 1862–3. (Journal, Vol. xxxiv.)
—— Map of. (Journal, Vol. xx.)
—— Map to illustrate Wallin's Journeys in. (Journal, Vol. xxiv.)

P

ARABIA.—Map of Part of. Showing the Route of Lieut.-Col. Pelly. (Journal, Vol. xxxv.)

—— Map of Northern and Central. To illustrate Mr. Blunt's Paper, "A Visit to Jebel Shammar." (Proceedings, Vol. ii., New Series.)

—— Map of Part of the South Coast of Arabia. (Journal, Vol. ix.)

—— Map of the Southern Coast of. Showing the Route of Capt. S. B. Miles and Werner Munzinger in 1870. (Journal, Vol. xli.)

—— Part of South-East Coast of. (Journal, Vol. xv.)

—— South-East Coast of. (Journal, Vol. xvi.)

ARABIA PETRÆA AND PALESTINE.—Map of Part of. (Journal, Vol. ix.)

ARAL SEA.—Map to illustrate Butakoff's Survey of the. (Journal, Vol. xxiii.)

ARAL, LAKE.—Southern Part of; according to the Survey of 1873. To illustrate Wood's Notes. (Journal, Vol. xlv.)

—— —— After Admiral Butakoff. To illustrate Wood's Notes on Lake Aral. (Journal, Vol. xlv.)

ARMENIA AND ASIA MINOR.—Map of. (Journal, Vol. vi.)

ARMENIA, KURDISTAN, AND UPPER MESOPOTAMIA.—Maps illustrating a Tour in. By J. G. Taylor, H.M. Consul for Kurdistan. (Journal, Vol. xxxviii.)

ASIA, CENTRAL.—Constructed from the latest English and Russian documents; adapted to Recent Astronomical Observations. By J. Arrowsmith. 1872. (Journal, Vol. xlv.)

—— —— Map of. To accompany the Paper, by Capt. H. Trotter, R.E., on the Geographical Results of Sir T. D. Forsyth's Mission to Kashghar, 1873–74. (Journal, Vol. xlviii.)

ASIA MINOR.—Map of part of. From Scutari to Vezir Köpri. (Journal, Vol. ix.)

—— —— Western portion of. (Journal, Vol. viii.)

—— —— Map of Routes in. (Journal, Vol. vii.)

ASIA WESTERN.—Sketch, showing the Routes of Lieuts. Conolly and Burnes. (Journal, Vol. iv.)

ASSAM OVER THE PATKOI RANGE INTO HOOKOONG.—Map showing the Route from. To illustrate the Paper by H. L. Jenkins, Esq. (Journal, Vol. xli.)

BAGHDAD TO BUSRAH.—Map to illustrate Mr. Loftus' Journey from. (Journal, Vol. xxvi.)

BELUCHISTAN AND EASTERN PERSIA.—Sketch Map of, to accompany the Papers by Col. F. J. Goldsmid, C.B., and J. W. Barns, Esq., C.E. (Journal, Vol. xxxvii.)

BENGAL, BAY OF.—Chart of the: showing the Currents of the S.W. Monsoon. by Lieut. J. A. Heathcote, H.M.I. Navy. (Journal, Vol. xxxii.)

BHAMO AND MOMEIN.—Map of the country between: showing the route of the expedition under the command of Major E. B. Sladen. (Journal, Vol. xli.)

BHAMO AND MUNG-MAU. Route Map between. Through the Hills of the Lenna Kahhyens, by Ney Elias, Esq., 1875. (Journal, Vol. xlvi.)

BHAWULPORE STATES (PUNJAB).—Map of the, to accompany the Paper by J. W. Barns, Esq., F.G.S. (Journal, Vol. xlii.)

BOLOR HIGHLANDS.—Map to accompany Paper on the. By M. Veniukof. (Proceedings, Vol. xiii.)

BOLOR MOUNTAINS, and the Upper Sources of the Amu Daria, explanatory Map to Article on the Pamir. By M. Veniukof. (Journal, Vol. xxxvi.)

BORNEO ISLAND.—Part of the N.W. Coast of Borneo, to illustrate the Paper of Spencer St. John, Esq., H.B.M. Consul-General for Borneo. (Journal, Vol. xxxii.)

—— NORTH. (Proceedings, Vol. iii., New Series, p. 256.)

BURMA, ETC.—Map to illustrate Capt. Yule's Paper on the Geography of. (Journal, Vol. xxvii.)

BUSTAR DEPENDENCY.—Sketch Map of the, by Capt. T. Holdich, R.E. (Proceedings, Vol. i., New Series.)

BUSHIR TO SHIRAZ, AND THENCE TO KAZERUN.—Map to illustrate General Monteith's and Consul Abbott's Route from. (Journal, Vol. xxvii.)

CAMBODIA.—Map of Part of the Province of Siemrab (Cambodia), to accompany the Paper by Dr. Bastian. (Journal, Vol. xxxv.)

—— ETC.—Map of Cambodia, the Lao Country, etc.: to illustrate the Route and Notes of M. Henri Mouhot, 1859–61. (Journal, Vol. xxxii.)

CARIA AND LYCIA.—Map of. By Mr. Hoskyn. (Journal, Vol. xii.)

CAUCASUS.—Map of the. (Journal, Vol. xxi.)

CHINA.—Sketch Map of the South-Western Frontiers of China, from a Map compiled by the French Missionaries. (Proceedings, Vol. xv.)

—— Map to illustrate the journey from Hankow to Tali-fu of Mr. A. R. Margary. (Journal, Vol. xlvi.)

—— Map showing the proposed Overland Trade Routes from India and British Burmah to. To accompany the Paper by J. Coryton, Esq. (Journal, Vol. xlv.)

—— CENTRAL AND SOUTHERN.—Map of, illustrating Mr. McCarthy's Journey from Chin-Kiang to Bhamo, 1877. (Proceedings, Vol. i., New Series.)

—— EASTERN.—Maps to accompany Papers on Journeys in, by G. J. Morrison, M.I.C.E., 1878. (Proceedings, Vol. ii., New Series.)

—— NORTH AND INNER MONGOLIA.—Route Map of Journey through, by Dr. Bushell. (Journal, Vol. xliv.)

—— SOUTH-EASTERN COAST OF.—From Sir Robert Dudley's Arcano del Mare. Vol. ii., 1647. (Journal, Vol. xliv.)

—— WESTERN AND EASTERN TIBET.—Route Map of Capt. W. J. Gill's Journey in. 1877. (Journal, Vol. xlviii.)

CHUSAN.—Map to illustrate Davis's Paper on. (Journal, Vol. xxiii.)

COCHIN.—Sketch to illustrate the Paper on. (Journal, Vol. iii.)

CONSTANTINOPLE TO MOSUL.—Route from. (Journal, Vol. x.)

COORG.—Map of. To accompany the Paper by George Bidie, M.B. (Journal, Vol. xxxix.)

CURIA MURIA ISLES.—Map of. (Journal, Vol. xi.)

CUTCH, RUNN OF, ETC.—Map to illustrate Sir H. Bartle E. Frere's Notes on the. (Journal, Vol. xl.)

DAMASCUS, HAURAN, AND LEBANON.—Map to illustrate the Rev. Mr. Porter's Paper on Damascus, Hauran, and Lebanon. (Journal, Vol. xxvi.)

EASTERN ARCHIPELAGO.—(Journal, Vol. xv.)

EASTERN TURKISTAN.—Sketch Map of: showing the Hydrography of the Pamir to the East, the true Courses of the Yarkand and Karakash Rivers, with all the Routes from Ladak across the Karakoram and adjacent Ranges. To illustrate the Paper of G. W. Hayward. (Journal, Vol. xl.)

Kandahar to India.—Sketch Map of a Portion of the march of the Tal—Chótiáli Field Force from Kandahar to India in the spring of 1879. Compiled from personal observation and from information obtained, by Lieut. R. C. Temple, b.s.c. (Journal, Vol. xlix.)

Kárún River.—Sketch of the. (Journal, Vol. xiv.)

Kashgar.—Map of the Route from Badakshan, across the Pamir Steppe to, with the Southern Branch of the Upper Oxus. From the Survey made by the Mirza, in 1868–69. To accompany the Paper by Major T. G. Montgomerie, r.e., f.r.g.s. (Journal, Vol. xli.)

Kashmere, &c.—Two Sections of the Map of George Ludwig von ——. Reduced to one fourth. (From a tracing sent to the R.G.S. by M. de Khanikof). (Proceedings, Vol. x.)

Kashmír.—Map of the Valley of. (Journal, Vol. vi.)

Kashmir.—Map of the valley of. From Surveys made by Capt. T. G. Montgomerie, under the direction of the Surveyor General of India. To illustrate the Notes of Capt. Godwin Austen and William Purdon, Esq., to which is added a Sketch of surrounding Countries. (Journal, Vol. xxxi.)

Khiva.—Khanate of. After Russian sources by Major Herbert Wood, r.e. (Journal, Vol. xlv.)

Khorassan.—Map of the Northern Frontier of. With parts of Irak and Mazandarán. To illustrate Reports by Capt. the Hon. G. Napier. (Journal, Vol. xlvi.)

Khuzistan.—Map of. (Journal, Vol. xvi.)

Kishm Island.—Map of. To accompany the Paper by Lieut. Col. Lewis Pelly. (Journal, Vol. xxxiv.)

Koladyn.—Map to illustrate Tickell's Voyage up the. (Journal, Vol. xxiv.)

Kong, or Cassia River.—Reduced from the large Map by Albert S. Bickmore, Esq., m.a. With Sketch Map illustrating Mr. Bickmore's Journey from Canton to Hankow. (Journal, Vol. xxxviii.)

Kooloo, Lahoul, and Spiti.—A Map to illustrate Capt. Harcourt's Paper on the Himalayan Valleys of. With a Sketch Map of the Passes from India to Eastern Turkistan. (Journal, Vol. xli.)

Korea, Strait of.—Tsu-sima Island in the Strait of Korea. To illustrate the Paper by Laurence Oliphant, Esq., 1863. (Journal, Vol. xxxiii.)

Kuldja District and the Russo-Chinese Frontier in Turkistan.—Reduced from Col. Walker's Map. (Proceedings, Vol. ii., New Series.)

Kumaón and Garhwál.—Map of. (Journal, Vol. xxi.)

Kurdistán.—Map of. (Journal, Vol. xi.)

—— Map of Part of. Illustrating the Journeys and Researches of Mr. Consul Taylor. (Journal, Vol. xxxv.)

Kurdistan and Part of Persia.—Map of. (Journal, Vol. viii.)

Kurrachee to Gwadur.—Map of the Coast from. Showing the Route traversed by Major Goldsmid and Party. (Journal, Vol. xxxiii.)

Leh (Ladak) to the City of Yarkund.—Summer Route from. By Capt. T. G. Montgomerie, r.e. (Journal, Vol. xxxvi.)

Leh and Ilchí.—Map of the Country between. Showing the Routes taken by Mr. Johnson, Civil-Assistant G. T. Survey, 1865. (Journal, Vol. xxxvii.)

Madras Presidency.—The Hill Districts in the. To accompany Mr. C. R. Markham's Paper. (Journal, Vol. xxxvi.)

MAGHIAN.—Map of. By M. Fedchenko. (Journal, Vol. xliii.)

MAHANUDDY RIVER (CENTRAL INDIA).—Sketch Map of the Basin of the. To accompany the Paper by R. Temple, Esq. (Journal, Vol. xxxv.)

MAHAVILLAGANGA RIVER, AT PERADENIA, CEYLON.—A View. (Journal, Vol. iii.)

MALABAR COAST.—Sketch to illustrate Capt. Carless's Paper on the Hurricane off the. (Journal, Vol. xix.)

MALAY ARCHIPELAGO.—Map to illustrate a Paper on the Physical Geography of the. By Alfred Russell Wallace, Esq., 1863. (Journal, Vol. xxxiii.)

MALDIVA ISLANDS.—From Capt. Horsburgh's Chart, 1814. (Journal, Vol. ii.)

MANCHURIA.—Map of the Russian Possessions in. To accompany the Paper by Rev. W. V. Lloyd. (Journal, Vol. xxxvii.)

—— Map to accompany the Notes on. By the Rev. Alexander Williamson. (Journal, Vol. xxxix.)

—— Map to accompany Notes of a Journey through. By the Archimandrite Palladius. (Journal, Vol. xlii.)

—— &c.—Map to illustrate the Routes of Messrs. Michie and Grant, the former from Tien-tsin to Moukden in Manchucia, the latter from Peking across the Desert of Gobi to Kiachta. (Journal, Vol. xxxiii.)

MEDITERRANEAN TO THE DEAD SEA.—Map showing the Levelling from. Executed by Capt. Wilson, R.E., under the direction of Sir Henry James, R.E., F.R.S., Director of the Ordnance Survey. (Journal, Vol. xxxvi.)

MENAM AND OTHER SIAMESE RIVERS.—Sketch of. From the Surveys and Observations of the American Missionaries. Communicated by Mr. Consul Parkes. 1855. (Proceedings, Vol. v.)

MESH-HED TO THE HERI RUD.—Dr. Forbes' Route from. (Journal, Vol. xiv.)

MESOPOTAMIA.—Trigonometrical Survey of a part of, from Sheriat-el-Beytha (on the Tigris) to Tel Ibrahim. To accompany the Paper by Lieut. J. B. Bewsher. (Journal, Vol. xxxvii.)

MIDIAN.—Map of the Land of. Constructed from Reconnaissances and Surveys made by Officers of the Egyptian General Staff, under the command of Capt. R. F. Burton, 1878. (Journal, Vol. xlix.)

MOKHÁ to SAN'Á.—Map of. (Journal, Vol. viii.)

MONGOLIA, WESTERN.—Map to illustrate a Journey through. By Ney Elias, Jun., F.R.G.S., July, 1872, to January, 1873. (Journal, Vol. xliii.)

NAKAB EL HAJAR.—Map of a Route to the Ruins of, in Arabia. (Journal, Vol. vii.)

NOR-ZAISAN LAKE, AND ITS NEIGHBOURHOOD (CHINESE TARTARY).—To illustrate the Paper of M. Abramof. (Journal, Vol. xxxv.)

OMAN, IN ARABIA.—Map of. (Journal, Vol. vii.)

OXUS, UPPER.—3 Sketches taken from Chinese Map. To illustrate Col. Yule's Papers. (Journal, Vol. xlii.)

—— UPPER REGION.—Photographic reduction of a Chinese Map of the Upper Oxus Region, with Autograph Transciptions by Julius Klaproth, to whom it belonged. (Journal, Vol. xlii.)

PALESTINE.—Physical Map of. To accompany the Paper by Major C. W. Wilson, R.E. (Journal, Vol. xliii.)

—— Map to illustrate Mr. Poole's Route in. (Journal, Vol. xxvi.)

PALESTINE.—Map to illustrate Robinson's Journey in. (Journal, Vol. xxiv.)

PAMIR STEPPE.—Map of the, and Neighbouring Districts. To illustrate the Letters of Col. Gordon and Members of the Kashgar Mission. (Proceedings, Vol. xviii.)

PAUMBUM PASSAGE.—Gulf of Manaar, 1833. (Journal, Vol. iv.)

PEKING.—Plan of the city of. From a Survey by Capt. Bouvier, of the French Engineers, 1862. To illustrate the Paper by W. Lockhart, Esq. (Journal, Vol. xxxvi.)

PERAK, AND ADJACENT NATIVE STATES.—Sketch Map of. To illustrate the Paper by W. Barrington D'Almeida. (Journal, Vol. xlvi.)

PERSIA.—Map to illustrate Routes from Teheran to Herat, and from Teheran to Bushire. By Capt. Claude Clerk. (Journal, Vol. xxxi.)

——— Routes in. (Journal, Vol. xi.)

——— Map to illustrate Consul Abbott's Routes in. (Journal, Vol. xxv.)

——— Section from Bushire to Teheran. To accompany the Paper by Major O. St. John. (Journal, Vol. xxxviii.)

——— AND INDIA.—Sketch to illustrate a Memoir, by E. Stirling, Esq., on the Political State of the Countries between Persia and India. (Journal, Vol. v.)

PERSIAN GULF.—Map of the Eastern Shores of the Persian Gulf. (Journal, Vol. v.)

PERSIA, EASTERN.—Map of. To illustrate the Paper by Major-Gen. Sir F. J. Goldsmid. (Journal, Vol. xliii.)

PISHIN VALLEY AND UPPER BASIN OF THE LORA.—Constructed from the surveys and reconnaissances executed by officers attached to the forces serving in Southern Afghanistan, 1879, collatted with Major Wilson's Map by W. J. Turner. (Proceedings, Vol. ii., New Series.)

RED SEA.—Map of the. (Journal, Vol. vi.)

RUSSIAN AND CHINESE FRONTIER.—Map of the. Illustrating the Journey of Semenof to the Tian-Shan Mountains and River Jaxartes, and Golubefs Issyk-kul Expedition. (Journal, Vol. xxxi.)

SAGHALIN.—The Island of. From Russian Authorities. To accompany the Paper by Col. Veniukof. (Journal, Vol. xlii.)

SARAWAK AND SINGAPÚR.—Meteorological Observations at. (Diagrams.) (Journal, Vol. xvi.)

SEISTAN.—Map of. To accompany the Paper by Major-Gen. Sir H. C. Rawlinson. (Journal, Vol. xliii.)

SHAN STATES.—Sketch Map to illustrate Journal of a Tour to Karen-ni, for the purpose of opening a Trading Road to the Shan Traders, from Mobyay and the adjacent Shan States, through Toungu. Protracted from the Notes, Bearings, etc., of Edward O'Riley, Esq. (Journal, Vol. xxxii.)

SHAN-TUNG.—Sketch Map showing the Mineral and Silk Districts of the Province of. (China.) To accompany the Paper by J. Markham, Esq., H.M. Consul at Chefoo. (Journal, Vol. xl.)

SIAM AND CAMBODIA.—Sketch Map from Bangkok in Siam, to Pelombing in Cambodia. To accompany the Journal of D. O. King, Esq., 1857–8. (Journal, Vol. xxx.)

——— AND THE ADJACENT STATES.—Sketch of. To illustrate Geographical Notes on Siam, by Harry Parkes, Esq., H.B.M. Consul at Amoy, 1855. (Proceedings, Vol. v.)

——— Map to illustrate Consul Parkes' Paper on. (Journal, Vol. xxvi.)

SIAM, GULF OF, AND ADJACENT DISTRICTS IN LAOS AND CAMBODIA.—To illustrate the Journey of Mr. H. G. Kennedy. (Journal, Vol. xxxvii.)

SIKHIM.—Map of. To illustrate Dr. Hooker's Paper. (Journal, Vol. xx.)

SINAI, MOUNT.—The Peninsula of. A Sketch from Observations on the ground, by the Rev. F. W. Holland, M.A. (Journal, Vol. xxxix.)

SULIMANI MOUNTAINS on the Afghan Frontier of British India. (Proceedings, Vol. i., New Series.)

SYRIA, ETC.—Map of. Showing the Routes of Dr. Charles T. Beke, 1861-2. (Journal, Vol. xxxii.)

TABRÍZ TO GILÁN.—Map of Route from. (Journal, Vol. x.)

THECHES, MOUNT (of Xenophon).—Sketch Map to accompany the Paper by M. Rorit, on the identification of. (Journal, Vol. xl.)

TIBET, &c.—Map of the head Waters of the Kin Char Kiang, Lan Tsan Kiang, Now Kiang, and Great¹ River of Tibet. Laid down from Chinese Maps by T. T. Cooper. (Proceedings, Vol. xiii.)

—— Maps showing the Route Survey from Nepal to Lhasa, and thence through the Upper Valley of the Brahmaputra, made by Pundit ——. From the Map compiled by Capt. T. G. Montgomerie, R.E. (Journal, Vol. xxxviii.)

—— Map to illustrate Strachey's Paper on. (Journal, Vol. xxiii.)

—— GREAT.—Map illustrating the Journey of the Pundit Nain Singh through, from Ladákh to Assam. To accompany the Paper by Capt. H. Trotter, R.E. (Journal, Vol. xlvii.)

—— AND NEPAL.—Map showing Routes of Native Explorers in. To illustrate the Papers by Mr. Markham and Lieut. Col. T. G. Montgomerie. (Journal, Vol. xlv.)

TIGRIS RIVER.—From Ctesiphon to Mósul. (Journal, Vol. ix.)

TRANS-INDUS.—Sketch Map of the Glaciers of the Mustakh Range (Trans-Indus) and Valley of Skardo, etc. Surveyed by Capt. H. H. Godwin Austen. (Journal, Vol. xxxiv.)

—— COUNTRIES, INCLUDING GILGIT, DILAIL, YASSIN, ETC.—By Geo. J. W. Hayward. (Journal, Vol. xli.)

—— FRONTIER.—Map showing Recent acquisitions to the Geography of the Districts bordering the British Trans-Indus Frontier between Peshawur and Dera Ismael Khan. (Journal, Vol. xxxii.)

TRANS-NARYN COUNTRY.—Map to illustrate Baron Osten Sacken's Route, from Vernoe to the. (Central Asia.) (Journal, Vol. xl.)

TRAVANCORE COAST AND BACK WATERS.—Map of Portion of the. Showing the Anchorage at Alipee. To accompany Mr. C. R. Markham's Paper. (Journal, Vol. xxxvi.)

TROY.—Map to accompany Dr. Forchhammer's Paper on the Topography of Troy. (Journal, Vol. xii.)

TULÚL EL SAFÁ.—Route Map of the. From Observations taken in May, 1871, by R. F. Burton, F.R.G.S., and C. F. Tyrrwhitt Drake. To illustrate Capt. R. F. Burton's Paper. (Journal, Vol. xlii.)

TURCOMAN STEPPE AND NORTHERN KHORASSAN.—To illustrate Sir H. Rawlinson's Paper, "The Road to Merv." (Proceedings, Vol. i., New Series.)

WURKALLAY BARRIER.—To accompany Mr. C. R. Markham's Paper. (Journal, Vol. xxxvi.)

YANG-TSZE-KIANG, THE, from Tung-Ting Lake to Chung-King.—To accompany the Paper by R. Swinhoe, Esq., H.M. Consul. (Journal, Vol. xl.)

V.—AFRICA.

AFRICA, CENTRAL, Map to illustrate Dr. Vogel's Journey to. (Journal, Vol. xxv.)

—— INTERIOR OF.—Dr. Livingstone's Explorations in. (Journal, Vol. xxvii.)

—— NORTH.—Map showing the Caravan Routes between Tripoli and Ghadamis. To accompany the Account of Ghadamis by C. H. Dickson, Esq. (Journal, Vol. xxx.)

—— —— Map of. To illustrate the Question, " Is the Quorra the Nigir of the Ancients ? " By W. Leake. (Journal, Vol. ii.)

—— —— Map to accompany a General Historical Description of the state of Human Society in Northern Central Africa, by Dr. H. Barth. (Journal, Vol. xxx.)

—— EAST CENTRAL.—Sketch of the supposed Route of Dr. Livingstone, and probable place of the attack by the Mavite, by J. Kirk, M.D., H.M. Vice-Consul, Zanzibar. (Proceedings, Vol. xi.)

—— EASTERN.—Map to illustrate the Explorations in. By Count Carl Krockow. (Journal, Vol. xxxvi.)

—— —— Map showing the Routes of some Native Caravans from the Coast into the Interior of. From information collected by the Rev. T. Wakefield, Missionary at Mambasa ; also of two Personal Journeys to the Southern Galla Country made by the Revs. T. Wakefield and C. New in 1865 and 1866-7. (Journal, Vol. xl.)

—— —— Map of the Routes in Eastern Africa between Zanzibar, the Great Lakes, and the Nile, Explored and Surveyed by Capt. J. H. Speke, 1857-63. (Journal, Vol. xxxiii.)

—— EAST.—Map of the Routes between Zanzibar and the Great Lakes in Eastern Africa, in 1857, 1858, and 1859, by Capts. R. F. Burton and J. H. Speke. (Journal, Vol. xxix.)

—— —— The East African Lakes, showing their relation to the Source of the Nile. With Map of the Lake Region :—1. According to Burton and Speke, May, 1858. 2. Speke, 1859. 3. Speke and Grant, 1863. 4. Sir S. W. Baker, 1864. (Journal, Vol. xxxvii.)

—— —— Map to illustrate the progress of the East Africa Expedition. (Journal, Vol. xxviii.)

—— —— Sketch Map of the Route of the R.G.S. East African Expedition from Dar-es-Salaam to Lake Nyassa, 1879. (Proceedings, Vol. ii., New Series.)

—— —— Map of the Route of the R.G.S. East African Expedition to Lakes Nyassa and Tanganyika, constructed from Mr. Thompson's Original Map, collated with the Routes of other Explorers, by W. J. Turner. (Proceedings, Vol. ii., New Series.)

—— Sketch Map of Native Routes from Dar-es-Salaam towards the head of Lake Nyassa. From Information obtained by Mr. Keith Johnson, R.G.S., Eastern African Expedition, 1879. (Proceedings, Vol. i. New Series.)

—— —— Sketch Map of Route from Lake Nyassa to Ugogo. By Mr. H. B. Cotterill. (Proceedings, Vol. xxii.)

—— EQUATORIAL.—Map illustrating M. Du Chaillu's Routes in, 1864-65 (Journal, Vol. xxxvi.)

—— WEST COAST OF.—To illustrate Capt. Belcher's Observations. (Journal, Vol. ii.)

—— —— Map of. (Journal, Vol. vi.)

—— South.—Map of: illustrating the Journey of Major Serpo Pinto from Benguella to Natal, 1877-79. (Proceedings, Vol. i., New Series.)

AFRICA, WEST COAST OF.—Map of Zulu, Amatonga, Natal, and Kaffir Land, from the Sketches of Messrs. Sanderson, Paxton, Rider, and Newling. To illustrate Papers by John Sanderson, Esq., 1861. (Journal, Vol. xxxii.)

—— —— Map to illustrate Mr. Anderson's Journey in. (Journal, Vol. xxv.)

—— —— Sketch to accompany a Trading Trip into the Orange River Free States, and the Country of the Transvaal Republic in 1851–52. By John Sanderson, Esq. (Journal, Vol. xxx.)

—— —— Sketch to illustrate the Paper by W. D. Cooley, Esq. (Journal, Vol. iii.)

—— —— Map of the Central Portion of. Illustrating Dr. Holub's Journeys, 1873–9. (Proceedings, Vol. ii., New Series.)

—— —— Map of. To illustrate the Paper by James Fox Wilson, Esq., and Dr. Livingstone's theory of Ancient Lakes. (Journal, Vol. xxxv.)

—— TEMPERATE. To illustrate a Paper by Sir Bartle Frere. (Proceedings, Vol. iii., New Series, p. 64.)

—— SOUTH-EAST.—Map to accompany a Journey from Inhambane to Zoutpansberg, in 1855–6, to which is added the parts of South Africa, adjacent, by J. McQueen, Esq. (Journal, Vol. xxxii.)

—— SOUTH-EASTERN.—Sketch Map of Part of. To illustrate the Journeys of Dr. Lacerda (1798), the Pombeiros (1806–11), and Major Monteiro. (1831–32). In Supplement to Journal, "The Lands of Cazembe," 1873.

—— SOUTHERN.—Outline Map of. To illustrate the Analysis of Capt. Owen's Voyage. (Journal, Vol. iii.)

—— Map of the S.W. portion of. (Journal, Vol. viii.)

—— WESTERN.—Map to illustrate Travels in the Yoruba and Nupe Countries. Performed by Daniel J. May, Esq., R.N., 1858. (Journal, Vol. xxx.)

ALBERT N'YANZA.—Map of. And of the Routes leading to its Discovery in 1864, by Samuel White Baker, Esq. (Proceedings, Vol. x.)

—— —— Map of the. And of the Routes leading to its Discovery in 1864, by Samuel W. Baker, Esq. (Journal, Vol. xxxvi.)

BAMANGWATO COUNTRY.—Map of the. To illustrate Capt. Patterson's Paper. (Proceedings, Vol. i., New Series.)

BARKLY TO GUBULUWAYO (South Africa).—Route Map of A. C. Bailie's Journey from. (Journal, Vol. xlviii.)

BENZERTA.—The Lakes of. (Journal, Vol. xvi.)

BERENICE.—View of the Ruins of. (Journal, Vol. vi.)

BINUÉ RIVER, UPPER.—Map of the. From a Survey by Mr. E. R. Flegel, of the Church Missionary Society's Expedition, 1879. (Proceedings, Vol. ii., New Series.)

BONAH TO KOSTANTINAH.—Map of Route from. (Journal, Vol. viii.)

BONNY AND BRASS RIVERS.—Chart of Creeks and Rivers between. Surveyed by R. D. Boler and R. Knight, Sept. 1874. (Journal, Vol. xlvi.)

CAMEROONS, MOUNT.—The Vicinity of. From a Drawing by the Rev. T. J. Comber, Baptist Missionary Society, 1877. (Proceedings, Vol. i., New Series.)

CAPE COLONY.—Map of. (Journal, Vol. vi.)

CAPE OF GOOD HOPE.—Chart of the Currents off the. To accompany Capt. Toynbee's Paper "On the Specific Gravity, Temperature, and Currents of the Sea," the result of a portion of five Consecutive yearly Voyages from England to India. Projected from the Log-books by S. Comm. C. George, Map Curator R.G.S. (Journal, Vol. xxxv.)

CAPE OF GOOD HOPE. Sketch of the Cape of Good Hope Colony. (Journal, Vol. v.)

CHAD, LAKE, AND NEIGHBOURING REGIONS.—To illustrate the Paper by Dr. Nachtigal. (Journal, Vol. xlvi.)

CHADDA RIVER.—Dr. Baikie's Trip up the. (Journal, Vol. xxv.)

CHOBE RIVER.—(Proceedings, Vol. iii., New Series, p. 256.)

CONGO RIVER.—Reduction of Lieut. Grandy's Map of his Route from Ambriz to the River Congo, 1873-4. (Journal, Vol. xlvi.)

—— Neighbourhood of San Salvador. (Proceedings, Vol. iii., New Series, p. 64.)

DAMARA LAND.—Map of the principal part of. Based on Prismatic Compass Triangulation checked by observed Latitudes. By C. J. Andersson, Esq., Cape Town, 1866. (Journal, Vol. xxxvi.)

DAR-ES-SALAM TO KILWA.—The Slave Caravan Route from. To accompany the Paper by Capt. F. Elton. (Journal, Vol. xliv.)

EGYPTIAN DESERT.—Map of the Egyptian Desert between Keneh and Suez, by J. Wilkinson, Esq. (Journal, Vol. ii.)

GAMBIA AND CASAMANZA RIVERS.—Sketch to illustrate Paper on the supposed junction of the Gambia and Casamanza Rivers. (Journal, Vol. iii.)

GASA COUNTRY.—Route Map of the. Illustrating the Journey of Umzila, King of Gasa. Reduced from the original Map constructed by Mr. St. Vincent Erskine. (Journal, Vol. xlv.)

JAMOOR RIVER.—Mouths of the. (Journal, Vol. xvi.)

JUBB AND HAINES RIVERS.—Lower Courses of the. (Journal, Vol. xiv.)

KAGÉI TO TABORA.—Map of Route from. By the Rev. C. T. Wilson. (Proceedings, Vol. ii., New Series.)

KILIMA-NDJARO MOUNTAINS.—Map of the Snowy Mountains, Kilima-ndjaro, illustrating the Paper of Baron C. Von der Decken. (Journal, Vol. xxxiv.)

KORDOFAN AND DARFUR.—Map of Routes in. Constructed from the reconnaissances made by Officers of the Egyptian General Staff, 1875-76, by W. J. Turner. (Journal, Vol. xlix.)

KWARA, YÉU, AND CHADA RIVERS.—(Journal, Vol. viii.) (See also Quorra and Niger.)

LIMPOPO RIVER.—Mouth of the. By St. Vincent W. Erskine. (Journal, Vol. xxxix.)

—— —— Map of Route from the Tati Settlement to Delagoa Bay. To illustrate the Paper by Capt. F. Elton. (Journal, Vol. xlii.)

—— AND ZAMBESI RIVERS.—Sketch Map of Mr. Baines' Routes between the. (Journal, Vol. xli.)

LUFIGI RIVER.—Map of the two main Mouths of the. From a Sketch by Capt. Wharton, H.M.S. "Shearwater." (Proceedings, Vol. xviii.)

MADAGASCAR.—Physical Map of. By the Rev. James Sibree, reduced from Dr. Mullens' Map. (Proceedings, Vol. i., New Series.)

—— Map to illustrate Col. Lloyd's Paper. (Journal, Vol. xx.)

—— Part of. From the latest Surveys by Joseph Mullens, D.D. (Journal, Vol. xlvi.)

—— The Central Provinces of. By Joseph Mullens, D.D. (Journal, Vol. xlv.)

MADAGASCAR, SOUTH-EAST, AND THE IBARA COUNTRY.—By Joseph Mullens, D.D. From the Surveys of Messrs. Sibree, Shaw, and Richardson. (Journal, Vol. xlvii.)

—— WEST-CENTRAL.—By Joseph Mullens, D.D. From Messrs. Grandidier, Sewell, &c. (Journal, Vol. xlvii.)

MAROCCO.—From Observations in 1830. (Journal, Vol. i.)

MOSELEKATSE.—Map to illustrate Mr. Moffat's Route to. (Journal, Vol. xxvi.)

NATAL. Map of the Colony of. To accompany the Paper by Dr. R. J. Mann. (Journal, Vol. xxxvi.)

N'GAMI, LAKE.—Map to illustrate the Route to. (Journal, Vol. xx.)

NIGER, RIVER.—Country of the. Map to accompany Notes of a Journey from Bida in Nupe, to Kano in Haussa. Performed by Dr. W. B. Baikie, R.N., 1862. (Journal, Vol. xxxvii.) (See also Quorra and Kwara.)

NILE and its Western Affluents, between the Albert Nyanza on the South, and the Sobat on the North. Founded on the Astronomical Observations, Bearings, and Distances, of John Petherick, Esq. (Journal, Vol. xxxv.)

—— Map of the, from Es-suan to Alleïs. (Journal, Vol. ix.)

—— Sections of the Valley of the Nile in Egypt. (Journal, Vol. ix.)

—— RIVER.—Sketch Map of Route from Gondokoro to Dufli, by J. Kemp, Esq., Sept., Oct., 1874. (Proceedings, Vol. xix.)

—— Sources of the. Rough Sketch of Countries North and South of the Equator on the Meridian of Khartúm. (Proceedings, Vol. v.)

—— Upper Countries of the Nile. To illustrate M. Linant's Journey. (Journal, Vol. ii.)

—— UPPER.—Map of the. To illustrate the Reports of Col. Gordon and M. Gessi, by W. J. Turner. (Proceedings, Vol. xxi.)

NYASSI, or the Great Lake of Southern Africa. (Journal, Vol. xv.)

NYASSI LAKE, THE SHIRE RIVER, &c.—From the MS. Map by Dr. Kirk. With Section. (Journal, Vol. xxxv.)

—— —— Sketch Map of. By Mr. E. D. Young, 1876. (Proceedings, Vol. xx.)

—— —— Route Survey of the Western Side of (Northern Portion). By Mr. James Stewart, C.E., 1879. (Proceedings, Vol. ii., New Series.)

—— —— Route Survey of the Western Side of. By Mr. Jas. Stewart, C.E., Livingstonia Mission, 1878. (Proceedings, Vol. i., New Series.)

—— AND TANGANYIKA.—Route Survey between. By Mr. Jas. Stewart, C.E., 1879. (Proceedings, Vol. ii., New Series.)

—— North end of. (Proceedings, Vol. iii., New Series, p. 320.)

OKAVANGO RIVER.—(Proceedings, Vol. iv., New Series, p. 44.)

OLD CALABAR, OR CROSS RIVER, THE.—(Journal, Vol. xiv.)

QUANZA RIVER.—Chart of the. From the Bar to the Livingstone Falls. Surveyed and Drawn by Carl Alexanderson, 1873–74. (Journal, Vol. xlvi.)

QUORRA, OR NIGER, RIVER.—Map of. (Journal, Vol. xi.)

—— —— The Course of the Quorra, the Joliba, or Niger of Park, from the Journals of Messrs. Richard and John Lander, with their Route from Badagry to the Northward, in 1830. (Journal, Vol. i.) (See also Kwara and Niger.)

RED SEA.—Map of the Red Sea, from the late Survey. (Journal, Vol. v.)

REGIO AROMATIFERA.—Sketch of the. To illustrate Mr. Cooley's Paper. (Journal, Vol. xix.).

RUFIGI RIVER.—Track and Soundings of Steam Cutter up the. By Capt. Sulivan, R.N., assisted by Sub-Lieut. F. J. Grassie, R.N., H.M.S. "London," 24th Feb., 1875. (Journal, Vol. xlv.)

RUFU, OR KINGANI RIVER (Eastern Africa).—Map of. To accompany the Paper by Frederick Holmwood, Esq. (Journal, Vol. xlvii.)

SCHWÁ.—Map to illustrate Dr. Beke's Excursion in. (Journal, Vol. xii.)

SENAAR.—Sketch of the Province of. (Journal, Vol. v.)

SHIRE AND ZAMBESI RIVERS.—The Course of the River Shire, below Lake Nyassa and the River Zambesi, below Kabrabasa. To illustrate the Papers of Dr. David Livingstone. (Journal, Vol. xxxi.)

SOCOTRA ISLAND.—Map of the. (Journal, Vol. v.)

SOUFFLEUR POINT, MAURITIUS.—(A View). (Journal, Vol. iii.)

SUAKIN to RA-SAI.—Map showing Route of the Electric Telegraph from. Reduced from the Map by the late Capt. L. Rokeby, R.N. (Journal, Vol. xliv.)

TAJURRAH TO ANKÓBAR.—Route from. (Journal, Vol. x.)

TANGANYIKA AND LOVALÈ.—Reduction of Lieut. Cameron's Preliminary Map of his Route and the adjacent Country between, 1874–5. With continuation from the Maps of Dr. Livingstone and other travellers. (Proceedings, Vol. xx.)

—— LAKE.—Map of. From Ujiji to its Southern extremity. Reduced from the Map by Lieut. V. Lovett Cameron, R.N. (Journal, Vol. xlv.)

—— —— From Ujiji to its Southern extremity. Reduced from the Map by Lieut. V. L. Cameron, R.N. (Proceedings, Vol. xix.)

TRANSVAAL AND THE SURROUNDING TERRITORIES.—By F. Jeppe, F.R.G.S. (Journal, Vol. xlvii.)

TRIPOLI TO GHADAMÍS.—Map to illustrate the Journey from. By Vice-Consul Dickson. (Journal, Vol. xxii.)

UNIAMESI, SEA OF, &c.—By the Rev. Messrs. Erhardt and Rebman, of the Church Missionary Society, 1855. (Proceedings, Vol. i.)

USAMBARA, SOUTHERN.—Map of Mr. Keith Johnston's Route in, 1879. Reduced from his original drawing. (Proceedings, Vol. i., New Series.)

—— —— Map of. By the Rev. J. P. Farler, B.A. (Proceedings, Vol. i., New Series.)

VEI LANGUAGE.—Inscriptions of the. (Journal, Vol. xx.)

—— —— Alphabet of the. (Journal, Vol. xx.)

VICTORIA NYANZA, LAKE.—1. Stanley's Map of the. Adapted to the Observations and Topography of Capt. Speke and Col. Grant by W. J. Turner.

2. Map of the Victoria Nyanza as delineated by Mr. H. M. Stanley. (Proceedings, Vol. xx.)

—— —— Map of the North-West Portion of the. Constructed from Col. Grant's Original Map and Bearings, adapted to the Astronomical Observations of Capt. Speke, by W. J. Turner. (Journal, Vol. xlvi.)

—— —— Map of the. Compiled from the Original Maps of Capt. Speke, Col. Grant, and Mr. Stanley; adapted to the Recorded Observations of Captain Speke by W. J. Turner. (Journal, Vol. xlvi.)

WHITE NILE, FROM KHARTUM TO RIGAF.—By Lieuts. Watson and Chippendall, R.E. (Journal, Vol. xlvi.)

—— —— FROM LARDO TO URONDOGANI.—Map of. By Col. Gordon, C.B., R.E. Surveyed in 1875–76. (Journal, Vol. xlvi.)

ZAMBESI REGION, CENTRAL. —(Proceedings, Vol. iii., New Series, p. 192.)

VI.—AMERICA AND WEST INDIES.

AMAZON RIVER.—Map of the. (Journal, Vol. vi.)

AMERICA, BRITISH NORTH.—Map to illustrate Capt. Synge's proposed Route through. (Journal, Vol. xxii.)

—— CENTRAL.—Map illustrating Fitz-Roy's Paper on. (Journal, Vol. xxiii.)

—— —— Map of. (Journal, Vol. xx.)

—— —— Map of Canal. (Journal, Vol. xxi.)

—— Discovery on N.E. Coast of. (Journal, Vol. x.)

—— NORTH.—Sketch showing the proposed Route of Capt. Back. (Journal, Vol. iii.)

—— —— Map of the Country between Lake Superior and Vancouver Island. To illustrate the Papers of the Exploring Expedition under the Command of Capt. John Palliser, 1857 to 1860. (Journal, Vol. xxx.)

—— SOUTH.—Chart of a Part of South America, Surveyed by Order of The Rt. Hon. the Lords Commissioners of the Admiralty, under the Direction of Capt. P. P. King, R.N., during the years 1826–30. (Journal, Vol. i.)

ANDES.—Map of the Bolivian Andes. (Journal, Vol. v.)

—— Map of the Mountains of Llanganati, in the Quitonian Andes, by Don Atanasio Guzman. To illustrate a Paper by Richard Spruce, Esq. (Journal, Vol. xxxi.)

—— Map of Proposed Line of Railway across the Andes, from Caldera to Fiambala. To accompany Report of Mr. E. A. Flint's Survey. Communicated by W. Wheelright Esq. (Journal, Vol. xxxi.)

—— Map to illustrate Extracts from the Narrative of a Route across the Southern Andes, by Don Guillermo Cox, 1862-3. (Journal, Vol. xxxiv.)

—— Map showing the Projected Railway Route from Buenos Ayres to Chile. To accompany the Paper by R. Crawford, Esq. (Journal, Vol. xliii.)

—— Map to illustrate Lloyd's Journey across the. (Journal, Vol. xxiv.)

—— Diagrams to illustrate T. J. Hutchinson's Paper, "Across the Andes from Callao." (Proceedings, Vol. xviii.)

ANEGADA, WITH ITS REEFS.—By R. H. Schomburgk. (Journal, Vol. ii.)

AQUIRY RIVER.—Map of the (an affluent of the Purûs). To accompany Notes by W. Chandless, Esq. (Journal, Vol. xxxvi.)

ARGENTINE REPUBLIC.—Map of part of the. To illustrate the Paper by Mr. Consul Hutchinson. (Journal Vol. xxxiv.)

ATACAMA DESERT OF (BOLIVIA).—Map of part of. To accompany the Paper by Mr. Josiah Harding. (Journal, Vol. xlvii.)

—— DISTRICT OF.—Showing the Territory in Dispute between Chili and Bolivia. (Proceedings, Vol. i., New Series.)

BOLIVIA.—Map of Part of. From the Surveys of J. B. Minchin. To illustrate the Paper by G. C. Musters (Retired Com. R.N.). (Journal, Vol. xlvii.)

BRAZIL.—Map of the Rivers Arinos, Juruena, and Tapajos. To accompany the Notes of W. Chandless, Esq., 1862. (Journal, Vol. xxxii.)

—— Map of the Rivers Canumá, Abacaxis, and Maué-assú and its

Tributaries. Reduced from the Original Map by W. Chandless, Esq. (Journal, Vol. xl.)

BRAZIL, NORTH-EAST.—Route Map of a Journey through. By James W. Wells, C.E. (Journal, Vol. xlvi.)

—— SOUTH.—The Valleys of the Tibagy and Ivahy, Province of the Paraná. By T. P. Bigg-Wither. (Journal, Vol. xlvi.)

BRITISH COLUMBIA.—1. Map of. Reduced from the Original Map by Mr. Alfred Waddington.

2. Sketch Map, showing Proposed Communication between Canada and British Columbia. To accompany the Paper by Mr. Alfred Waddington. (Journal, Vol. xxxviii.)

—— —— Part of. To illustrate the Papers of Mr. Justice Begbie, Com. Mayne, R.N., Lieut. Palmer, R.E., and Mr. Downie, 1861. (Journal, Vol. xxxi.)

—— —— Outline Map of Part of. By Lieut. H. S. Palmer, R.E. Reconnaissance Sketch of Part of Cariboo by Lieut. H. S. Palmer, R.E. (Journal, Vol. xxxiv.)

—— NORTH AMERICAN BOUNDARY.—By Capt. S. Anderson, R.E., Chief Astronomer, North American Boundary Commission. (Journal, Vol. xlvi.)

—— GUAYANA.—Map of. (Journal, Vol. vii.)

—— —— Map of. (Journal, Vol. vi.)

—— —— Map of a Portion of. (Journal, Vol. xv.)

—— —— Part of. (Journal, Vol. iv.)

—— —— Huts of the Warrows. (A View.) (Journal, Vol. iv.)

—— GUIANA —Sketch Map of. By J. E. Alexander, H.P. (Journal, Vol. ii.)

—— —— Sketch Map of a Portion of the Essequebo and Potaro Rivers. Showing the Position of Kaieteur Fall. To accompany the Paper by C. B. Brown, Esq. (Journal, Vol. xli.)

—— —— Reduction of the Map of. Compiled from the Surveys executed under Her Majesty's Commission from 1841 to 1844, and under the Direction of the Royal Geographical Society from 1835 to 1839, by Sir R. H. Schomburgk. Revised and Corrected. (Proceedings, Vol. ii., New Series.)

CALIFORNIA.—Sketch of the Coast of Upper California (Journal, Vol. v.)

CARTHAGENA TO BOGOTO.—Section of South America, from Carthagena to Bogoto.—A Spanish MS. found among Mr. Lloyd's Papers. Authority unknown. (Journal, Vol. i.)

CENTRAL AMERICA.—Map of. (Journal, Vol. xi.)

COLUMBUS.—Map to illustrate Capt. Becher's Landfall of. (Journal, Vol. xxvi.)

COOMAROW FALL.—Massaroony River. (View.) (Journal, Vol. iv.)

CORDOBA TO LA RIOJA.—Route from. South America. (Journal, Vol. ix.)

COSTARRICA.—Map of. (Journal, Vol. vi.)

CUZCO.—Map of the Environs of. (Journal, Vol. vi.)

—— Plan of. Ancient and Modern. (Journal, Vol. xli.)

DARIEN.—Map of Part of the Isthmus of. To accompany the Paper by M. Lucien de Puydt. (Journal, Vol. xxxviii.)

—— Map to illustrate Provost's Survey of the Isthmus of. (Journal, Vol. xxiv.)

PERU.—Map showing the Course of the Rivers, S. Gavan and Esquilaya in the Province of Carabaya. To accompany the Paper by Sr. Raimondi. (Journal, Vol. xxxvii.)

—— Map showing the Junction of the Rivers Mantaro and Apurimac. To accompany the Paper by Prof. A. Raimondi. (Journal, Vol. xxxviii.)

—— SOUTHERN.—Map of. (Journal, Vol. xxi.)

—— —— Map of. To accompany Mr. Markham's Paper. (Journal, Vol. xliv.)

PURUS, RIVER.—Mr. Markham's Route to the. (Journal, Vol. xxv.)

—— —— Map of the. From near its source to its mouth. By W. Chandless, Esq. (Journal, Vol. xxxvi.)

RIO NEGRO.—Map to illustrate Wallace's Paper on the. (Journal, Vol. xxii.i)

—— —— OF PATAGONIA.—Map of. (Journal, Vol. vi.)

SAMANÁ.—Map to illustrate Schomburgk's Paper on. (Journal, Vol. xxiii.)

SANTA CRUZ RIVER.—Map of. (Journal, Vol. vii.)

TABASCO AND ITS TRIBUTARIES.—Part of the. (Journal, Vol. xv.)

TERRA COTTA.—Heads in. (Journal, Vol. vii.)

UNITED STATES.—Map of the South-Western Portion of the, and of Sonora and Chihuahua. To illustrate the Paper by Dr. W. A. Bell. (Journal, Vol. xxxix.)

URUGUAY.—Estancia de San Jorge. From a Survey by Don Juan Frugoni, Durazno, 1867. (Proceedings, Vol. ii., New Series.)

USUMASINTA RIVER.—Sketch of the Course of the, Central America. To illustrate Col. Galindo's Paper. (Journal, Vol. iii.)

VANCOUVER ISLAND.—Sketch of the Country between Albernie Canal and Nanaimo. Showing the Line of Road proposed by Com. Mayne, R.N. 1861. (Journal, Vol. xxxii.)

—— —— Map of. To illustrate the Paper of Dr. C. Forbes, R.N. (Journal, Vol. xxxiv.)

—— —— AND PART OF BRITISH COLUMBIA.—Map of. To accompany the Paper by R. Brown, Esq. (Journal, Vol. xxxix.)

—— —— Map to illustrate Lieut.-Col. Grant's Paper on. (Journal, Vol. xxvii.)

VIRGIN ISLANDS.—Map of the. (Journal, Vol. v.)

WEST INDIES.—1. Bahama Islands. Antonia de Herrera, 1601.
2. Bahama Islands. Modern. To accompany Mr. Major's Paper.
3. Watling Island. To accompany Mr. Major's Paper. (Journal, Vol. xli.)

WILLIAM THE FOURTH'S CATARACT.—View of. (Journal, Vol. vi.)

YNCAS.—Ttahuantin-Suyu or the Empire of the (except Quito and Chile) in its four great divisions of Chincha-Suyu, Cunti-Suyu, Anti-Suyu, Colla-Suyu, with their Tribes and Ayllus or Lineages; also the Routes of the Ynca Conquerers. By Clements R. Markham, C.B. (Journal, Vol. xlii.)

YUKON OR KWICH-PAK RIVER.—Map of the. To illustrate Mr. Whymper's Paper. (Journal, Vol. xxxviii.)

VII.—AUSTRALASIA.

AUSTRALIA.—Map of. (Journal, Vol. viii.)

—— Central.—Map to illustrate Diaries of Exploration of, by John McDouall Stuart, Esq., 1860 and 1861. (Journal, Vol. xxxi.)

—— Map to accompany the Diary of Messrs. Burke and Wills, across Australia to the Gulf of Carpentaria; also Mr. Howitt's Journal to Cooper's Creek. Constructed chiefly from the Observations and Field-book of W. J. Wills, Esq., 1861. (Journal, Vol. xxxii.)

—— EASTERN.—Map of: on which are Delineated the Routes of Messrs. Burke and Wills, McKinlay, Landsborough and Walker, &c. (Journal, Vol. xxxiii.)

—— MORETON BAY, &c.—Sketch Map to illustrate Mr. H. S. Russell's Papers. (Journal, Vol. xv.)

—— NORTH-EAST.—Map to illustrate the Winds of. To accompany the Paper by Dr. A. Rattray, M.D., R.N. (Journal, Vol. xxxviii.)

—— —— Map to illustrate the Climate and Physical Geography of North-East Australia. To accompany the Paper by Dr. A. Rattray, M.D., R.N. (Journal, Vol. xxxviii.)

—— —— Map illustrating the Overland Expedition from Port Denison to Cape York under the Command of F. and A. Jardine, Esqs. To accompany Mr. Richardson's Paper. (Journal, Vol. xxxvi.)

—— Dr. Leichardt's Exploration in. (Journal, Vol. xvi.)

—— Map of Capt. Sturt's Route. (Journal, Vol. xvii.)

—— NORTH.—Map to complete Diaries of Exploration across Australia (from South to North) by John McDouall Stuart, Esq., 1861 and 1862. (Journal, Vol. xxxiii.)

—— Map of the N.W. Coast. (Journal, Vol. viii.)

—— NORTH-WESTERN.—Map of. To illustrate the Journal of Exploring Expedition, Commanded by F. T. Gregory, Esq., 1861. (Journal, Vol. xxxii.)

—— Map to illustrate the Route of the North Australian Expedition, and Mr. Wilson's Paper on the Physical Geography of N.W. Australia. (Journal, Vol. xxviii.)

—— SOUTH.—Sketch to illustrate Extracts of Explorations made by Surv.-Gen. Freeling, Mr. S. Hack, and others in South Australia, 1857. (Proceedings, Vol. ii.)

—— Range of Southern Dialects of. (Journal, Vol xv.)

—— Map of the Explorations from Beltana Station (South Australia), to the City of Perth (Western Australia), by Ernest Giles, 1875. (Journal, Vol xlvi.)

—— Map of the South-East Portion of Australia, showing the Progress of Discovery in the Interior of New South Wales to 1832. (Journal, Vol. ii.)

—— Map of the South-Eastern Portion of. (Journal, Vol. vii.)

—— WESTERN.—Map to illustrate Mr. Austin's Explorations in. (Journal, Vol. xxvi.)

—— —— From the Latest Documents received in the Colonial Office, 1832. (Journal, Vol. ii.)

—— —— Map showing the Explorations to the Eastward and Southward of Hampton Plains. By Alexander Forrest, Assistant Surveyor, 1871. (Journal, Vol. xlii.)

AUSTRALIA, WESTERN.—Map showing the Route of the Exploring Expedition through the Centre of, from Champion Bay, on the West Coast, to the Overland Telegraph Lines between Adelaide and Port Darwin. Commanded by John Forrest, 1874. (Journal, Vol. xlv.)

BARCOO AND WARREGO.—Mr. Kennedy's Expedition to the. (Journal, Vol. xxii.)

FLINDERS' RANGE, AUSTRALIA.—Country to the E. of. (Journal, Vol. xiv.)

—— RIVER.—Portion of the. To illustrate the Observations of Com. Norman, R.N. (Journal, Vol. xxxiii.)

LIVERPOOL PLAINS AND MORETON BAY.—Map of the Country between. By Com. H. G. Hamilton, R.N. (Journal, Vol. xiii.)

MELVILLE AND BATHURST ISLANDS.—With Coburg Peninsula. (Journal, Vol. iv.)

MURRAY RIVER.—Country near the Mouth of the River Murray, Australia. (Journal, Vol. iii.)

NEW GUINEA.—Chart of the South-East Coast of. To accompany the Paper by Capt. J. Moresby, R.N. (Journal, Vol. xliv.)

—— —— Map of the Fly River. Drawn from the Original Charts made by Signor L. M. D'Albertis by W. J. Turner. (Proceedings, Vol. i., New Series.)

—— —— EASTERN.—Map of. To accompany the Paper by Capt. J. Moresby, R.N. (Journal, Vol. xlv.)

NEW ZEALAND.—Map of the Provinces of Canterbury and Otago. To illustrate the Papers of Mr. James M'Kerrow, Dr. J. Haast, and Dr. Hector. (Journal, Vol. xxxiv.)

—— —— Routes near West Coast of Nelson District. By John Rochfort, Esq., in 1859. (Journal, Vol. xxxii.)

—— —— Chart of. (Journal, Vol. ii.)

—— —— Map of the Province of Canterbury, showing the Five Routes between the East and West Coasts, with Sections of the Routes. To accompany the Paper by Dr. J. Haast. (Journal, Vol. xxxvii.)

—— —— Middle Island of. (Journal, Vol. xxi.)

—— —— Middle Island of. (Journal, Vol. xx.)

OTAGO.—Map to illustrate Mr. Thomson's Survey of. (Journal, Vol. xxviii.)

PERTH TO EUCLA AND ADELAIDE.—Map showing the Overland Tracks from. By John Forrest, Government Surveyor, 1870. (Journal, Vol. xli.)

—— —— RUSSEL RANGE (Australia).—Map to illustrate the Route of the Expedition from. Also of the Settlers' Expedition from Perth to the Gascoigne River, and of the Expedition to the Murchison River. (Journal, Vol. xxii.)

SOUTHERN ALPS.—Map of the. In the Province of Canterbury, New Zealand. Reduced from the large Map by Julius Haast, Ph.D., F.R.S. (Journal, Vol. xl.)

TENIMBER ISLANDS.—Map of the. After Guyot's General Map of the Assistant Residency Banda. Illustrating the recent Discovery of Egeron Strait. To accompany the Paper by Prof. P. J. Veth. (Journal, Vol. xlviii.)

VIII.—ATLANTIC OCEAN AND ISLANDS.

Ascension Island.—View from the Mountain Road in the Island of Ascension. (Journal, Vol. v.)

Atlantic Ocean.—With Contour Lines showing approximately the depth of water in fathoms. (Proceedings, Vol. xxi.)

—— —— Sections of. Between St. Thomas and Tenerife. 2. St. Thomas to Bermuda. 3. Bermuda to Halifax. 4. Bermuda to New York. 5. Bermuda to Azores, Azores to Madeira. 6. Section of Equatorial Atlantic. 7. Section of South Atlantic. 8. Section of Mid-Atlantic, taken nearly North and South. 9. Section of North Atlantic, taken nearly North and South. (Proceedings, Vol. xviii.)

—— —— Deep Sea Sections. To illustrate the Paper by Capt. Sherard Osborn, R.N. (Journal, Vol. xli.)

—— —— Sections of. To illustrate a Paper "On the Distribution of Salt in the Ocean, as indicated by the Specific Gravity of its Waters." By J. Y. Buchanan, Chemist and Physicist in the "Challenger" Expedition. (Journal, Vol. xlvii.)

—— and Mediterranean.—2 Diagrams showing the Temperature of. To illustrate the Paper by Dr. Carpenter "On the Temperature of the Deep-Sea Bottom, and the Conditions by which it is determined." (Proceedings, Vol. xxi.)

—— Ocean.—Northern Portion of. With Contour Lines showing approximately the depth of water in fathoms. (Proceedings, Vol. xxi.)

—— —— North.—Surveys of H.M.S. "Bulldog" in the. To illustrate the Paper by Capt. Sir F. Leopold McClintock, R.N., F.R.G.S. (Proceedings, Vol. v.)

—— —— Section of. Between Disco and Valentia. (Proceedings, Vol. xxi.)

—— —— Surface Temperatures of the. Between Shetland and Greenland, collected by Admiral Irminger. (Journal, Vol. xl.)

Azores.—Island of St. Mary. (Journal, Vol. xv.)

Davis Strait and the Atlantic Ocean.—Soundings of H.M.S. "Valorous," 1875. (Proceedings, Vol. xx.)

Formigas Bank, Azores.—Sketch to illustrate Capt. Vidal's Paper on the. (Journal, Vol. xix.)

Gulf Stream.—Diagram of the. To illustrate the Paper by A. G. Findlay. (Proceedings, Vol. xiii.)

IX.—PACIFIC OCEAN AND ISLANDS.

Behring Strait.—Map to illustrate Capt. Collinson's Voyage through. (Journal, Vol. xxv.)

Chatham Islands.—Map of. (Journal, Vol. xi.)

Fiji Islands.—Dr. Macdonald's Explorations in the. (Journal, Vol. xxvii.)

New Britain, N.E. Portion.—(Proceedings, Vol. iii., New Series, p. 128.)

Pacific Ocean, etc.—12 Sections showing the Temperature of various Parts of the. To illustrate the Summary of Recent Observations on Ocean

Temperature made in H.M.S. "Challenger" and U.S.S. "Tuscarora"; with their bearing on the Doctrine of a General Oceanic Circulation sustained by difference of Temperature. By W. B. Carpenter, M.D., LL.D., Corresponding Member of the Institute of France. (Proceedings, Vol. xix.)

PACIFIC OCEAN, CENTRAL.—Section of. To illustrate a Paper on "The Distribution of Salt in the Ocean, as Indicated by the Specific Gravity of its Waters." By J. Y. Buchanan, Chemist and Physicist in the "Challenger" Expedition. (Journal, Vol. xlvii.)

RAPA-NUI, OR EASTER ISLAND.—Chart of. To accompany the Paper by J. L. Palmer, Esq., R.N. (Journal, Vol. xl.)

SANDWICH ISLANDS.—Chart of the. To accompany the Paper by the Bishop of Honolulu. (Journal, Vol. xxxviii.)

SOLOMON, NEW HEBRIDES, AND SANTA CRUZ GROUPS.—To illustrate the Paper by Lieut. A. H. Markham, R.N. (Journal, Vol. xlii.)

X.—INDIAN OCEAN ISLANDS.

COCOS OR KEELING ISLANDS.—Map of the: exhibiting the changes that have taken place since 1836. (Proceedings, Vol. i., New Series.)

PETER BOTTE MOUNTAIN.—Ascent of the. (View.) (Journal, Vol. iii.)

ALPHABETICAL LIST

OF THE

AUTHORS OF PAPERS IN THE ROYAL GEOGRAPHICAL SOCIETY'S 'JOURNALS' AND 'PROCEEDINGS.'

O'RILEY, Edward. xxxii. 164. Proceedings, Vol. vi. 83.

ORR, John. xi. 192.

OSBORN, Adm. Sherard, C.B. xxvii. 133; xxviii. 371; xxxvi. 279; xli. 46. Proceedings, Vol. i. 104, 305; iii. 55; ix. 42; xii. 92; xv. 28; xvi. 227; xvii. 172.

OSTEN SACKEN, Baron. xl. 250. Proceedings, Vol. xiv. 221.

OSWELL, W. C. xx. 143; xxii. 163.

OWEN, Captain, R.N. i. 66; ii. 81.

OXENHAM, E. L. xlv. 170. Proceedings, Vol. xix. 244.

PAGE, E. Legh. viii. 317.

PALGRAVE, W. Gifford. xxxiv. 111. Proceedings, Vol. viii. 63; xvi. 223.

PALLADIUS, Archimandrite. xlii. 142.

PALLISER, Capt. xxx. 267. Proceedings, Vol. ii. 38, 146, 228; iii. iv. 73.

PALMER, Lieut., R.E. xxxi. 224; xxxiv. 171. Proceedings, Vol. iv. 33; viii. 87.

PALMER, John Linton, R.N. xl. 167. Proceedings, Vol. xiv. 108.

PARISH, Sir Woodbine. iii. 94; iv. 182; vi. 136.

PARISH, Capt. A. xxvi. 154. Proceedings, Vol. i. 36.

PARKES, Sir Harry. xxiv. 306; xxvi. 71. Proceedings, Vol. i. 13.

PARKYNS, Mansfield. xx. 254.

PARRY, F. xliv. 152.

PATTERSON, Capt., R. R. Proceedings (N.S.), Vol. i. 240, 509.

PAYER, Julius. xlv. 1. Proceedings, Vol. xix. 17.

PELLY, Sir Lewis. xxxiv. 251; xxxv. 169, 231. Proceedings, Vol. viii. 18; ix. 293.

PENEY, Dr. Proceedings, Vol. vi. 18.

PENTLAND, J. B. v. 70; viii. 427.

PERRY, Gerald Raoul. Proceedings, Vol. vi. 74.

PESCHUROF, M. xxviii. 376. Proceedings, Vol. ii. 153; iii. 92.

PETERMANN, Dr. A. xviii. 89; xx. 232; xxii. 118; xxiii. 129. Proceedings, Vol. ix. 90, 114.

PETHERICK, Consul. xxxv. 289. Proceedings, Vols. iv. 39, 223; v. 27, 40, 41; vi. 18; vii. 20; viii. 122.

PEYTIER, M. viii. 423.

PHILIPPI, Dr., R.A. xxv. 158.

PHILLIPS, Geo. xliv. 97. Proceedings, Vol. xviii. 168.

PHILLIPS, Capt., R.N. iii. 275.

PHILPOTS, E. P. Proceedings, Vol. xiii. 372.

PIM, Capt. Bedford, R.N. Proceedings, Vol. vi. 75, 112.

PINTO, Major Serpa. Proceedings (N.S.), Vol. i. 481.

POEY, Andrés. xxv. 291.

POLLINGTON, Viscount. x. 445.

POOLE, H. xxvi. 55. Proceedings, Vol. i. 221.

PORTER, Rev. J. L. xxvi. 43.

POSTON, Hon. C. Proceedings, Vol. xix. 302.

POWELL, W. Proceedings (N.S.), Vol. iii. 84.

POWER, Mrs. Col. v. 243.

POWER, John. xxviii. 349.

PREVOST, Commr., R.N. xxiv. 249.

PRICHARD, Dr. J. C. ix. 192.

PRITCHETT, G. xxx. 64. Proceedings, Vol. iii. 93.

PROUT, Major H. G. xlix. 392.

PRUDHOE, Lord. v. 38.

PUNDIT, The. xxxviii. 129; xlvii. 86. Proceedings, Vol. xxi. 325.

PURDON, Wm. xxxi. 14. Proceedings, Vol. iv. 31.

PUYDT, M. Lucien de. xxxviii. 69. Proceedings, Vol. xii. 63.

QUIN, Capt. Michael, R.N. xxvi. 232.

RAE, Dr. John. xxii. 73; xxv. 246. Proceedings, Vol. v. 80; vii. 102.

RAFINESQUE, C. S. xi. 165.

RAFN, Professor. xiv. 316.

RAIMONDI, Don Antonio. xxxvii. 116; xxxviii. 413. Proceedings, Vol. xi. 102; xiii. 112.

RANDELL, W. R. xxxi. 145. Proceedings, Vol. iv. 94.

RATTRAY, A. xxxviii. 370; xlii. 431. Proceedings, Vol. xii. 313.

RAWLINSON, Sir Henry, K.C.B. ix. 26; x. 1, 65; xii. 112; xxvii. 185; xlii. 482; xliii. 272. Proceedings, Vol. i. 39, 280, 351; v. 219; x. 134; xiii. 10; xvii. 92, 108, 162; xviii. 414; (N.S.) i. 106, 161.

READE, Winwood. Proceedings, Vol. vii. 106.

R

VETCH, Capt. vii. 1; viii. 157.
VETH, Professor. Proceedings (N.S.), Vol. i. 759.
VIDAL, Capt., R.N. i. 51; xix. 160.
VIGNE, T. G. ix. 512.
VOGEL, Dr. xxi. 130; xxiv. 276; xxv. 237. Proceedings, Vol. ii. 30, 79.
VON BAER, Professor. viii. 210, 411.
VON DER DECKEN, Baron. Proceedings, Vol. viii. 5; x. 28, 109.
VON HAMMER, Baron. xii. 261.
VON KROKOW, Count. xxxvi. 198.
VON MALTZAN, Baron. Proceedings, Vol. xvi. 115.
VON MULLER, Baron. xx. 275.
VON WILDENBRUCH, Colonel. xx. 227.
VON WRANGELL, Admiral. xviii. 19, 24.
VON WREDE, Baron. xiv. 107.

WADDINGTON, A. xxxviii. 118. Proceedings, Vol. xii. 121.
WAKEFIELD, Rev. J. xl. 303. Proceedings, Vol. xvi. 125.
WALDEGROVE, Capt., R.N. iii. 156, 168.
WALKER, Mr. (Australia). Proceedings, Vol. vii. 5, 6, 84.
WALKER, A. Proceedings, Vol. ix. 33.
WALKER, Col. J. T. xxxii. 303.
WALKER, Capt. J. B. Proceedings, Vol. xvi. 135.
WALKER, R. B. N. Proceedings, Vol. xvii. 354.
WALLACE, A. R. xxiii. 212; xxx. 172; xxxii. 127; xxxiii. 217. Proceedings, Vol. i. 193; ii. 163; iii. 358; vi. 43; vii. 206; xxi. 505.
WALLICH, Dr. Proceedings, Vol. vii. 53.
WALLIN, Dr. G. A. xx. 293; xxiv. 115; xxv. 260.
WARBURTON, Col. Egerton. Proceedings, Vol. v. 124; xviii. 183; xix. 41.
WAREHAM, Mr. xii. 21.
WARREN, Capt. C. xlviii. 283. Proceedings, Vol. xix. 155.
WASHINGTON, Capt., R.N. i. 123; vii. 172; viii. 235, 448.
WATSON, R. G. Proceedings, Vol. vi. 103.
WATSON, Lieut. xlvi. 417, 424.
WATTS, W. L. xlvi. 1. Proceedings, Vol. xx. 21.
WEBB, Capt. W. S. iv. 376.

WELLS, J. W. xlvi. 308.
WELLSTED, Lieut., I.N. v. 129, 286; vi. 96; vii. 20, 102.
WEYPRECHT, Lieut. xlv. 19.
WHEELWRIGHT, W. xxxi. 155. Proceedings, Vol. iv. 45.
WHITE, Robert. Proceedings, Vol. i. 27.
WHITE, T. P. Proceedings, Vol. xiii. 352.
WHITELOCK, Lieut., I.N. viii. 170.
WHITLEY, N. Proceedings, Vol. xiii. 229.
WHITNEY, Asa. xxi. 86.
WHYMPER, F. xxxviii. 219. Proceedings, Vol. xii. 186.
WHYTE, W. A. Proceedings, Vol. xiv. 243.
WICKHAM, G. H. Proceedings, Vol. xiii. 58.
WICKHAM, Capt., R.N. viii. 460; xii. 79.
WILKINSON, Sir Gardner. ix. 431; xxv. 206.
WILKINSON, J. ii. 28.
WILKINSON, J. R. Proceedings, Vol. xiii. 134.
WILLIAMSON, Rev. A. xxxix. 1. Proceedings, Vol. xiii. 26.
WILSON, Rev. C. T. Proceedings (N. S.), Vol. ii. 353.
WILSON, Major C. W. xliii. 206. Proceedings, Vol. xvii. 326.
WILSON, Col. D. iii. 283.
WILSON, Capt. J. C., R.N. xxxvi. 244.
WILSON, J. Fox. xxxv. 106. Proceedings, Vol. ix. 106.
WILSON, Capt. J. R. xiii. 118.
WILSON, J. S. xxviii. 137.
WOLFE, Lieut. J., R.N. iii. 77.
WOOD, Lieut., I.N. vi. 29; x. 530.
WOOD, Major Herbert. xlv. 367.
WORTABET, Dr. xxxii. 100.
WRANGELL, Admiral von. xviii. 19, 24.

YORKE, Colonel Philip. xxi. 35
YOUNG, Sir Allen. Proceedings, Vol. v. 70; ix. 296.
YOUNG, E. D., R.N. xxxviii. 111. Proceedings, Vol. xii. 79; xx. 451; xxi. 225.
YULE, Col. H., C.B. xxvii. 54; xlii. 438. Proceedings, Vol. i. 269; x. 270.

ZAHRTMANN, Admiral. v. 102.

GEOGRAPHY

AT THE

BRITISH ASSOCIATION.

From 1832 to 1850 Geography was considered with Geology, sometimes with a separate President for the geographical papers. After 1850 Geography and Ethnology formed a separate Section E. After 1869 Ethnology was placed in a sub-section of Section D, and since that year Section E has been for Geography alone.

PRESIDENTS.

GEOGRAPHICAL BRANCH OF SECTION C.

1831. *York*	..	No sections.
1832. *Oxford* ..	..	⎫
1833. *Cambridge* ..	..	⎪ No separate President for the geographical
1834. *Edinburgh* ..	..	⎬ branch.
1855. *Dublin* ..	..	⎭
1836. *Bristol* ..	..	Mr. R. I. Murchison, F.R.S.
1837. *Liverpool* ..	..	Mr G. B. Greenough, F.R.S.
1838. *Newcastle* ..	..	Lord Prudhoe, Captain, R.N.
1839. *Birmingham*	..	Mr. G. B. Greenough, F.R.S.
1840. *Glasgow* ..	..	Mr. G. B. Greenough, F.R.S.
1841. *Plymouth* ..	..	⎫
1842. *Manchester*	..	⎪
1843. *Cork*	..	⎬ No separate President for the geographical
1844. *York*	..	⎪ branch.
1845. *Cambridge* ..	..	⎭
1846. *Southampton*	..	Mr. G. B. Greenough, F.R.S.
1847. *Oxford* ..	..	⎫
1848. *Swansea* ..	..	⎪ No separate President for the geographical
1849. *Birmingham*	..	⎬ branch.
1850. *Edinburgh* ..	..	⎭

PRESIDENTS

OF THE

GEOGRAPHICAL SECTION

OF THE

BRITISH ASSOCIATION.

(SECTION E).

1851.	*Ipswich*	Sir Roderick Murchison, F.R.S.
1852.	*Belfast*	Colonel Chesney, F.R.S.
1853.	*Hull*	Mr. R. G. Latham, F.R.S.
1854.	*Liverpool*	Sir Roderick Murchison, F.R.S.
1855.	*Glasgow*	Sir John Richardson, C.B., F.R.S.
1856.	*Cheltenham* ..	Sir Henry Rawlinson, K.C.B., F.R.S.
1857.	*Dublin*	Rev. Dr. J. H. Todd.
1858.	*Leeds*	Sir Roderick Murchison, F.R.S.
1859.	*Aberdeen*	Admiral Sir James C. Ross, F.R.S.
1860.	*Oxford*	Sir Roderick Murchison, F.R.S.
1861.	*Manchester* ..	Mr. John Crawfurd, F.R.S.
1862.	*Cambridge*	Mr. Francis Galton, F.R.S.
1863.	*Newcastle*	Sir Roderick Murchison, F.R.S.
1864.	*Bath*	Sir Roderick Murchison, F.R.S.
1865.	*Birmingham* ..	Sir Henry Rawlinson, K.C.B., F.R.S.
1866.	*Nottingham* ..	Sir Charles Nicholson, *Bart.*
1867.	*Dundee*	Sir Samuel Baker.
1868.	*Norwich*	Captain Richards, R.N., C.B., F.R.S.
1869.	*Exeter*	Sir H. Bartle Frere, G.C.S.I., K.C.B.
1870.	*Liverpool*	Sir Roderick Murchison, K.C.B., F.R.S.
1871.	*Edinburgh*	Colonel H. Yule, C.B.
1872.	*Brighton*	Mr. Francis Galton, F.R.S.
1873.	*Bradford*	Sir Rutherford Alcock, K.C.B.
1874.	*Belfast*	Lieut.-Colonel Wilson, C.B., F.R.S.
1875.	*Bristol*	Lieut.-General R. Strachey, C.S.I., F.R.S.
1876.	*Glasgow*	Captain Evans, R.N., C.B., F.R.S.
1877.	*Plymouth*	Admiral Sir E. Ommanney, C.B., F.R.S.
1878.	*Dublin*	Sir Wyville Thomson, F.R.S.
1879.	*Sheffield*	Mr. Clements Markham, C.B., F.R.S.
1880.	*Swansea*	Lieut.-General Sir J. H. Lefroy, K.C.M.G., F.R.S.
1881.	*York*	Sir Joseph D. Hooker, K.C.S.I., C.B., F.R.S.

SECRETARIES OF SECTION E.

Geography & Ethnology.

1851. *Ipswich* ..	.. Dr. Norton Shaw,	Rev. J. Donaldson, Mr. Cull, (*Ethn.*)
1852. *Belfast* '..	.. ,, ,,	Mr. Mac Adam, Mr. Cull, (*Ethn.*)
1853. *Hull* ..	.. ,, ,,	Rev. H. W. Kemp, Mr. Cull, (*Ethn.*)
1854. *Liverpool*	.. ,, ,,	Rev. H. Higgins, Dr. Ihne, Mr. Cull, (*Ethn.*)
1855. *Glasgow*..	.. ,, ,,	Dr. Blackie, Mr. Cull, (*Ethn.*)
1856. *Cheltenham*	.. ,, ,,	Mr. Hartland, W. H. Rumsey. Mr. Cull, (*Ethn.*)
1857. *Dublin* ..	.. ,, ,,	Mr. Ferguson, Dr. Madden. Mr. Cull, (*Ethn.*)
1858. *Leeds* ..	.. ,, ,,	Mr. F. Galton, Dr. O'Callaghan, T. Wright, (*Ethn.*)
1859. *Aberdeen*	.. ,, ,,	Prof. Geddes, Mr. Cull, (*Ethn.*)
1860. *Oxford* ..	.. ,, ,,	Captain Burrows, R.N., Dr. Lemprière, Dr. Hunt, (*Ethn.*)
1861. *Manchester*	.. ,, ,,	W. Spottiswoode, J. Kingsley, Dr. Hunt, (*Ethn.*)
1862. *Cambridge*	.. ,, ,,	Rev. J. Glover, J. W. Clarke, Dr. Hunt, (*Ethn.*)
1863. *Newcastle*	.. C. R. Markham	R. W. Watson, C. Carter Blake, (*Ethn.*)
1864. *Bath* ..	.. ,, ,,	H. W. Bates, Capt. Murchison, T. Wright, (*Ethn.*)
1865. *Birmingham*..	,, ,,	H. W. Bates, S. Evans, G. Jabet, T. Wright, (*Ethn.*)
1866. *Nottingham*	.. ,, ,,	H. W. Bates, R. H. Major, Rev. E. T. Cusins, D. W. Nash, T. Wright, (*Ethn.*)
1867. *Dundee.* ..	.. H. W. Bates,	Cyril Graham, S. J. Mackie, R. Sturrock, (*Ethn.*)
1868. *Norwich* ..	.. C. R. Markham,	H. W. Bates, T. Baines, T. Wright, (*Ethn.*)

(*Geography.*)

1869. *Exeter* ..	.. C. R. Markham,	H. W. Bates, J. H. Thomas.
1870. *Liverpool*	.. ,, ,,	,, ,, A. Mott, D. Buxton.
1871. *Edinburgh*	.. ,, ,,	A. Keith Johnston, A. Buchan, J. H. Thomas.
1872. *Brighton*..	.. H. W. Bates,	A. Keith Johnston, Rev. J. Newton, J. H. Thomas.
1873. *Bradford*..	.. C. R. Markham,	A. Keith Johnston, H. W. Bates.
1874. *Belfast* ..	.. E. C. Rye,	E. G. Ravenstein, J. H. Thomas.
1875. *Bristol* ..	.. H. W. Bates,	E. C. Rye, F. Tuckett.
1876. *Glasgow* ..	.. ,,	,, R. O. Wood.
1877. *Plymouth*	.. ,,	,, F. E. Fox.
1878. *Dublin* ..	.. E. C. Rye, John Coles.	
1879. *Sheffield* ..	.. H. W. Bates,	E. C. Rye, C. E. D. Black.
1880. *Swansea* ..	.. ,,	,,

THE

HAKLUYT SOCIETY

(1847-1881.)

Presidents.

1847. Sir Roderick Murchison, Bart., K.C.B., F.R.S.
1871. Right Honourable Sir David Dundas.
1877 ⎫
to ⎬ Colonel H. Yule, C.B.
1881.⎭

Secretaries.

1847. Mr. Desborough Cooley.
1849. Mr. R. H. Major.
1859 ⎫
to ⎬ Mr. Clements Markham, C.B., F.R.S.
1881.⎭

1881.

President.

Colonel H. YULE, C.B., F.R.G.S.

Vice-Presidents.

Admiral C. R. DRINKWATER BETHUNE, C.B., F.R.G.S.
Major-General Sir HENRY RAWLINSON, K.C.B., F.R.G.S.

Council.

W. A. TYSSEN AMHERST, Esq., M.P., F.R.G.S.
Rev. Dr. G. P. BADGER, D.C.L., F.R.G.S.
J. BARROW, Esq., F.R.S., F.R.G.S.
WALTER DE GRAY BIRCH, Esq.
E. H. BUNBURY, Esq., F.R.G.S.
Adm. Sir R. COLLINSON, K.C.B., F.R.G.S.
The Earl of DUCIE, F.R.S., F.R.G.S.
Captain F. B. HANKEY, R.N.
Lieut.-Gen. Sir J. HENRY LEFROY, C.B., K.C.M.G., F.R.G.S.

R. H. MAJOR, Esq., F.S.A., F.R.G.S.
Rear-Admiral MAYNE, C.B., F.R.G.S.
E. DELMAR MORGAN, Esq., F.R.G.S.
Admiral Sir ERASMUS OMMANNEY, C.B., F.R.S., F.R.G.S.
Lord ARTHUR RUSSELL, M.P., For. Sec. R.G.S.
The Lord STANLEY OF ALDERLEY.
EDWARD THOMAS, Esq., F.R.S.
Lieut.-Gen. Sir HENRY THUILLIER, C.S.I., F.R.S., F.R.G.S.

Honorary Secretary—C. R. MARKHAM, C.B., F.R.S., Sec. R.G.S.

Bankers—Messrs. RANSOM, BOUVERIE, AND Co., 1, Pall Mall East.

THE HAKLUYT SOCIETY, which is established for the purpose of printing rare or unpublished Voyages and Travels, aims at opening by this means an easier access to the sources of a branch of knowledge, which yields to none in importance, and is superior to most in agreeable variety. The narratives of travellers and navigators make us acquainted with the earth, its inhabitants and productions; they exhibit the growth of intercourse among mankind, with its effects on civilisation, and, while instructing, they at the same time awaken attention, by recounting the toils and adventures of those who first explored unknown and distant regions.

The advantage of an Association of this kind consists not merely in its system of literary co-operation, but also in its economy. The acquirements, taste, and discrimination of a number of individuals, who feel an interest in the same pursuit, are thus brought to act in voluntary combination, and the ordinary charges of publication are also avoided, so that the volumes produced are distributed among the Members (who can alone obtain them) at little more than the cost of printing and paper. The Society expends the whole of its funds in the preparation of works for the Members; and since the cost of each copy varies inversely as the whole number of copies printed, it is obvious that the members are gainers individually by the prosperity of the Society, and the consequent vigour of its operations. The number of Members is now 240.

Gentlemen desirous of becoming Members of the Hakluyt Society should intimate their intention to the Secretary, Mr. CLEMENTS R. MARKHAM, C.B., F.R.S., 21, *Eccleston Square, S.W.*, or to the Society's Agent for the delivery of its volumes, Mr. RICHARDS, 37, *Great Queen Street, Lincoln's Inn Fields;* when their names will be recorded, and on payment of their subscription of 1*l.* 1*s.* to Mr. Richards, they will receive the volumes issued for the year.

New Members have, at present (1881), *the privilege of purchasing the publications of the Society for previous years for* 25*l.* 1*s.* 6*d.* Members wishing to purchase back volumes may, with the consent of the Council, be supplied with them at the rate of 10*s.* each volume, when they require any number less than one quarter of the whole series, and at the rate of 8*s.* 6*d.* a volume when they require any number more than a quarter of the whole series.

The Members are requested to bear in mind that the power of the Council to make advantageous arrangements will depend in a great measure on the prompt payment of the subscriptions, which are payable in advance on the 1st of January, and are received by Mr. RICHARDS, 37, Great Queen Street, Lincoln's Inn Fields. Post-Office Orders should be made payable to Mr. THOMAS RICHARDS, at the *West Central Office, High Holborn.*

WORKS ALREADY ISSUED.

1.—THE OBSERVATIONS OF SIR RICHARD HAWKINS, KNT.,

In his Voyage into the South Sea in 1593. Reprinted from the edition of 1622, and edited by Capt. C. R. Drinkwater Bethune, R.N., C.B.
Issued for 1848. (*First Edition out of print. See No.* 57.)

2.—SELECT LETTERS OF COLUMBUS.

With Original Documents relating to the Discovery of the New World. Translated and Edited by R. H. Major, Esq., of the British Museum.
Issued for 1849. (*First Edition out of print. See No.* 43.)

3.—The Discoverie of the Empire of Guiana,

By Sir Walter Raleigh, Knt. Edited, with copious Explanatory Notes, and a Biographical Memoir, by Sir Robert H. Schomburgk, Phil.D., &c.

Issued for 1850.

4.—Sir Francis Drake his Voyage, 1595.

By Thomas Maynarde, together with the Spanish Account of Drake's attack on Puerto Rico. Edited from the Original MSS. by W. D. Cooley, Esq.

Issued for 1850.

5.—Narratives of Early Voyages

Undertaken for the Discovery of a Passage to Cathaia and India, by the North-west, with Selections from the Records of the worshipful Fellowship of the Merchants of London, trading into the East Indies ; and from MSS. in the Library of the British Museum, now first published ; by Thomas Rundall, Esq. *Issued for* 1851.

6.—The Historie of Travaile into Virginia Britannia,

Expressing the Cosmographie and Commodities of the Country, together with the manners and customs of the people, gathered and observed as well by those who went first thither as collected by William Strachey, Gent., the first Secretary of the Colony ; now first Edited from the original manuscript in the British Museum, by R. H. Major, Esq., of the British Museum.

Issued for 1851.

7.—Divers Voyages touching the Discovery of America

And the Islands adjacent, collected and published by Richard Hakluyt, Prebendary of Bristol in the year 1582. Edited, with Notes and an Introduction, by John Winter Jones, Esq., of the British Museum.

Issued for 1852.

8.—A Collection of Documents on Japan.

With a Commentary by Thomas Rundall, Esq. *Issued for* 1852.

9.—The Discovery and Conquest of Florida,

By Don Ferdinando de Soto. Translated out of Portuguese by Richard Hakluyt ; and Edited, with notes and an introduction, by W. B. Rye, Esq., of the British Museum. *Issued for* 1853.

10.—Notes upon Russia,

Being a Translation from the Earliest Account of that Country, entitled Rerum Muscoviticarum Commentarii, by the Baron Sigismund von Herberstein, Ambassador from the Court of Germany to the Grand Prince Vasiley Ivanovich, in the years 1517 and 1526. Two Volumes. Translated and Edited, with Notes and an Introduction, by R. H. Major, Esq., of the British Museum. Vol. 1. *Issued for* 1853.

11.—The Geography of Hudson's Bay.

Being the Remarks of Captain W. Coats, in many Voyages to that locality, between the years 1727 and 1751. With an Appendix, containing Extracts from the Log of Captain Middleton on his Voyage for the Discovery of the North-west Passage, in H.M.S. 'Furnace,' in 1741-2. Edited by John Barrow, Esq., F.R.S., F.S.A. *Issued for* 1854.

12.—NOTES UPON RUSSIA. Vol. 2.

Issued for 1854.

13.—THREE VOYAGES BY THE NORTH-EAST,

Towards Cathay and China, undertaken by the Dutch in the years 1594, 1595, and 1596, with their Discovery of Spitzbergen, their residence of ten months in Novaya Zemlya, and their safe return in two open boats. By Gerrit de Veer. Edited by C. T. Beke, Esq., Ph.D., F.S.A.
(*First Edition out of print. See No. 54.*) *Issued for* 1855.

14-15.—THE HISTORY OF THE GREAT AND MIGHTY KINGDOM OF CHINA AND THE SITUATION THEREOF.

Compiled by the Padre Juan Gonzalez de Mendoza. And now Reprinted from the Early Translation of R. Parke. Edited by Sir George T. Staunton, Bart. With an Introduction by R. H. Major, Esq. 2 vols.
Issued for 1855.

16.—THE WORLD ENCOMPASSED BY SIR FRANCIS DRAKE.

Being his next Voyage to that to Nombre de Dios. Collated, with an unpublished Manuscript of Francis Fletcher, Chaplain to the Expedition. With Appendices illustrative of the same Voyage, and Introduction by W. S. W. Vaux, Esq., M.A. *Issued for* 1856.

17.—THE HISTORY OF THE TARTAR CONQUERORS WHO SUBDUED CHINA.

From the French of the Père D'Orleans, 1688. Translated and Edited by the Earl of Ellesmere. With an Introduction by R. H. Major, Esq.
Issued for 1856.

18.—A COLLECTION OF EARLY DOCUMENTS ON SPITZBERGEN AND GREENLAND,

Consisting of: a Translation from the German of F. Martin's important work on Spitzbergen, now very rare; a Translation from Isaac de la Peyrère's Relation de Greenland; and a rare piece entitled "God's Power and Providence showed in the miraculous preservation and deliverance of eight Englishmen left by mischance in Greenland, anno 1630, nine months and twelve days, faithfully reported by Edward Pelham." Edited, with Notes, by Adam White, Esq., of the British Museum. *Issued for* 1857.

19.—THE VOYAGE OF SIR HENRY MIDDLETON TO BANTAM AND THE MALUCO ISLANDS.

From the rare Edition of 1606. Edited by Bolton Corney, Esq.
Issued for 1857.

20.—RUSSIA AT THE CLOSE OF THE SIXTEENTH CENTURY.

Comprising "The Russe Commonwealth" by Dr. Giles Fletcher, and Sir Jerome Horsey's Travels, now first printed entire from his manuscript in the British Museum. Edited by E. A. Bond, Esq., of the British Museum.
Issued for 1858.

21.—THE TRAVELS OF GIROLAMO BENZONI IN AMERICA, IN 1542–56.

Translated and Edited by Admiral W. H. Smyth, F.R.S., F.S.A.
Issued for 1858.

22.—INDIA IN THE FIFTEENTH CENTURY.

Being a Collection of Narratives of Voyages to India in the century preceding the Portuguese discovery of the Cape of Good Hope; from Latin, Persian, Russian, and Italian Sources, now first translated into English. Edited, with an Introduction, by R. H. Major, Esq., F.S.A.
Issued for 1859.

23.—NARRATIVE OF A VOYAGE TO THE WEST INDIES AND MEXICO,

In the years 1599–1602, with Maps and Illustrations. By Samuel Champlain. Translated from the original and unpublished Manuscript, with a Biographical Notice and Notes by Alice Wilmere.   *Issued for* 1859.

24.—EXPEDITIONS INTO THE VALLEY OF THE AMAZONS

During the Sixteenth and Seventeenth Centuries: containing the Journey of Gonzalo Pizarro, from the Royal Commentaries of Garcilasso Inca de la Vega; the Voyage of Francisco de Orellana, from the General History of Herrera; and the Voyage of Cristoval de Acuña, from an exceedingly scarce narrative written by himself in 1641.   Edited and Translated by Clements R. Markham, Esq.   *Issued for* 1860.

25.—EARLY INDICATIONS OF AUSTRALIA.

A Collection of Documents shewing the Early Discoveries of Australia to the time of Captain Cook.   Edited by R. H. Major, Esq., of the British Museum, F.S.A.   *Issued for* 1860.

26.—THE EMBASSY OF RUY GONZALEZ DE CLAVIJO TO THE COURT OF TIMOUR, 1403–6.

Translated, for the first time, with Notes, a Preface, and an Introductory Life of Timour Beg.   By Clements R. Markham, Esq.   *Issued for* 1861.

27.—HENRY HUDSON THE NAVIGATOR.

The Original Documents in which his career is recorded.   Collected, partly Translated, and Annotated, with an Introduction by George Asher, LL.D.
Issued for 1861.

28.—THE EXPEDITION OF URSUA AND AGUIRRE,

In search of El Dorado and Omagua, A.D. 1560–61.   Translated from the "Sexta Noticia Historiale" of Fray Pedro Simon, by W. Bollaert, Esq.; with an Introduction by Clements R. Markham, Esq.   *Issued for* 1862.

29.—THE LIFE AND ACTS OF DON ALONZO ENRIQUEZ DE GUZMAN.

Translated from a Manuscript in the National Library at Madrid, and edited, with Notes and an Introduction, by Clements R. Markham, Esq.
Issued for 1862.

30.—DISCOVERIES OF THE WORLD BY GALVANO,

From their first original unto the year of our Lord 1555. Reprinted, with the original Portuguese text, and edited by Vice-Admiral Bethune, C.B.
Issued for 1863.

31.—MARVELS DESCRIBED BY FRIAR JORDANUS,

Of the Order of Preachers, native of Severac, and Bishop of Columbum; from a parchment manuscript of the Fourteenth Century, in Latin, the text of which has recently been Translated and Edited by Colonel H. Yule, C.B., F.R.G.S., late of H.M. Bengal Engineers. *Issued for* 1863.

32.—THE TRAVELS OF LUDOVICO DI VARTHEMA

In Syria, Arabia, Persia, India, &c., during the Sixteenth Century. Translated by J. Winter Jones, Esq., F.S.A., and edited, with Notes and an Introduction, by the Rev. George Percy Badger. *Issued for* 1864.

33.—THE TRAVELS OF CIEZA DE LEON IN 1532–50

From the Gulf of Darien to the City of La Plata, contained in the first part of his Chronicle of Peru (Antwerp 1554). Translated and edited, with Notes and an Introduction, by Clements R. Markham, Esq. *Issued for* 1864.

34.—THE NARRATIVE OF PASCUAL DE ANDAGOYA.

Containing the earliest notice of Peru. Translated and edited, with Notes and an Introduction, by Clements R. Markham, Esq. *Issued for* 1865.

35.—THE COASTS OF EAST AFRICA AND MALABAR

In the beginning of the Sixteenth Century, by Duarte Barbosa. Translated from an early Spanish manuscript by the Hon. Henry Stanley.
Issued for 1865.

36.—CATHAY AND THE WAY THITHER. Vol. 2.

A Collection of all minor notices of China, previous to the Sixteenth Century. Translated and edited by Colonel H. Yule, C.B.   Vol. 1. *Issued for* 1866.

37.—CATHAY AND THE WAY THITHER. Vol. 2.

Issued for 1866.

38.—THE THREE VOYAGES OF SIR MARTIN FROBISHER.

With a Selection from Letters now in the State Paper Office. Edited by Rear-Admiral Collinsou, C.B. *Issued for* 1867.

39.—THE PHILIPPINE ISLANDS.

Moluccas, Siam, Cambodia, Japan, and China, at the close of the 16th century. By Antonia de Morga. Translated from the Spanish, with Notes, by Lord Stanley of Alderley. *Issued for* 1868.

40.—THE FIFTH LETTER OF HERNAN CORTES.

To the Emperor Charles V., containing an Account of his Expedition to Honduras in 1525–26. Translated from the Spanish by Don Pascual de Gayangos. *Issued for* 1868.

41.—THE ROYAL COMMENTARIES OF THE YNCAS.

By the Ynca Garcilasso de la Vega. Translated and Edited, with Notes and an Introduction, by Clements R. Markham, Esq. Vol. 1.

Issued for 1869.

42.—THE THREE VOYAGES OF VASCO DA GAMA

And his Viceroyalty, from the Lendas da India of Caspar Correa; accompanied by original documents. Translated and Edited by the Lord Stanley of Alderley. *Issued for* 1869.

43.—SELECT LETTERS OF CHRISTOPHER COLUMBUS,

With other Original Documents, relating to his Four Voyages to the New World. Translated and edited by R. H. Major, F.S.A., &c. 2nd Edit.

Issued for 1870.

44.—HISTORY OF THE IMÂMS AND SEYYIDS OF 'OMAN,

By Salîl-Ibn-Razîk, from A.D. 661–1856. Translated from the original Arabic, and edited, with Notes, Appendices, and an Introduction, continuing the History down to 1870, by George Percy Badger, F.R.G.S.

Issued for 1870.

45.—THE ROYAL COMMENTARIES OF THE YNCAS. Vol. 2.

Issued for 1871.

46.—THE CANARIAN,

Or Book of the Conquest and Conversion of the Canarians in the year 1402, by Messire Jean de Bethencourt, Kt. Composed by Pierre Bontier and Jean le Verrier. Translated and Edited, with Notes and an Introduction, by R. H. Major, F.S.A. *Issued for* 1871.

47.—REPORTS ON THE DISCOVERY OF PERU;

Translated and Edited, with Notes and an Introduction, by Clements R. Markham, C.B. *Issued for* 1872.

48.—NARRATIVES OF THE RITES AND LAWS OF THE YNCAS;

Translated from the original Spanish Manuscripts, and Edited, with Notes and an Introduction, by Clements R. Markham, C.B., F.R.S.

Issued for 1872.

49.—TRAVELS TO TANA AND PERSIA,

By Josasa Barbaro and Ambrogio Contarini; Edited by Lord Stanley of Alderley; and Narratives of other Italian Travels in Persia, Translated and Edited by Charles Grey, Esq. *Issued for* 1873.

50.—VOYAGES OF THE ZENI

To the Northern Seas in the Fourteenth Century. Translated and Edited by R. H. Major, F.S.A. *Issued for* 1873.

51.—THE CAPTIVITY OF HANS STADE OF HESSE IN 1547–55

Among the Wild Tribes of Eastern Brazil; translated by Albert Tootal, Esq., and annotated by Richard F. Burton. *Issued for* 1874.

52.—The First Voyage Round the World by Magellan,

Translated from the Accounts of Pigasetta and other contemporary writers. With Notes and an Introduction by Lord Stanley of Alderley.
Issued for 1874.

53.—The Commentaries of the Great Afonso Dalboquerque,

Second Viceroy of India. Translated from the Portuguese Edition of 1774; with Notes and Introduction by Walter de Gray Birch, Esq., F.R.S.L. Vol. 1.
Issued for 1875.

54.—Three Voyages by the North-East.

Second Edition of Gerrit de Veer's Three Voyages to the North East by Barents. Edited, with an Introduction, by Lieut. Koolemans Beynen, of the Royal Dutch Navy. *Issued for* 1876.

55.—The Commentaries of the Great Alfonso Dalboquerque.
Vol. 2. *Issued for* 1875.

56.—The Voyages of Sir James Lancaster.

With Abstracts of Journal of Voyages preserved in the India Office, and the Voyage of Captain John Knight to seek the N.W. Passage. Edited by Clements R. Markham, c.b., f.r.s. *Issued for* 1877.

57.—Second Edition of the Observations of Sir Richard Hawkins, Kt.,

In his Voyage into the South Sea in 1593, with the Voyages of his grandfather William, his father Sir John, and his cousin William Hawkins. Edited by Clements R. Markham, c.b., f.r.s. *Issued for* 1877.

58.—The Bondage and Travels of Johann Schiltberger,

From his capture at the battle of Nicopolis in 1396 to his escape and return to Europe in 1427: translated, from the Heidelberg MS. edited in 1859 by Professor Karl Freidrich Neumann, by Commander J. Buchan Telfer, R.N.; with Notes by Professor B. Bruun, and a Preface, Introduction, and Notes by the Translator and Editor. *Issued for* 1878.

59.—The Voyages and Works of John Davis the Navigator.

Edited, with an Introduction and Notes, by Captain Albert H. Markham, R.N., F.R.G.S. *Issued for* 1878.

60.—The Commentaries of the Great Afonso Dalboquerque.
Vol. 3. *Issued for* 1879.

61.—The Natural and Moral History of the Indies,

By Father Joseph de Acosta: edited, with Notes and an Introduction, by Clements R. Markham, c.b., f.r.s. Vol. 1. *Issued for* 1879.

62.—History of the Indies by Acosta. Vol. 2.
Issued for 1880.

OTHER WORKS UNDERTAKEN BY EDITORS.

Voyages of William Baffin. Edited by Clements R. Markham, C.B., F.R.S. (*Nearly ready.*)

Father Francisco Alvarez. Narrative of the Portuguese Embassy to Abyssinia. 1520. Translated and Edited by Lord Stanley of Alderley. (*Nearly ready.*)

A Manuscript History of Bermuda, in the British Museum (*Sloane*, 750). Edited by Lieut.-General Sir J. Henry Lefroy, K.C.M.G., C.B.
(*In the Press.*)

Rosmital's Embassy to England, Spain, &c., in 1466. Edited by R. C. Graves, Esq.

The Journal of the Pilot Gallego, and other Documents relating to the Voyages of Mendana. Translated and edited by W. A. Tyssen Amherst, Esq.

Voyages of John Huigen von Linschoten to the East Indies. Edited by Arthur Burnell, Esq., LL.D.

Voyages and Travels of Anthony Jenkinson. Edited by E. Delmar Morgan, Esq.

WORKS SUGGESTED TO THE COUNCIL FOR PUBLICATION.

Journal of the Jesuit Desideri in Tibet.

Inedited Letters, &c., of Sir Thomas Roe during his Embassy to India.

The Topographia Christiana of Cosmas Indicopleustes.

Bernhard de Breydenbach, 1483–84, A.D. Travels in the Holy Land.

Felix Fabri, 1483. Wanderings in the Holy Land, Egypt, &c.

El Edrisi's Geography.

Voyage made by Captain Jaques Cartier in 1535 and 1536 to the isles of Canada, Hochlega, and Saguenay.

Ca da Mosto. Voyages along the Western Coast of Africa in 1454 : translated from the Italian text of 1507.

Leo Africanus.

J. dos Santos. The History of Eastern Ethiopia. 1607.

Joam de Castro. Account of a Voyage made by the Portuguese in 1541, from the city of Goa to Suez.

John and Sebastian Cabot. Their Voyages to America.

Willoughby and Chancellor. Their Voyages to the North-east, with the Voyages of Burroughs, Pett, and Jackman; and the Embassy of Sir Dudley Digges to Russia.

Icelandic Sagas narrating the Discovery of America.

The Voyages of the Earl of Cumberland, from the Records prepared by order of the Countess of Pembroke.

La Argentina. An account of the Discovery of the Provinces of Rio de la Plata from 1512 to the time of Domingo Martinez de Irala; by Ruiz Diaz de Guzman.

For EU product safety concerns, contact us at Calle de José Abascal, 56–1°, 28003 Madrid, Spain or eugpsr@cambridge.org.

www.ingramcontent.com/pod-product-compliance
Ingram Content Group UK Ltd.
Pitfield, Milton Keynes, MK11 3LW, UK
UKHW010342140625
459647UK00010B/777